CRITICAL ESSAYS ON
JAMES JOYCE

Critical Essays on
James Joyce

Critical Essays on James Joyce

Bernard Benstock

G. K. Hall & Co. • Boston, Massachusetts

Published by G. K. Hall & Co.
A publishing subsidiary of ITT

Copyright © 1985 by Bernard Benstock

All rights reserved.

Library of Congress Cataloging in Publication Data

Main entry under title:

Critical essays on James Joyce.

Bibliography: p.
Includes index.
1. Joyce, James, 1882–1941–Criticism and
interpretation–Addresses, essays, lectures.
I. Benstock, Bernard.
PR6019.09Z5276   1985   823′.912   84–12987
ISBN 0–8161–8751–7

This publication is printed on permanent/durable acid-free paper
MANUFACTURED IN THE UNITED STATES OF AMERICA

CRITICAL ESSAYS ON MODERN BRITISH LITERATURE

The new critical essays series on modern British literature attempts to provide a variety of approaches to the modern classical writers of Britain and Ireland, and the best contemporary authors. The formats of the volumes in the series vary with the thematic designs of individual editors, and with the amount and nature of existing reviews, criticism, and scholarship. In general, the series seeks to represent the best in published criticism, augmented, where appropriate, by original essays by recognized authorities. It is hoped that each volume will be unique in developing a new overall perspective on its particular author.

The editor of this volume, Bernard Benstock, has been a central figure in nearly three decades of Joyce scholarship. He is uniquely qualified to undertake this compendium of representative and salient works which comprise the history of Joyce scholarship from its inception in the works of Joyce's own selected apostles (those who knew him and were personally chosen by Joyce to present an exegesis of his works to the world) to successive waves of critical responses. Benstock uses a chronological format to survey the varieties and dominant tendencies through the history of Joyce criticism, including the period of collaborative ventures in collections of essays, the broad tendencies of successive shifts of critical opinion, the rivalry of American and European scholarship, and the contemporary redefinition of newly trained and oriented French contemporary critical theory followers.

The book will appeal to both Joyce scholars, who will have a chance to reread seminal works in a new context, and to new serious students of Joyce. It succeeds in making a new statement about a very popular author and his critics.

Zack Bowen, GENERAL EDITOR

University of Delaware

CONTENTS

INTRODUCTION

Assimilating James Joyce

As we move through the last quarter of the century, it is no longer sufficient to consider James Joyce as the major writer of the epoch. Joyce's work stands as an epicenter against which all the international literature of the century is measured and distanced: a milestone in the advancement and subsequent retrenchment of the modernist movement; a touchstone for the constant evaluation and re-evaluation of all major literary talents; a lodestone that has attracted coteries and imitators, as well as functioned as a guiding course for several generations of writers; and a millstone around the necks of lesser practitioners of the literary arts and critics incapable of dealing with extraordinary circumstances and overwhelming demands. Even if we acknowledge the excesses of such an estimation of Joyce's position in modern letters, enormous efforts will be required for even minor qualifications of them. References to Joyce in lectures and commentaries and reviews have become a commonplace, even when Joyce himself is not the subject. When Joyce is the subject, the explications and observations and controversies have become legion, and it is apparent that early in the 1980s the fourth generation of Joyce criticism has emerged and is making its impact as something decidedly new.

Anyone still capable of wondering aloud whether the last word on Joyce has not already been published demonstrates an ignorance of the scope of the problem comparable to assuming that the Model T Ford is the last word in locomotive possibilities. Each generation redefines the set of Joycean problems, and every Joyce text—not only the inexhaustible *Ulysses* and *Finnegans Wake*—reactivates critical responses and approaches. For every critic who has attempted to nail shut a particular area of consideration, dozens immediately appear with crowbars to pull up the floorboards. It is not surprising at this stage to encounter new analysts who survey the Joyce scene and announce that the important work now needs to begin. Nor are all of these iconoclasts necessarily newcomers to the Joyce lists: some are veterans of earlier campaigns who have seriously re-evaluated their own thinking, and undertaken ex-

1

tensive renovations of their attitudes. Various books and articles on Joyce have essentially disappeared from view, usually because the authors have ridden their hobbyhorses to death and failed to comprehend the extensive complexities of Joyce's work. Yet, over the past seven decades, as the essays in this collection attest, an enduring body of critical examination has built up and been retained, regardless of the vagaries of critical trends.

The existence of a "Joyce Industry" has appalled some members of the academic and literary professions, probably because they assumed that theirs was a "gentlemanly" endeavor of strictly individual employment. No coordinated establishment exists, as the diversity of these essays demonstrate, for regardless of how cohesive a Joycean community may become, the individuated approaches that the scholar-critic undertakes in the isolation of the study or den become apparent in the published work. A community—or several interrelated communities—has emerged during the past two decades, to share problems and pool resources, a communal effort that has made the work of each of us much easier and lessened the possibility of certain errors that take root in isolation.

Joyce himself was responsible for the first efforts to put Joycean scholarship into mature operation, as he engaged friends and fellow writers, as well as critics and even a biographer, to undertake the investigation that he considered necessary for his literary output. On one hand these efforts were a matter of public relations and publicity, bringing *Ulysses* and *Finnegans Wake* in particular into prominence and himself into the limelight; on the other hand he was determined to serve the posterity of his creations by keeping the professors busy for centuries to come—as he coyly intimated. He was not above providing explications upon request, and although undoubtedly amused by over-enthusiasms and even critical egregiousness, he nonetheless encouraged serious scholarship even when these texts were still very new.

Joyce's publication problems with several of his books made him wary of the luxury of the writer unconcerned with the marketing of his work and the conscientious creation of a reputation. *Dubliners* took ten years before one of the two publishing houses that had contracted to publish it finally did so, after numerous objections and attempts at censorship, as well as the burning of the typescript by an incensed printer. *Ulysses*, having run afoul of the League for the Suppression of Vice in the United States, was privately printed for Joyce by Sylvia Beach's Paris bookshop, Shakespeare and Company, only to have copies burned on English docks and confiscated at American customs. And *Finnegans Wake*, carefully constructed to fly by those nets, proved instead an early casualty of World War Two, when even the awaited masterpiece of a renowned author was rendered insignificant by the monumental conflict. Only *A Portrait of the Artist as a Young Man* of all of

Joyce's major writings had relatively smooth sailing, although Joyce himself agonized over his own delay in completing the work that should have fulfilled the promise of fame within ten years—the actual publication coming two years late. Under the pressure of these adversities the author undertook his own advertising campaign, and considering his insistence that his intricate and obscure work be comprehended by his readers, he also undertook to educate the cadre that would enlighten the reading public.

Joyce's relationships with other writers who were his contemporaries were often complex, but not necessarily ambiguous. Behind the scenes an Edward Garnett as a reader for Duckworth managed to have *A Portrait* rejected, but Ezra Pound, whom Joyce had already befriended, gave it a fine review once it was in print. Arnold Bennett reviewed *Ulysses* quite favorably, and Virginia Woolf had expressed enthusiasm for the early episodes, even considering the impossible task of having it published by the Hogarth Press. She later reacted against its excesses, but nonetheless maintained a serious regard for it as a major accomplishment, and even worried whether Joyce would be able to complete *Finnegans Wake*, that he might have brought himself to the edge of an abyss and was unable to see the possibility of writing anything beyond the *Wake*. Pound also began to despair of *Ulysses*, never quite comfortable when the focus shifted from the intellectual Stephen to the prosaic Leopold Bloom, but it was the *Wake* that broke the camel's back, and he denounced it on Radio Rome as a "bourgeois novel." T. S. Eliot, also brought into confluence with Joyce by his friend Pound, proved to be invaluable as a prestigious editor, using the pages of his own *Dial* to establish *Ulysses* within a framework that was congenial to his own critical theories. And in France the author of *Ulysses* was pleased to engage such prominent literati as Valery Larbaud and the conservative Louis Gillet as "sponsors."

I

The history of the early reception of Joyce's books is a predictably uneven one, and the reviews reprinted here are in themselves a microcosm of that history. Ezra Pound, of course, cannot be denied his seminal role in appreciating and advocating Joyce's early writing—so much so that he can even be forgiven the dual lapses of taste in embracing Mussolini and dismissing *Finnegans Wake*. (Only the sponsorship by Arthur Symons of *Chamber Music* ranks chronologically ahead of Pound's initiating efforts.) Pound had access to the London review, the *Egoist*, and he opened its pages to Joyce for serial publication of *A Portrait* and of *Ulysses*; the financial support subsequently given to Joyce by its editor, Harriet Shaw Weaver, outweighs all other kinds of assistance that Joyce ever received. Pound's short review, "Dubliners and Mr James Joyce," gives the impression of deliriously locking the barn door after the horse has wildly run free, and in many ways is an elaborate justification of Pound's own theses, rather than a review of Joyce's volume of fifteen stories. His admiration of Joyce's "clear hard prose" positions Joyce so firmly within Pound's own camp that it obviously does dual service in praising Joyce and justifying Pound simultaneously. There is a sense in Pound's review that he is still attempting to dictate to Joyce the terms of the contract which will bind him to Pound, even though *Dubliners* is already complete and published and *A Portrait* in the process of being serialized in the *Egoist*. Consequently, Joyce may not be impressionistic, must be a realist, may not be parochially Irish, must be international, even "continental." As long as Joyce lived up to the terms of that contractual arrangement he retained Pound's blessings.

Almost three years later, when the well-known novelist H. G. Wells reveiwed *A Portrait of the Artist as a Young Man* (first in England in the *Nation*, 24 February 1917, and then in America in the *New Republic*, 10 March 1917), Joyce was still a relatively unknown author. Unlike the conspirator Pound engaging a co-conspirator, Wells writes as a master surveying a contingent of field hands, and if one reads the closing sentence of his first paragraph as a superlative, he seems to be designating Joyce's *Portrait* as the best novel of 1916. Only when we look carefully at the other contenders (Caradoc Evans, Thomas Burke), does the honor seem diminished. The reference to the first two "chapters" of Dorothy Richardson's *Pilgrimage* ("amusing experiments" likened to the painting of the Futurists) offers a real basis for comparison with Joyce, but Wells apparently saw no connection and ignored any such comparison. Instead, he makes the Irish connection, with Swift in particular, that Pound had played down so emphatically. Joyce has since had his enjoyment in countering Wells's accusation of "cloacal obsession," citing the English rather than the Irish who are obsessed with building water closets, but Wells's close attention to that facet of *A Portrait* still strikes us as open and attentive to a vital aspect of the novel. George Bernard Shaw was far from original when he noted that *Ulysses* showed the Irish their own filth and served as a form of enforced toilet training for his nation. Wells takes pains not to gloss over the unpleasantness, despite his own displeasure.

Wells's perspective remains fascinating many decades later: he offers no indication that he and Joyce are in any way contemporaries, and it is not the author Joyce that he is reviewing (as Pound did), but the text itself. Every aspect of *A Portrait* disturbs him, from the raw materials to the innovative techniques, from the concentration on Stephen that he admires to the Irishness of the book that awakens his English liberalism to the serious dangers emanating from that rebellious isle. Without having to contend with a formidable Joyce, but confronting a first novel by a neophyte, Wells manages to reveal more about himself in his handling of *A Portrait*, and he writes one of the first critiques of Joyce that suggests what many have later uncomfortably discerned: that the greatness of Joyce's literary creativity is often in direct proportion to the degree that he disturbs and even unnerves his reader. T. S. Eliot, a bare half-dozen years later, cannot help but approach *Ulysses* as a monument erected by a masterbuilder, and must find other ways of subverting it to conform with his own position.

One might well argue that by the autumn of 1923 Eliot had more than enough time to come to terms with *Ulysses*, much of which had been available for him in installments for years, and that the scant pages of "review" mask his particular unease with the monster. Despite its too-apparent limitations, "*Ulysses*, Order, and Myth" has retained its stature as the important findings of a major critic examining the masterpiece of a prestigious writer, and is often referred to as a "seminal" essay. Eliot brackets his observations between encomiums that have become memorable: *Ulysses* is praised as "the most important expression which the present age has found" and as "a step toward making the modern world possible for art." The opening statement requires no qualifiers, but the closing is based on the assumption that the modern world has been a source of complaint for T. S. Eliot, and for Joyce as well, he assumes. What Eliot feels he "discovered" in *Ulysses*, the presence of Homer's *Odyssey* in Joyce's text, has become the abiding commonplace in Joyce studies; wave after wave of commentators have stressed, dismissed, reasserted, discredited and reassessed the place of the Homeric in the Joycean scheme. For Eliot it was central in having provided the mythic context that resisted the formlessness of the modern world: the "realism" that appealed to Pound and Wells has no claim on Eliot, and he is adept in carrying along with him a close companion in Wyndham Lewis (in his reference to *Tarr*) in case Joyce does not exactly serve the purpose Eliot has outlined for *Ulysses*. The assertions of a powerful voice have helped Eliot's essay weather the changing attitudes of Joyce's readers toward the primacy—or even the relevance—of the Homeric role in the Joycean text.

By 1939 it was no longer conceivable for a critic of the eminence of Edmund Wilson to pass off a six-paragraph review of the new Joyce work. Joyce's tomes defied journalistic reviewing, and Wilson approached *Finnegans Wake* with a full kit of critical tools. "The Dream of H. C. Earwicker" carried over two issues of the *New Yorker*, and earned Wilson respectful acknowledgment (howbeit with a correction) from Joyce himself. In many ways Wilson determined the path of critical apprehension of the *Wake* for a long time to come: his reading of the narrative has a solid novelistic orientation; his approach is so sane, so logical, so careful to grasp essentials. Unlike Eliot, Wilson casually dismisses the importance of the *Odyssey* to *Ulysses*, seeing it merely as scaffolding, and in the same sense he is quite casual about Wakean scaffolding (Vico, for example), and prefers to read *Finnegans Wake* as the story of the Earwickers as *Ulysses* was the story of the Blooms and Stephen Dedalus. Yet, although he tends to credit Joyce with breaking from Flaubertian naturalism, he also expresses his disappointment that Earwicker is not naturalistically portrayed, that characterization in the *Wake* is not as sharpedged as in the previous novel. Aware that the tale told in *Finnegans Wake* rises ineffably into "universal history," Wilson cannot quite reconcile his hunger for reality and Joyce's generous servings of sheer poetry, considering Joyce always to have been "deficient in dramatic and narrative sense." He was not the first to worry over Joyce as "overingenious," nor the last of those who read the various drafts of the *Wake* and pontificated on the interim stage at which Joyce should have halted before excessive excess took over. Wilson's enthusiasms, however, are infectious, and along with Harry Levin he can probably be credited with the Americanization of Joyce studies, a situation that has had uncomfortable international repercussions.

In his long footnote, appended to the reprinting of the June 1939 version of "The Dream of H. C. Earwicker," Wilson acknowledges the interest in the *Wake* by such American critics as Levin (who published the first full-length study of the Joyce corpus in 1941, only months after Joyce's corpse was laid to rest in a Zurich grave), John Peale Bishop, and Thornton Wilder. While Joyce's Europe was preoccupied with the War, a small segment of America was preoccupied with studying Joyce, a preoccupation that has persisted to an overdeveloped degree. It was not the dignified efforts of these critics, however, that propelled *Wake* studies into full form, but an unseemly dispute between Joseph Campbell and Thornton Wilder over plagiarism from Joyce's *Wake* in *The Skin of Our Teeth* which guaranteed the publication of the Joseph Campbell-Henry Morton Robinson *Skeleton Key to Finnegans Wake*. Campbell mined the *Wake* for its mythic materials, and for many years the *Key* was the indispensable guide.

II

Wilson's reference to *Our Exagmination Round His Factification for Incamination of Work in Progress* reminds us of the basically European roots not only for Joyce but for Joyce exegesis. At a time when *Ulysses* was legally unavailable in most of the English-speaking world and somewhat incomprehensible even where available, and the *Wake* already appearing in periodicals as segments of an untitled Work in Progress, Joyce himself was coercing and / or encouraging various annotators and commentators, both on the complete *Ulysses* and the incomplete *Wake*. The 1929 *Exagmination* gave a dozen Paris-based writers an opportunity to taste and assess a soupçon of the eventual "new Irish stew" that Joyce was still concocting. Probably the most enduring of these twelve essays, and in some measure because of his own elevation to prominence, is Samuel Beckett's scrupulously titled "Dante ... Bruno. Vico .. Joyce." In effect, Beckett writes *as the author* of Work in Progress, assuming an auctorial authority in contradistinction to the critical authority of an Eliot or a Wilson, so that the area of contention is that between the reader and the text, rather than between the critic and the author. For Beckett, Joyce is neither "deficient" nor "overingenious," but the reader is admonished: "if you don't understand it, Ladies and Gentlemen, it is because you are too decadent to receive it." Although he asserts an unequivocal authority, Beckett cannot at the time pretend to a complete knowledge of the partially written work, but the portions of the work quoted are expected ineluctably to stand for the whole and to have a solid permanence. And Giambattista Vico is also expected to have an invested authority as Beckett's fulcrum into the Joycean text—when Joyce himself downgraded the importance of Vico, indicating that he used Vico "for all he was worth," he corroborated more than diminished the Viconian significance that Beckett introduced. At the center of Beckett's evocative magic, between applications of Vico and Dante and the invocation of Joyce's language, resides the central critical nugget that all readers have taken away as treasure from the essay: "Here form *is* content, content *is* form. . . . His writing is not *about* something; *it is that something itself*."

Almost co-eval with the publication of the dozen exegeses of the Work in Progress was Stuart Gilbert's exegesis in *James Joyce's Ulysses*, a study of the previous work that is as different from that of Beckett and Company as *Ulysses* now seems from *Finnegans Wake*. As Gilbert's second chapter, reprinted here, immediately demonstrates, the approach to the Joycean text is painstakingly careful and verges on simplification. Gilbert's role is to chart the terrain, avoiding major obstacles and bypassing the whirlpools: he attempts to rescue *Ulysses* from charges of obscurity (much less obscenity), suggesting that all difficult matters can eventually be cleared up by a critical perspective of "sweet reasonableness." Systematically he explicates passage after passage, quoting extensively from and footnoting the Shakespeare and Company text that few of his readers could then possess (or now afford), and displays one of the two schema that Joyce had drawn up and offered to his chosen explicators. The coherence of the chart of structural units and complementary guides speaks for itself (where there is a map there is terra cognita), and Joyce is swiftly abstracted by Stuart Gilbert from the evil companionship of the excessive schools of modernism, with one of the orderly, structured poems of *Pomes Penyeach* offered as the proper companion to *Ulysses*. Nor was the study of *Ulysses* published four years later by Frank Budgen, *James Joyce and the Making of Ulysses*, any more intended to disquiet the nervous reader. Budgen substitutes for Gilbert's tone of intelligent complicity with the text one of companionable complicity with its author: Joyce emerges as a witty conversationalist, informative and logical, whose diligent efforts as a novelist are concomitant with his perceptive and humane stature as a person. Budgen followed his anecdotal analyses of *Ulysses* with reminiscences of Joyce, and followed him into the far murkier area of *Finnegans Wake* as well, maintaining his calm demeanor in undertaking commentary in that area.

Unlike Beckett, Budgen throws down no challenge to the prospective reader of *Finnegans Wake* but quietly assumes that since the same person who wrote *Ulysses* also wrote the *Wake*, the path into that work should be a straight one. Joyce for him is a man who wrote a book, a man who lived in a city, who discussed various topics with him—an approachable author. He eschews erudition or portentousness, and is content to make simple statements without embarrassment: *"Finnegans Wake* is a resurrection myth." He cuts a swathe through the dream world and the myth, finding the characters who populate the Chapelizod locale, and although he shows his discomfort with the absence of "story" in the *Wake*, Budgen imposes a clear-eyed control of the materials to intuit its multifarious tale. Published only months after Joyce's death, "Joyce's Chapters of Going Forth by Day" reveals itself in its closing paragraph as an elegy and a eulogy for James Joyce, the writer who "wrote out of the center of his consciousness where his own experience was at one with that of his fellow men." Throughout his writings about Joyce, Frank Budgen has retained his position as a concerned amateur, never scholar or critic or teacher, and here he confronts the *Wake* very much in his own guise, revealing his vantagepoint as a painter and as a sailor, even as an Englishman and a Socialist. The *Wake* in his hands becomes his text, as Joyce had been his companion, and he tells the "story" as he reads it in the book of himself. As one of the first essays written about Joyce after the writer's death, it shows its detachment from the active control of the author, and harbingers a new spate of critical approaches that accept the absence of the author. Joyce is no longer there to pass judgment on his judges, to praise a perceptive comment or correct a mis-identification. A new era of Joyce criticism had begun, one in which the professional academic would play the major role.

A second generation of Joyce commentators began to publish in the late 1940s and early 1950s, generally within the confines of American academia. In an important sense they were the first true Joyceans, a corps of teachers who encouraged their students to read and write about Joyce, while they themselves maintained a continuous interest throughout the next decades in Joyce studies. Along with William York Tindall, Richard M. Kain sparked this new era with the publication of *Fabulous Voyager*, and it is significant that in the opening chapter of this study of *Ulysses* he announces that the time is "ripe for a *reconsideration* of this important monument of modern culture," while referring back to the phalanx of commentators who were the pioneers. In his contention that both *Ulysses* and *Finnegans Wake* have as their basic themes "social criticism and philosophic relativity," Kain identifies himself with those who, like László Moholy-Nagy, insisted that Joyce "contained multitudes," that his was a cosmic vision, an embracing of all mankind, as Frank Budgen had stressed. Kain is polite but firm in his stand against Harry Levin's charge that Joyce was lacking in humanity and philosophy, and no more enthusiastic in what he considered Stuart Gilbert's emphasis on Joyce's narrow aesthetics. There is no doubt as one reads Richard Kain's opening essay that Joyce criticism is no longer a field in which each practitioner carves out an individual area for investigation, but an arena in which sides line up for combat. Denied a place within the Great Tradition by a traditionalist F. R. Leavis, Joyce is encompassed within an even greater one by Richard Kain, and singled out as the supreme modern artist aware of the monumental changes that were shattering the status quo of bourgeois values in the twentieth century. In the chill environment of cold-war America, Joyce achieved an apotheosis for his humanistic stature that had not been attempted before nor duplicated since.

III

"The complex personality of Joyce awaits a definitive biographer," wrote Richard Kain in 1947, expressing a need that was becoming universally acknowledged. Joyce himself had set Herbert S. Gorman the task in the 1920s, not so much to set the record straight as to set the hunt in the directions that Joyce wanted explored. Gorman's "authorized" biographies fought Joyce's battles for him, presenting those "facts" which corroborated his role as an artist of determined integrity, but kept his "complex personality" a private matter for himself alone. The Richard Ellmann biography of 1959 set out to be definitive, and was untouched by Joyce's particular authority. It has served the professional exceedingly well, despite certain limitations: some have argued that it failed to expose a fully rounded Joyce, or to determine the sexual or spiritual complexities of Joyce's personality. What the biography succeeded in doing was establishing with tenacity the parallel tracks of Joyce's life and Joyce's work, specifically revealing itself throughout its 800 pages as the biography of a *writer*. To do so Ellmann used Joyce's fiction as biographical evidence and Joyce's life as material for confronting the fictional texts. Ellmann also conferred with many of those alive at the time who knew Joyce, but did not necessarily privilege their testaments, fusing them instead with the testimonies from Joyce's letters and from the Joyce texts. (A first volume of the letters was edited by Stuart Gilbert and published in 1957, with Ellmann incorporating that collection within his three-volume publication in 1966: the first generation of the coterie again supplanted by the second generation.) In revising *James Joyce* for the 1982 centenary year Ellmann apparently found very few new facts—those who knew Joyce personally have become extremely scarce, but Joyce's published work remains a mine of information, as attested by the applicability of the essay in the biography, "The Backgrounds of 'The Dead.'"

Despite various dissenting voices, even among the admirers of Joyce's work, the strongly expansive views held by Budgen and Kain, Tindall and Ellmann, held sway well into the 1950s. "Positive readings" of the Joycean texts, and especially of the inconclusive closures that distinguish most of his works, were coupled with enthusiastic evaluations of the major characters that Joyce created. Stephen Dedalus and Leopold Bloom and Molly Bloom, as well as Humphrey Chimpden Earwicker and Anna Livia Plurabelle, were often seen as either personae of the artist himself or of mankind in general (although Joyce's own designation of Bloom as a "good man" never managed to win over Ezra Pound). The writings of Hugh Kenner, however, culminating with the 1956 publication of *Dublin's Joyce*, provided a chilling antidote to what some saw as a tendency toward critical pollyannaism; Kenner has been implicated in leading a movement of detractors of Stephen Dedalus, contending that as a young man this version of the artist was a cold prig. The overly close identification of Stephen with his creator had caused some confused and uncritical readings, essentially denying Joyce his own perspective on his past self and his range of perceptions in developing character within the demands of a fictional set of circumstances. Kenner's corrective was not always well-accepted, but even his detractors became aware of the intensive force of Kenner's critical observations, and Kenner himself was capable of taking a close look at his past criticism and of altering his concepts as he rethought and reworked his observations. His perspectives on *A Portrait* have undergone his own assessment and reassessment from the first publication in 1948 until the 1977 "Cubist *Portrait*," in which he nonetheless casts a cold eye at the young Stephen, "a tedious cliché, weary, disdainful, sterile." Kenner dismantles the "autobiographical paradigm" that has served for so long as the accepted method of reading *A Portrait of the Artist as a Young Man*, and remains tentative in the paradigm he maps out in its place. In asserting that Joyce contains multitudes, Kenner suggests something more esoteric than the Whitmanesque containing of multitudes that Moholoy-Nagy has contended.

The explosion in Joyce studies was a phenomenon of the 1960s, ushered in by the establishment of two journals that have continued ever since as conduits and clearing houses for work in the field: *A Wake Newslitter*, begun in 1961 by Clive Hart and Fritz Senn, and the *James Joyce Quarterly*, begun in 1963 by Thomas F. Staley. By focusing almost exclusively on *Finnegans Wake*, the *Newslitter* concentrated on the exegetical minutiae that for a long time seemed the essentials for understanding the *Wake*, yet it was quickly apparent that some sort of systematic approach was needed for handling a text that often invited eccentric explication. Toward that end Clive Hart laid down the ground rules in "The Elephant in the Belly," a position paper that intimates the convoluted state of *Wake* studies even at that early date. Hart's dicta remain over the past two decades as standard criteria, although the dichotomy of critical apprehension persists: overly literal dealings with the fanciful materials of the *Wake* produce stodgy scholarship, while overly fanciful readings of the literal words result in idiosyncratic interpretations. Hart is insistent on retaining the sane proportions of both variants, of holding on to the verifications of Joyce's intentions without dropping the imaginative possibilities that Joyce set loose as well. In steering between the Scylla of scholarship and the Charybdis of reader-response, Hart prefers to navigate nearer to Scylla, all the while showing himself mesmerized by the poetic whirlpool. He acknowledges an attitude that has held firm even in the present age of theories deriving from "the French schools": that Joyce in particular commanded his intentions with such a firm hand that it would take a brave, if not reckless, pilot who would ignore the Joycean charts. (Because it ran so intentionally against the current schools, Louis Mink's recent *Finnegans Wake Gazetteer*, insisting on its purposeful adherence to intentionalism, has not received the attention that it would have had if it been published a decade earlier.)

More than anyone else Fritz Senn has been responsible for returning Joyce to the European continent, in internationalizing Joyce studies and making the Joyce Industry a multi-national. With Thomas F. Staley he conceived of the idea of a bi-annual Joyce symposium, the first of which gave form to a James Joyce Foundation as well, and from his vantage point in Zurich he has been a magnet drawing in Joyceans from all over the world. His work has been the scrupulous charting of the Joyce minefields, including the monitoring of translations of Joyce's texts into the various European languages. Senn embodies a tendency of the new generation of commentators never to allow a previously explored area to pass into perpetuity without reexamination: every turn of previous exploration is turned and turned again under his gaze, even the presumably fixed terrain of Homeric correspondences in *Ulysses* that Stuart Gilbert had exhaustively encompassed. "Perhaps the most pervasive Homeric features in *Ulysses* are not the one to one relationships that Stuart Gilbert began to chart for us" a Senn sentence commences, allowing for a closed book to be reopened, a closed issue reintroduced. Rather than setting up a collator that sets Homer's book against Joyce's, Senn creates a palimpsest, superimposing the two upon each other (and not necessarily in chronological sequence: Joyce is allowed to recreate Homer's text while crafting his own), to which he adds Skeat's *Ety-*

mological Dictionary as well, and numerous translations of Homer and numerous translations of Joyce's words back into their root language. Senn's method proves as polytropic as his material. In the tension between the cosmic view of Joyce's epic works and the "esoteric symbolism" that implies the painstaking craft of the maker of mosaics, Senn constrains both facets of the contradiction, as his gambit announces: "Joyce's works can be seen, with equal validity, either as one great whole or as a series of self-contained units." Like many Joyce critics of his generation Fritz Senn worked his way back from the complexities of *Finnegans Wake* to the previously unrecognized complexities of the entire Joyce canon.

The ability of a Fritz Senn to encompass all of Joyce's works, including *Finnegans Wake*, has been shared by several other accomplished Joyce scholars, although the complexities of the unique problems of the various works have resulted in specialists concentrating in special areas of the field. From the outset Father Robert Boyle has worked with equal ease on each Joyce text, from the poems of *Chamber Music* through the poetics of *Finnegans Wake*, usually bringing observations on one to bear on the others. His expertise on Catholicism, and his privileged position as a Jesuit priest, superimposed on his scholarly skills a varied degree of approaches to Joyce that, in conjunction with the scholarship of his colleague, William Noon, S. J., provided a corrective to and an expansion of the often limited perspectives of those who could not approximate Joyce's own experiences. The lauding of Joyce as the High Priest of Modernism and the awareness of Joyce as a self-professed apostate fail to take into consideration that Joyce, as Boyle contends, brought "many centuries of Catholic tradition to bear on his vision of literary art" as he came "face to face with the ultimate mystery of human existence." Unlike other Catholic writers on Joyce, Boyle refuses to hedge on Joyce's apostasy or return Joyce to the Church he left. Boyle invariably adds dimensions to the Joycean configuration, rather than delimit it, and his exploitation of the sexual ramifications in the Joyce works constantly amplifies the ecclesiastical characteristics that he explicates. It is also characteristic of the best commentary of this period that Boyle concentrates so deliberately on Joyce's language—and not just on language *en gros*, but on words, on the individual word. In isolating Joyce's "terms," Boyle returns them to their Catholic origins and displaces them from the "marketplace" connotations which they have accidentally acquired, but he does not fail to sense the uniquely Joycean irony in their reapplication in *Ulysses* and the *Wake*. The gap between the student of theology and the "priest of eternal imagination" narrows under Father Boyle's analytical application.

Boyle's "Miracle in Black Ink" and Senn's "Book of Many Turns" were both papers given at a conference on the 50th anniversary of the publication of *Ulysses* staged at the University of Tulsa, and subsequently published first in the *James Joyce Quarterly* and then in book form. The conference was the first of a series in America that have since regularly supplemented the international symposia in European cities, and together with the consequent publications characterize the industriousness and cooperation of Joycean practitioners. The concept of group effort in Joyce studies developed apparently of its own accord, the realization of the interdependence of scholars and critics working on interrelated aspects of the complex territory. Toward that end Clive Hart planned a volume on the fifteen stories of *Dubliners*, inviting a different writer to contribute on each of the stories. (No single book on *Dubliners* by an individual author had as yet been published, and when one was made available, it proved to be a disappointment, primarily because the writer so obviously operated within a vacuum without access to Joycean colleagues.) The essay on "The Dead" in Hart's *James Joyce's Dubliners* retains much of the intellectual atmosphere of the Sixties as it pertained to an interest in Joyce: a major preoccupation with the sanctity of the text, so that Joyce's words and his phrases are reproduced at every juncture; an eclectic critical approach that blends sociological and psychological perspectives; and a determination that every nook and cranny of the story be investigated, every nugget held up for examination. Nor have Joyce's symbolic structures been overlooked, but traced with such tenacity that faint-hearted reviewers gasped at the excesses, a reaction that failed to deter the symbol hunters who, since the era of William York Tindall, have remained relentless, even though some of their symbols seemed far from esoteric.

The collective activities of Joycean colleagues continued on into the early Seventies, suggesting to some detractors the consolidation of an Establishment in control, although many new enthusiasts were constantly being added: these were often the students of the professors of the previous generation, and there was actually very little of the "closed society" about the Joycean Community, although there was certainly a continually augumenting American cast to its make-up. The most significant characteristics of the Hart volume was the eclecticism of the participants themselves, several of whom had previously written almost exclusively on *Finnegans Wake* but were here focusing on the presumably "easier" volume of Joyce stories. The community expanded; their interests and concerns expanded; and the assumption that every facet of James Joyce's art deserved—and required—equally careful scrutiny took definite hold. The phenomenon of the collective effort had various forms during the late Sixties and early Seventies (Hart followed up his *Dubliners* essays with a volume on *Ulysses*, coedited with David Hayman; Senn and Michael Begnal collected essays for *A Conceptual Guide to Finnegans Wake*—in both cases a different critic wrote on each of the chapters—and Staley and Benstock published collections on *Ulysses* and *A Portrait*, varying "approaches" by several writers to the totality of each of the Joyce texts). By the end of the Seventies and the beginning of the Eighties the collective volumes have become rare, and a return to "individuated" approaches may seem to be highly prevalent, as new concepts of critical theory permeate the Joyce profession.

IV

It was only a matter of time before the revolutionary changes in literary theory emanating from France would affect Joyce studies, and Joyce has indeed become the happy hunting ground of new critical approaches. Some of the effects have been drastic, comparable to the British shopkeepers who precipitously retired when their currency went decimal or the Swedish drivers who gave up driving when their country changed to the right side of the road. Some Joyce commentators have dug in their heels and retained their "traditional" critical tools, insisting that the newer criticism at its best only reaffirms through unnecessarily arduous contortions the basic results that they had arrived at through straightforward methods; others have moved quickly into the employment of new tools despite their past commitments; and still others have picked over the new offerings and chosen for themselves those aspects which blended well with their own established ideas. But most importantly a new generation has entered the field as a product of a new and different system of education. The applications to James Joyce are now extensive and fortunately diverse. In particular the Joyce texts have always lent themselves well to concentration on language, on complex psychoanalytical insights, on structural analyses, and on the variety of narrational techniques.

Wake studies may well be the major recipient of a new lease on life due to the infusion of new critical possibilities, a needed rescue from the doldrums of the past decade. The enthusiasm of the 1960s, when one heard of "central theories" about to be advanced and "major breakthroughs" in explication, disintegrated rather mysteriously, and a sense that the piling up of data, of word lists in foreign languages and annotations and place names, brought the reader no nearer to a comfortable understanding—not only *of* the text, but *with* the text. In his essay on the "Nodality and Infra-Structure of *Finnegans Wake*" David Hayman returns to Beckett's admonition that the *Wake* "is not *about* something; *it is that something itself*." Hayman has the immense value of his own credentials as one of the most important *Wake* detectives of the past two decades, and he abandons none of his previous weapons as he takes up the cudgels for his nodal theory. He relies on his own important *A First-Draft Version of Finnegans Wake* as supportive evidence, balancing between the original generative development of the work and the newer awareness of primary, secondary and tertiary nodes already evident in the notes and early drafts. There is a breath of fresh air in Hayman's reapproaching the *Wake* distinctly different from a great deal of tired trampling through the terrain that has marked recent criticism. That Hayman stays consistently and doggedly with the Joyce text characterizes the best element of the application of new theories to the old vintage.

Fresh avenues into the *Wake* are particularly appreciated, but all parts of the Joyce canon should be re-examined periodically, and the new poetics in its various guises offers a complete set of "beginnings," even into Joyce's earliest published efforts. Thomas F. Staley, as editor of the *James Joyce Quarterly* for more than twenty years, has been particularly sensitive to changes and innovations, and in "A Beginning: Signification, Story, and Discourse in Joyce's 'The Sisters,'" he draws upon European schemes of critical approach. Yet, like Hayman, he lays the groundwork in the critical foundations that have formed under *Dubliners* scholarship over the years, his footnotes moving both back into traditional avenues and laterally across continents to newly opening boulevards. As Staley assimilates he also questions and discards: only those theoretical determinations demonstratively applicable to the Joyce text are retained. Hayman's retention of the generative method is honored by Staley with equal insistence as he correlates Joyce's initial assessment of his own material, moving deftly from the nineteenth-century "realism" into the twentieth century, giving priority to "the word over the world," but also giving "special attention to the correspondence between word and world." By concentrating exclusively on the opening paragraph of the opening story of *Dubliners* Staley performs the requisitive acts of Joycean investigation, close readings of all facets of a Joyce text, with particular attention to the "full range of the linguistic activity of the text." In his close readings Staley replicates the techniques of his own teacher, Father Robert Boyle, as he finds the ritual language of "The Sisters" particularly potent, and the relationship between the boy narrator and the priest who had been his mentor—an ambiguous relationship that has worried many critics of the story—dependent on the language the boy has inherited and reapplied to the situation of the failed cleric's life and death.

In his citation of Wolfgang Iser, Staley acknowledges one of the major European theorists and suggests the problem of criticism that develops initially as theory and then undergoes the process of application to a writer like James Joyce. Joyce's position at the epicenter of Modernism has meant that critics whose training has not been specifically in Joyce studies nonetheless find themselves dealing extensively with the Joyce canon—and Iser is one of several who have done important work in bringing their theories to bear on the texts, particularly *Ulysses*. It is interesting that Iser picks up the *Ulysses* problem exactly where it began, with T. S. Eliot's Homeric concerns, ontogeny quite literally recapitulating philogeny. But he cuts through a morass of difficulties that have grown up around the "Oxen of the Sun" chapter by critics who have been too rigid in their treatment of it and by critics who have thrown up their hands in horror at its excesses. Iser undertakes to grapple with the potentialities of meaning that the reader expects to have actualization in the world of reality, cautioning that the "actualization of this potential is not left to the discretion of the individual reader," but has its bases in Joyce's stylistic manipulations in the chapter. His meticulous reading of the text concludes that "style reproduces only aspects of reality and not . . . reality itself." *Ulysses* breaks with the traditional attempt of the novel to capture reality, positing more realities than it can itself contain, but through the multivarious styles and pastiches of style (as in "Oxen of the Sun") offers a plethora of possibilities. Iser understands what more literal readers of *Ulysses* avoid, that Joyce highlighted the "inadequacy of style as regards the presentation of reality," exposing "the intangibility and expansibility of observable reality." The view that *Ulysses* is patterned upon and therefore constrained by some map of the Dublin of 1904 finds no favor with Iser, who views Joyce revealing "the characteristic quality of style—namely, that it imposes form on an essentially formless reality."

Wrenching Joyce away from the traditional center, as Iser does in marking the break with conventional assumptions about reality that characterize *Ulysses*, might seem unnecessary for an author so often credited as the leader of the "Revolution of the Word," but as Margot Norris maintains, Joyce has for a long time been the property of "conservative critics, who have dominated *Wake* criticism for the last thirty years." In the decade since this diagnosis, her own work on *Finnegans Wake* has established itself as an important radical interpretation of the *Wake*, and her diagnosis is as precise as it is damning when she contends that "the limitation of this conservative, novelistic approach to the work is most evident in its lack of progress toward establishing clearly the intellectual orientation of the work." The history of *Wake* commentary has, with some isolated exceptions and, as Norris implies, the tentative intimations of the Exagminators, been the attempt to impose a realistic frame around the "marryvoising moodmoulded cyclewheeling history" that is *Finnegans Wake*. Norris liberates the work from the frame, acknowledging instead its total and constant "freeplay of elements," "the expression of a decentered universe." In lieu of a narrative line that confines the freeplay within a plot, she maintains that "the formal elements of the work, plot, character, and point of view, are not anchored to a single point of reference, do not refer back to a center. This condition produces that curious flux and uncertainty in the work which is sensed intuitively by the reader." Just as Wolfgang Iser considers *Ulysses* a book of many facets of realities moving outward from the limited confines of a single text, suggesting further realities that it cannot itself contain, so Margot Norris brings her study of the bricolage

collected by Joyce in the *Finnegans Wake* grab bag-napsack to the conclusion that Joyce extended the perimeters of the *Wake* beyond its
covers to the critiques that he commissioned and encouraged on the
Wake after its completion.

Seeds sown by Hayman and Norris for radical interpretations of
the *Wake* in the Seventies have had only a few sproutings in the Eighties,
since conservative criticism has essentially held firm, but several new
interpreters have recently appeared. In her various considerations of the
Wake (as well as *Ulysses*), Shari Benstock amasses the threads of several new modes of criticism, and in "Nightletters" she shares Margot
Norris's enthusiasm for the illuminating responses to Joyce that are offered by Jacques Derrida, and she corroborates Norris's decision that
"Wakean events are subject to multiple recapitulations on all narrative
levels." Whereas conservative criticism has sought to close up *Finnegans
Wake* into finite meanings and a structured set of circumstances, Shari
Benstock and several others have attempted to open the work into wider
dimensions and greater sets of component elements—not only has the
book no beginning and no end, it also has no *middle*. Benstock adds to
linguistic and psychoanalytical perspectives an insistently feminine criticism, locating the woman in her various manifestations at the core of
a nonetheless decentered configuration. Focusing on the all-important
letter in the *Wake*, she avoids previous attempts to "read" the letter,
to translate it into everyday language, acknowledging that there is no
single letter, nor one single reading of any variant of that letter, instead
reading the Joyce *text* that alludes to and foregrounds the fragments of
a letter. "The writing of *Finnegans Wake*," she concludes, "both inhabits
and is inhabited by women, by ALP and Issy, who are present in the
transparent space of the hymeneal folds, in the silences of the historically
interweaved, overlapped, and spiralling story, who constitute the absent
center of the *Wake* universe, who are to be found inside the mirror, in
the bar between the conscious and the unconscious, between dreaming
and waking, between signifier and signified—both inside and outside the
fabric they weave." Her conclusions are a far distance from and at variance with the schools of thought that still are moored at firm docks
(*"Finnegans Wake* is a dream") or sail about in the rough seas fishing
for foreign words and annotations and influences and a central thesis.

V

The essays in this volume have been chosen to present a *flow* of
critical ideas on the major Joyce texts, a loosely chronological ordering
of nineteen essays of various proportions covering fifty years of criticism.
Literal chronology has been somewhat violated in order to create a
readable text that reveals the variety of approaches as well as the inter-
connectness of approaches to Joyce's work, with the preceding intro-

ductory essay as a "guide" to the interrelationships and a historical survey into which these selected segments fit. Nor have the selections been packaged according to the individual Joyce works, the assumption being that once we move out of the linear time frame in which the books arrived at certain junctures into the hands of their readers, *Dubliners, A Portrait, Ulysses,* and *Finnegans Wake* assume the consistency of a single literary entity, and the critical focus on one rather than all of them is forced by the necessity of concentration and a workable field of inquiry. The essays stand on their own merits, are exempla of hundreds of other essays with which they form an amalgam, and interlock into a multivarious critical configuration. We have reached an age in Joyce commentary when it is no more possible to reproduce anything more than a highly selective sampler of Joyce criticism than it is to affix a bibliography of Joyce studies to a volume of essays, since any such bibliography requires a book publication of its own.

BERNARD BENSTOCK

University of Tulsa

EARLY ASSESSMENTS

Dubliners and Mr James Joyce   Ezra Pound*

Freedom from sloppiness is so rare in contemporary English prose that one might well say simply, 'Mr Joyce's book of short stories is prose free from sloppiness,' and leave the intelligent reader ready to run from his study, immediately to spend three and sixpence on the volume.[1]

Unfortunately one's credit as a critic is insufficient to produce this result.

The readers of *The Egoist*, having had Mr Joyce under their eyes for some months, will scarcely need to have his qualities pointed out to them. Both they and the paper have been very fortunate in his collaboration.

Mr Joyce writes a clear hard prose. He deals with subjective things, but he presents them with such clarity of outline that he might be dealing with locomotives or with builders' specifications. For that reason one can read Mr Joyce without feeling that one is conferring a favour. I must put this thing my own way. I know about 168 authors. About once a year I read something contemporary without feeling that I am softening the path for poor Jones or poor Fulano de Tal.

I can lay down a good piece of French writing and pick up a piece of writing by Mr Joyce without feeling as if my head were being stuffed through a cushion. There are still impressionists about and I dare say they claim Mr Joyce. I admire impressionist writers. English prose writers who haven't got as far as impressionism (that is to say, 95 per cent of English writers of prose and verse) are a bore.

Impressionism has, however, two meanings, or perhaps I had better say, the word "impressionism" gives two different "impressions."

There is a school of prose writers, and of verse writers for that matter, whose forerunner was Stendhal and whose founder was Flaubert. The followers of Flaubert deal in exact presentation. They are often so intent on exact presentation that they neglect intensity, selection, and

*This review of *Dubliners* first appeared in the *Egoist*, 1, No. 14 (15 June 1914).

concentration. They are perhaps the most clarifying and they have been perhaps the most beneficial force in modern writing.

There is another set, mostly of verse writers, who founded themselves not upon anybody's writing but upon the pictures of Monet. Every movement in painting picks up a few writers who try to imitate in words what someone has done in paint. Thus one writer saw a picture by Monet and talked of "pink pigs blossoming on a hillside," and a later writer talked of 'slate-blue' hair and "raspberry-coloured flanks."

These "impressionists" who write in imitation of Monet's softness instead of writing in imitation of Flaubert's definiteness, are a bore, a grimy, or perhaps I should say, a rosy, floribund bore.

The spirit of a decade strikes properly upon all of the arts. There are "parallel movements." Their causes and their effects may not seem, superficially, similar.

This mimicking of painting ten or twenty years late, is not in the least the same as the "literary movement" parallel to the painting movement imitated.

The force that leads a poet to leave out a moral reflection may lead a painter to leave out representation. The resultant poem may not suggest the resultant painting.

Mr Joyce's merit, I will not say his chief merit but his most engaging merit, is that he carefully avoids telling you a lot that you don't want to know. He presents his people swiftly and vividly, he does not sentimentalize over them, he does not weave convolutions. He is a realist. He does not believe "life" would be all right if we stopped vivisection or if we instituted a new sort of "economics." He gives the thing as it is. He is not bound by the tiresome convention that any part of life, to be interesting, must be shaped into the conventional form of a "story." Since De Maupassant we have had so many people trying to write "stories" and so few people presenting life. Life for the most part does not happen in neat little diagrams and nothing is more tiresome than the continual pretence that it does.

Mr Joyce's *Araby*, for instance, is much better than a "story," it is a vivid waiting.

It is surprising that Mr Joyce is Irish. One is so tired of the Irish or "Celtic" imagination (or "phantasy" as I think they now call it) flopping about. Mr Joyce does not flop about. He defines. He is not an institution for the promotion of Irish peasant industries. He accepts an international standard of prose writing and lives up to it.

He gives us Dublin as it presumably is. He does not descend to farce. He does not rely upon Dickensian caricature. He gives us things as they are, not only for Dublin, but for every city. Erase the local names and a few specifically local allusions, and a few historic events of the past, and substitute a few different local names, allusions and events, and these stories could be retold of any town.

That is to say, the author is quite capable of dealing with things about him, and dealing directly, yet these details do not engross him, he is capable of getting at the universal element beneath them.

The main situations of *Madame Bovary* or of *Doña Perfecta* do not depend on local colour or upon local detail, that is their strength. Good writing, good presentation can be specifically local, but it must not depend on locality. Mr Joyce does not present "types" but individuals. I mean he deals with common emotions which run through all races. He does not bank on "Irish character." Roughly speaking, Irish literature has gone through three phases in our time, the shamrock period, the dove-grey period, and the Kiltartan period. I think there is a new phase in the works of Mr Joyce. He writes as a contemporary of continental writers. I do not mean that he writes as a faddist, mad for the last note, he does not imitate Strindberg, for instance, or Bang. He is not ploughing the underworld for horror. He is not presenting a macabre subjectivity. He is classic in that he deals with normal things and with normal people. A committee room, Little Chandler, a nonentity, a boarding house full of clerks—these are his subjects and he treats them all in such a manner that they are worthy subjects of art.

Francis Jammes, Charles Vildrac and D. H. Lawrence have written short narratives in verse, trying, it would seem, to present situations as clearly as prose writers have done, yet more briefly. Mr Joyce is engaged in a similar condensation. He has kept to prose, not needing the privilege supposedly accorded to verse to justify his method.

I think that he excels most of the impressionist writers because of his more rigorous selection, because of his exclusion of all unnecessary detail.

There is a very clear demarcation between unnecessary detail and irrelevant detail. An impressionist friend of mine talks to me a good deal about "preparing effects," and on that score he justifies much unnecessary detail, which is not "irrelevant," but which ends by being wearisome and by putting one out of conceit with his narrative.

Mr Joyce's more rigorous selection of the presented detail marks him, I think, as belonging to my own generation, that is, to the "nineteen-tens," not to the decade between "the nineties" and to-day.

At any rate these stories and the novel now appearing in serial form are such as to win for Mr Joyce a very definite place among English contemporary prose writers, not merely a place in the "Novels of the Week" column, and our writers of good clear prose are so few that we cannot afford to confuse or to overlook them.

Note

1. *Dubliners*, by James Joyce, Grant Richards.

James Joyce   H. G. Wells*

An eminent novelist was asked recently by some troublesome newspaper what he thought of the literature of 1916. He answered publicly and loudly that he had heard of no literature in 1916; for his own part he had been reading "science." This was kind neither to our literary nor our scientific activities. It was not intelligent to make an opposition between literature and science. It is no more legitimate than an opposition between literature and "classics" or between literature and history. Good writing about the actualities of the war too has been abundant, that was only to be expected; it is an ungracious thing in the home critic to sit at a confused feast and bewail its poverty when he ought to be sorting out his discoveries. Criticism may analyze, it may appraise and attack, but when it comes to the mere grumbling of veterans no longer capable of novel perceptions, away with it! There is indeed small justification for grumbling at the writing of the present time. Quite apart from the books and stories about the war, a brilliant literature in itself, from that artless assured immortal Arthur Green (the Story of a Prisoner of War) up to the already active historians, there is a great amount of fresh and experimental writing that cannot be ignored by anyone still alive to literary interests. There are, for instance, Miss Richardson's Pointed Roofs, and Backwater, amusing experiments to write as the Futurists paint, and Mr. Caradoc Evan's invention in My People, and Capel Sion, of a new method of grimness, a pseudo-Welsh idiom that is as pleasing in its grotesque force to the intelligent story-reader as it must be maddening to every sensitive Welsh patriot. Nowhere have I seen anything like adequate praise for the romantic force and beauty of Mr. Thomas Burke's Limehouse Nights. In the earlier 'nineties when Henley was alive and discovering was in fashion that book would have made a very big reputation indeed. Even more considerable is A Portrait of the Artist as a Young Man, by James Joyce. It is a book to buy and read and lock up, but it is not a book to miss. Its claim to be literature is as good as the claim of the last book of Gulliver's Travels.

It is no good trying to minimize a characteristic that seems to be deliberately obtruded. Like Swift and another living Irish writer, Mr. Joyce has a cloacal obsession. He would bring back into the general picture of life aspects which modern drainage and modern decorum have taken out of ordinary intercourse and conversation. Coarse, unfamiliar words are scattered about the book unpleasantly, and it may seem to many, needlessly. If the reader is squeamish upon these matters, then there is nothing for it but to shun this book, but if he will pick his way, as one has to do at times on the outskirts of some picturesque

*This review of A Portrait of the Artist as a Young Man appeared in the New Republic, 10 (March 1917).

Italian village with a view and a church and all sorts of things of that sort to tempt one, then it is quite worth while. And even upon this unsavory aspect of Swift and himself, Mr. Joyce is suddenly illuminating. He tells at several points how his hero Stephen is swayed and shocked and disgusted by harsh and loud *sounds*, and how he is stirred to intense emotion by music and the rhythms of beautiful words. But no sort of smell offends him like that. He finds olfactory sensations interesting or aesthetically displeasing, but they do not make him sick or excited as sounds do. This is a quite understandable turn over from the more normal state of affairs. Long ago I remember pointing out in a review the difference in the sensory basis of the stories of Robert Louis Stevenson and Sir J. M. Barrie; the former visualized and saw his story primarily as picture, the latter mainly heard it. We shall do Mr. Joyce an injustice if we attribute a normal sensory basis to him and then accuse him of deliberate offense.

But that is by the way. The value of Mr. Joyce's book has little to do with its incidental insanitary condition. Like some of the best novels in the world it is the story of an education; it is by far the most living and convincing picture that exists of an Irish Catholic upbringing. It is a mosaic of jagged fragments that does altogether render with extreme completeness the growth of a rather secretive, imaginative boy in Dublin. The technique is startling, but on the whole it succeeds. Like so many Irish writers from Sterne to Shaw Mr. Joyce is a bold experimentalist with paragraph and punctuation. He breaks away from scene to scene without a hint of the change of time and place; at the end he passes suddenly from the third person to the first; he uses no inverted commas to mark off his speeches. The first trick I found sometimes tiresome here and there, but then my own disposition, perhaps acquired at the blackboard, is to mark off and underline rather fussily, and I do not know whether I was so much put off the thing myself as anxious, which after all is not my business, about its effect on those others; the second trick, I will admit, seems entirely justified in this particular instance by its success; the third reduces Mr. Joyce to a free use of dashes. One conversation in this book is a superb success, the one in which Mr. Dedalus carves the Christmas turkey; I write with all due deliberation that Sterne himself could not have done it better; but most of the talk flickers blindingly with these dashes, one has the same wincing feeling of being flicked at that one used to have in the early cinema shows. I think Mr. Joyce has failed to discredit the inverted comma.

The interest of the book depends entirely upon its quintessential and unfailing reality. One believes in Stephen Dedalus as one believes in few characters in fiction. And the peculiar lie of the interest for the intelligent reader is the convincing revelation it makes of the limitations of a great mass of Irishmen. Mr. Joyce tells us unsparingly of the adolescence of this youngster under conditions that have passed almost altogether out of English life. There is an immense shyness, a profound secrecy, about matters of sex, with its inevitable accompaniment of nightmare revelations and furtive scribblings in unpleasant places, and there is a living belief in a real hell. The description of Stephen listening without a doubt to two fiery sermons on that tremendous theme, his agonies of fear, not disgust at dirtiness such as unorthodox children feel but just fear, his terror-inspired confession of his sins of impurity to a strange priest in a distant part of the city, is like nothing in any boy's experience who has been trained under modern conditions. Compare its stuffy horror with Conrad's account of how under analogous circumstances Lord Jim wept. And a second thing of immense significance is the fact that everyone in this Dublin story, every human being, accepts as a matter of course, as a thing in nature like the sky and the sea, that the English are to be hated. There is no discrimination in the hatred, there is no gleam of recognition that a considerable number of Englishmen have displayed a very earnest disposition to put matters right with Ireland, there is an absolute absence of any idea of a discussed settlement, any notion of helping the slow-witted Englishman in his three-cornered puzzle between North and South. It is just hate, a cant cultivated to the pitch of monomania, an ungenerous violent direction of the mind. That is the political atmosphere in which Stephen Dedalus grows up, and in which his essentially responsive mind orients itself. I am afraid it is only too true an account of the atmosphere in which a number of brilliant young Irishmen have grown up. What is the good of pretending that the extreme Irish "patriot" is an equivalent and parallel of the English or American liberal? He is narrower and intenser than any English Tory. He will be the natural ally of the Tory in delaying British social and economic reconstruction after the war. He will play into the hands of the Tories by threatening an outbreak and providing the excuse for a militarist reaction in England. It is time the American observer faced the truth of that. No reason is that why England should not do justice to Ireland, but excellent reason for bearing in mind that these bright-green young people across the Channel are something quite different from the liberal English in training and tradition, and absolutely set against helping them. No single book has ever shown how different they are, as completely as this most memorable novel.

Ulysses, Order, and Myth   T. S. Eliot*

Mr. Joyce's book has been out long enough for no more general expression of praise, or expostulation with its detractors, to be necessary; and it has not been out long enough for any attempt at a complete measurement of its place and significance to be possible. All that one can usefully do at this time, and it is a great deal to do, for such a book, is to elucidate any aspect of the book—and the number of aspects is indefinite—which has not yet been fixed. I hold this book to be the most important expression which the present age has found; it is a book to which we are all indebted, and from which none of us can escape. These are postulates for anything that I have to say about it, and I have no wish to waste the reader's time by elaborating my eulogies; it has given me all the surprise, delight, and terror that I can require, and I will leave it at that.

Among all the criticisms I have seen of the book, I have seen nothing—unless we except, in its way, M. Valéry Larbaud's valuable paper which is rather an Introduction than a criticism—which seemed to me to appreciate the significance of the method employed—the parallel to the *Odyssey*, and the use of appropriate styles and symbols to each division. Yet one might expect this to be the first peculiarity to attract attention; but it has been treated as an amusing dodge, or scaffolding erected by the author for the purpose of disposing his realistic tale, of no interest in the completed structure. The criticism which Mr. Aldington directed upon *Ulysses* several years ago seems to me to fail by this oversight—but, as Mr. Aldington wrote before the complete work had appeared, fails more honorably than the attempts of those who had the whole book before them. Mr. Aldington treated Mr. Joyce as a prophet of chaos; and wailed at the flood of Dadaism which his prescient eye saw bursting forth at the tap of the magician's rod. Of course, the influence which Mr. Joyce's book may have is from my point of view an irrelevance. A very great book may have a very bad influence indeed; and a mediocre book may be in the event most salutary. The next generation is responsible for its own soul; a man of genius is responsible to his peers, not to a studio full of uneducated and undisciplined coxcombs. Still, Mr. Aldington's pathetic solicitude for the half-witted seems to me to carry certain implications about the nature of the book itself to which I cannot assent; and this is the important issue. He finds the book, if I understand him, to be an invitation to chaos, and an expression of feelings which are perverse, partial, and a distortion of reality. But unless I quote Mr. Aldington's words I am likely to falsify. "I say, moreover," he says,[1] "that when Mr. Joyce, with his marvellous gifts, uses them to

*This essay first appeared in the *Dial*, 75 (Nov. 1923), and is reprinted with permission from Faber & Faber and Harcourt Brace Jovanovich.

disgust us with mankind, he is doing something which is false and a libel on humanity." It is somewhat similar to the opinion of the urbane Thackeray upon Swift. "As for the moral, I think it horrible, shameful, unmanly, blasphemous: and giant and great as this Dean is, I say we should hoot him." (This, of the conclusion of the Voyage to the Houyhn- hnms—which seems to me one of the greatest triumphs that the human soul has ever achieved.—It is true that Thackeray later pays Swift one of the finest tributes that a man has ever given or received: "So great a man he seems to me that thinking of him is like thinking of an empire falling." And Mr. Aldington, in his time, is almost equally generous.)

Whether it is possible to libel humanity (in distinction to libel in the usual sense, which is libeling an individual or a group in contrast with the rest of humanity) is a question for philosophical societies to discuss; but of course if *Ulysses* were a "libel" it would simply be a forged document, a powerless fraud, which would never have extracted from Mr. Aldington a moment's attention. I do not wish to linger over this point: the interesting question is that begged by Mr. Aldington when he refers to Mr. Joyce's "great *undisciplined* talent."

I think that Mr. Aldington and I are more or less agreed as to what we want in principle, and agreed to call it classicism. It is because of this agreement that I have chosen Mr. Aldington to attack on the pres- ent issue. We are agreed as to what we want, but not as to how to get it, or as to what contemporary writing exhibits a tendency in that direc- tion. We agree, I hope, that "classicism" is not an alternative to "ro- manticism," as of political parties, Conservative and Liberal, Republican and Democrat, on a "turn-the-rascals-out" platform. It is a goal toward which all good literature strives, so far as it is good, according to the possibilities of its place and time. One can be "classical," in a sense, by turning away from nine-tenths of the material which lies at hand and selecting only mummified stuff from a museum—like some contemporary writers, about whom one could say some nasty things in this connection, if it were worth while (Mr. Aldington is not one of them). Or one can be classical in tendency by doing the best one can with the material at hand. The confusion springs from the fact that the term is applied to literature and to the whole complex of interests and modes of behavior and society of which literature is a part; and it has not the same bearing in both applications. It is much easier to be a classicist in literary criti- cism than in creative art—because in criticism you are responsible only for what you want, and in creation you are responsible for what you can do with material which you must simply accept. And in this material I include the emotions and feelings of the writer himself, which, for that writer, are simply material which he must accept—not virtues to be enlarged or vices to be diminished. The question, then, about Mr. Joyce, is: how much living material does he deal with, and how does he deal with it: deal with, not as a legislator or exhorter, but as an artist?

It is here that Mr. Joyce's parallel use of the *Odyssey* has a great importance. It has the importance of a scientific discovery. No one else has built a novel upon such a foundation before: it has never before been necessary. I am not begging the question in calling *Ulysses* a "novel"; and if you call it an epic it will not matter. If it is not a novel, that is simply because the novel is a form which will no longer serve; it is because the novel, instead of being a form, was simply the expression of an age which had not sufficiently lost all form to feel the need of something stricter. Mr. Joyce has written one novel—the *Portrait*; Mr. Wyndham Lewis has written one novel—*Tarr*. I do not suppose that either of them will ever write another "novel." The novel ended with Flaubert and with James. It is, I think, because Mr. Joyce and Mr. Lewis, being "in advance" of their time, felt a conscious or probably unconscious dissatisfaction with the form, that their novels are more formless than those of a dozen clever writers who are unaware of its obsolescence.

In using the myth, in manipulating a continuous parallel between contemporaneity and antiquity, Mr. Joyce is pursuing a method which others must pursue after him. They will not be imitators, any more than the scientist who uses the discoveries of an Einstein in pursuing his own, independent, further investigations. It is simply a way of controlling, of ordering, of giving a shape and a significance to the immense panorama of futility and anarchy which is contemporary history. It is a method already adumbrated by Mr. Yeats, and of the need for which I believe Mr. Yeats to have been the first contemporary to be conscious. It is a method for which the horoscope is auspicious. Psychology (such as it is, and whether our reaction to it be comic or serious), ethnology, and *The Golden Bough* have concurred to make possible what was impossible even a few years ago. Instead of narrative method, we may now use the mythical method. It is, I seriously believe, a step toward making the modern world possible for art, toward that order and form which Mr. Aldington so earnestly desires. And only those who have won their own discipline in secret and without aid, in a world which offers very little assistance to that end, can be of any use in furthering this advance.

Note

1. *English Review*, April, 1921.

The Dream of H. C. Earwicker
Edmund Wilson*

James Joyce's *Ulysses* was an attempt to present directly the thoughts and feelings of a group of Dubliners through the whole course of a summer day. *Finnegans Wake* is a complementary attempt to render the dream fantasies and the half-unconscious sensations experienced by a single person in the course of a night's sleep.

This presents a more difficult problem to the reader as well as to the writer. In *Ulysses*, the reader was allowed to perceive the real objective world in which the Blooms and Dedalus lived, and their situation and relationships in that world, so that its distortions or liquefactions under the stress of special psychological states still usually remained intelligible. But in *Finnegans Wake* we are not supplied with any objective data until the next to the last chapter, when the hero— and then only rather dimly—wakes up for a short time toward morning; and we are dealing with states of consciousness which, though they sometimes have something in common with the drunken imaginations of the Night Town scene in *Ulysses* or the free associations of Mrs. Bloom's insomniac reveries, are even more confused and fluid than these; so that it becomes on a first reading the reader's prime preoccupation to puzzle out who the dreamer is and what has been happening to him. And since Joyce has spent seventeen years elaborating and complicating this puzzle, it is hardly to be expected that one reading will suffice to unravel it completely.

Let me try to establish, however, some of the most important facts which provide the realistic foundation for this immense poem of sleep. The hero of *Finnegans Wake* is a man of Scandinavian blood, with what is apparently an adapted Scandinavian name: Humphrey Chimpden Earwicker, who keeps a pub called The Bristol in Dublin. He is somewhere between fifty and sixty, blond and ruddy, with a walrus mustache, very strong but of late years pretty fat. When embarrassed, he has a tendency to stutter. He has tried his hand at a number of occupations; has run for office and has gone through a bankruptcy. He is married to a woman named Ann, a former salesgirl, who is more or less illiterate and whose maiden name seems to have begun with Mac. They are both Protestants in a community of Catholics, he an Episcopalian and she a Presbyterian; and by reason both of his religion and of his queer-sounding foreign name, he feels himself, like Bloom in *Ulysses*, something of an alien among his neighbors. The Earwickers have three children—a girl named Isobel, who has evidently passed adolescence,

*This review of *Finnegans Wake* first appeared in the *New Republic*, 99 (28 June 1939 and 12 July 1939) and is reprinted with permission from Farrar, Straus & Giroux.

and two younger boys, twins: Kevin and Jerry. There are also a maid-of-all-work called Kate and a man about the place called Tom.

It is a Saturday night in summer, after a disorderly evening in the pub. Somebody—probably Earwicker himself—has been prevailed upon to sing a song: later, when it was closing time, he had to put a man outside, who abused him and threw stones at the window. There has also been a thunderstorm. Earwicker has been drinking off and on all day and has perhaps gone to bed a little drunk. At any rate, his night is troubled. At first he dreams about the day before, with a bad conscience and a sense of humiliation: then, as the night darkens and he sinks more deeply into sleep, he has to labor through a nightmare oppression.

He and his wife are sleeping together; but he has no longer any interest in her as a woman. He is preoccupied now with his children. His wife is apparently much younger than he, was only a girl when he married her; so that it is easy for him to confuse his first feelings for her with something like an erotic emotion which is now being aroused by his daughter. And his affection for his favorite son is even acquiring homosexual associations. Little Kevin is relatively sedate: named after the ascetic St. Kevin, he may be destined for the Catholic priesthood. Jerry (Shem) is more volatile and has given evidences of a taste for writing; and it is Jerry rather than Kevin (Shaun) with whom the father has tended to identify himself.

To tell the story in this way, however, is to present it the wrong way around. It depends for its dramatic effect on our not finding out till almost the end—pages 555-90, in which Earwicker partially wakes up—that the flights of erotic fantasy and the horrors of guilt of his dream have been inspired by his feelings for his children. The pub is on the edge of the Phoenix Park, between it and the River Liffey and not far from the suburb of Chapelizod, which is said to have been the birthplace of Iseult. At the very beginning of the dream, we find Earwicker figuring as Tristram; and through the whole night he is wooing Iseult; he carries her off, he marries her. The Freudian censor has intervened to change *Isobel* into *Iseult la Belle*—as well as to turn the ana (upper)–Liffey, which figures in the dream as a woman, into *Anna Livia Plurabelle*. The idea of incest between father and daughter is developed on page 115; the transition from Isobel to Iseult is indicated in the "Icy-la-Belle" of page 246; and the sister of the twins is designated by her family nickname "Izzy" on page 431. But, though the boys have been given their real names and planted pretty clearly—on pages 26-27—it is not until almost the end—on page 556—that a definite identification of Earwicker's daughter with Iseult is made. In the same way, it is not until the passage on pages 564-65 that we are led to connect with Earwicker's son the homosexual motif which has first broken into his dream with the ominous incident of the father's accosting a soldier in the park and subsequently being razzed by the police, and which works free toward morning—page 474—to the idea, not related to actuality, of "some chubby boybold love of an angel."

In the meantime, the incest taboo and the homosexuality taboo have together—as in the development of Greek tragedy out of the old myths of cannibalism and incest—given rise, during Earwicker's effortful night, to a whole mythology, a whole morality. He is Tristram stealing Iseult, yes; but—at the suggestion of an Adam's mantelpiece in the bedroom where he is sleeping—he is also Adam, who has forfeited by his sin the Paradise of the Phoenix Park; at the suggestion of a copy of Raphael's picture of Michael subduing Satan which hangs on the bedroom wall, he is an archangel wrestling with the Devil. And he has fallen not merely as Adam but also as Humpty Dumpty (he is fat and his first name is Humphrey); as the hero of the ballad of *Finnegan's Wake*, who fell off a scaffold while building a house (but came to life again at the sound of the word 'Whisky'); and as Napoleon (an obelisk dedicated to Wellington is a feature of the Phoenix Park, though there is apparently no Wellington Museum). Since the landmarks of the life of Swift still keep their prestige in Dublin, he is Swift, who loved Stella and Vanessa with the obstructed love of a father and whose mind was finally blotted by madness: Swift's cryptic name for Stella, "Ppt," punctuates the whole book.

And Earwicker is also making up in sleep for an habitual feeling of helplessness due to his belonging to a racial and religious minority. He is sometimes the first Danish conqueror of Ireland, who sailed up that very Liffey; sometimes Oliver Cromwell, that other hated heathen invader.

But it is Joyce's further aim to create, through Earwicker's mythopœic dream, a set of symbols even more general and basic. He has had the idea of making Earwicker, resolved into his elemental components, include the whole of humanity. The river, with its feminine personality, Anna Livia Plurabelle, comes to represent the feminine principle itself. At one time or another all the women who figure in Earwicker's fantasy are merged into this stream of life which, always renewed, never pausing, flows through the world built by men. The daughter, still a little girl, is early identified with a cloud, which will come down to earth as rain and turn into the rapid young river; the Anna Livia Plurabelle chapter describes a lively woman's coming-of-age; in the end, the mature river, broader and slower now, will move toward her father, the sea. The corresponding masculine principle is symbolized by the Hill of Howth, which rises at the mouth of the Liffey; and the idea of the hill as a citadel and the idea of the city as a male construction associate themselves with this: the man is a hill that stands firm while the river runs away at his feet; he is a fortress, he is Dublin, he is all the cities of the world.

And if Earwicker is animated in sleep by the principles of both the sexes, he has also a double existence in the rôles of both Youth and Old Age. Canalizing his youthful impulses in a vision of himself as his favorite son, he dreams himself endowed with a resilience to go out and try life again; exalted by a purity of idealism which has not yet been tainted by experience, and yet bubbling with roguish drolleries, blithely beloved by the girls. On the other hand, foreshadowing his own decline, he sees the vision of a chorus of old men, who, drivelingly reminiscent, at the same time gloat and scold at the thought of the vigorous young Tristram kissing Iseult on the other side of the bushes, and exclaim in admiration—an expansion of Earwicker's feelings at the sight of his own sleeping son—over the form of the sleeping Earwicker (Shaun-Jerry). The old men are named Matthew Gregory, Marcus Lyons, Luke Tarpey and Johnny MacDougall; and they are identified variously with the four apostles, the Four Masters (early sages of Irish legend), the Four Waves of Irish mythology, the four courts of Dublin, and the four provinces of Ireland (Johnny MacDougall is evidently Ulster: he always follows at some distance behind the others). These fathers are always associated with a gray ass and sycamore trees, and have perhaps been suggested to Earwicker by four sycamore trees on the Liffey, among which a neighbor's donkey has been grazing. All of these major motifs are woven in and out from beginning to end of the book, and each at a given point receives a complete development: the woman-river in pages 196–216—the well-known Anna Livia Plurabelle chapter; the male city-fortress-hill in pages 532–54 (already published separately as *Haveth Childers Everywhere*); the Young Man in the chapters about Shaun, pages 403–73; and the Old Men, providing a contrast, just before, in 383–99.

There are also a stone and an elm on opposite sides of the Liffey, which represent the death principle and the life principle (Ygdrasil). The tree has several graciously rustling solos (a notable one at the end, beginning on page 619), and in the Anna Livia Plurabelle chapter she has a long conversation with the stone, which blends with the gossip of two old washerwomen drying clothes on the riverbank. This dialogue is only one of many dialogues which are really always the same disputation, and in which one of the parties, like the stone, is always hard-boiled, immobile and prosaic, while the other is sensitive, alive, rather light-mindedly chattering or chirping. The tougher of the two parties in these interchanges is always browbeating or bullying the other. Sometimes they are Satan and Saint Michael; sometimes they are transmogrified antitheses derived from Aesop's fables: the Mookse and the Gripes (the Fox and the Grapes), the Ondt and the Gracehoper (the Ant and the Grasshopper); but all these dualisms are evidently connected with the diverse temperaments of Earwicker's twins (who sometimes appear as Cain and Abel), and represent the diverse elements in the character of Earwicker himself, as these struggle within his own consciousness, the aggressive side sometimes reflecting certain powers in the external world—the force of hostile opinion or the police—which he now fears, now feels he can stand up to. The various pairs, however, shift their balance and melt into one another so readily that it is impossible to give any account of them which will cover all the cases in the book.

Besides all this, just as Joyce in *Ulysses* laid the *Odyssey* under requisition to help provide a structure for his material—material which, once it had begun to gush from the rock of Joyce's sealed personality at the blow of the Aaron's rod of free association, threatened to rise and submerge the artist like the flood which the sorcerer's apprentice let loose by his bedeviled broom; so in the face of an even more formidable danger, he has here brought in the historical theory of the eighteenth-century philosopher, Giambattista Vico, to help him to organize *Finnegans Wake*. It was Vico's idea that civilizations always pass through three definite phases: a phase when people imagine gods, a phase when they make up myths about heroes, and a phase when they see things in terms of real men. It will be noted that the figures mentioned above divide themselves among these three categories of beings. Vico further believed that history moved in cycles and that it was always repeating itself, which—to the frequent exasperation of the reader—*Finnegans Wake* is also made to do. And there is also a good deal more out of Vico, which you can find out about in *Our Exagmination*[1] but which seems even more idle and forced than the most forced and idle aspects of the Odysseyan parallel in *Ulysses*. The fact that there is a Vico Road in the Dublin suburb Dalkey—"The Vico Road goes round and round to meet where terms begin"—gives Joyce a peg in actuality on which to hang all this theory.

There is one important respect in which Joyce may seem to depart from Vico. Vico, so far as is known, did not believe in progress: his cycles did not spiral toward an earthly goal; his hope for salvation was in heaven. But the cycles of *Finnegans Wake* do result in a definite progression. As Earwicker lives through from darkness to light, he does slough off his feeling of guilt. By morning the Devil has been vanquished by Michael; Youth has bounded free of Age; the Phoenix of Vico and the Phoenix Park has risen from its ashes to new flight; Tristram has built a castle (Howth Castle) for his bride; and Iseult, once the object of an outlawed love, now married and growing older, turns naturally and comfortably at last into the lawful wife in the bed beside him, whom Earwicker is making an effort not to jab with his knees; the tumult and turbidity of Saturday night run clear in the peace of Sunday morning; the soul, which has been buried in sleep, is resurrected, refreshed, to life.

Yet if one looks at the book as a whole, one finds that the larger cycle does return upon itself. This will be seen when I discuss the last pages. In the meantime, let me merely point out that we do not find in *Finnegans Wake* any climax of exaltation comparable either to the scene where Stephen Dedalus realizes his artist's vocation or to Molly Bloom's great affirmative. The later book represents an aging phase in the constant human subject with which the series of Joyce's books has dealt. This subject—which must never be lost sight of, though in this case it is easy to do so—is the nexus of intimate relationships involved in a family situation. We find it first in the *Portrait of an Artist* in the attitude of Dedalus toward his family, and in the delicate but vital displacement in the relations of the young married couple who figure in the short story called *The Dead*. In *Exiles*, another young married couple come back from abroad with a son, and a more serious displacement takes place when the wife meets an old lover. In *Ulyssess*, the relations of man and wife, by this time almost middle-aged, have been affected by more serious readjustments, and they are related in a complex way to the relations of the Blooms to their children, of Dedalus to his parents, and of both the Blooms to Dedalus. Now, in *Finnegans Wake*, the husband and wife have reached an age at which, from the emotional point of view, they seem hardly important to one another, and at which the chief source of interest is the attitude of the father toward the children— "the child we all love to place our hope in," as Earwicker thinks in the last moments before the rising sun wakes him up. (We have already had intimations of this relationship in the adoptively paternal instincts of Bloom toward the spiritually parentless Dedalus; in Joyce's little lyric poems, poignant to the point of anguish, that deal with his own children; and in the poem called *Ecce Puer*, in which the family cycle appears.)

Here this family situation has been explored more profoundly by Joyce than in any of his previous books. In sleep, the conventions and institutions with which we discipline and give shape to our lives are allowed partly to dissolve and evaporate, so as partly to set free the impulses of the common human plasm out of which human creatures are made; and then the sexual instincts of the man and the woman, the child's instinct and the parent's instinct, the masculine and feminine principles themselves, come into play in confusing ways, shadow forth disturbing relationships, which yet spring from the prime processes of life. *Finnegans Wake* carries even farther the kind of insight into such human relations which was already carried far in *Ulysses*; and it advances with an astounding stride the attempt to find the universally human in ordinary specialized experience which was implied in the earlier book by the Odysseyan parallel. Joyce will now try to build up inductively the whole of human history and myth from the impulses, conscious and dormant, the unrealized potentialities, of a single human being, who is to be a man even more obscure and even less well-endowed, even less civilized and aspiring, than was Leopold Bloom in *Ulysses.*

Finnegans Wake, in conception as well as in execution, is one of the boldest books ever written.

II

In order to get anything out of *Finnegans Wake,* you must grasp a queer literary convention. It has been said by T. S. Eliot that Joyce is the greatest master of language in English since Milton. Eliot has also pointed out that Milton is mainly a writer for the *ear.* Now Joyce through a large part of his adult life has been almost as blind as Milton; and he has ended, just as Milton did, by dealing principally in auditory sensations. There is as little visualization in *Finnegans Wake* as in *Samson Agonistes.* Our first criticism, therefore, is likely to be that nothing is *seen* in Earwicker's dream. It is, after all, not uncommon in dreams to have the illusion of seeing people and places as clearly as when we are awake; and in the dream literature with which we are already familiar—*Alice in Wonderland, The Temptation of Saint Anthony*—the dreamers are visited by plain apparitions, not merely by invisible voices. But we must assume with *Finnegans Wake* that Earwicker's imagination, like Joyce's, is almost entirely auditory and verbal. We have been partly prepared by *Ulysses,* in which we listen to the thoughts of the characters but do not see them very distinctly.

But there is another and more serious difficulty to be got over. We are continually being distracted from identifying and following Earwicker, the humble proprietor of a public house, who is to encompass the whole microcosm of the dream, by the intrusion of all sorts of elements—foreign languages, literary allusions, historical information—which could not possibly have been in Earwicker's mind. The principle on which Joyce is operating may evidently be stated as follows. If the artist is to render directly all the feelings and fancies of a sleeper, primitive, inarticulate, infinitely imprecise as they are, he must create a literary medium of unexampled richness and freedom. Now it is also Joyce's purpose in *Finnegans Wake* to bring out in Earwicker's consciousness the processes of universal history: the languages, the cycles of society, the typical relationships of legend, are, he is trying to show us, all implicit in every human being. He has, as I have indicated, been careful to hook up his hero realistically with the main themes of his universal fantasia: the Bible stories, the Battle of Waterloo, Tristram and Iseult, and so forth. But since Earwicker's implications *are* shown to be universal, the author has the right to summon all the resources of his superior knowledge in order to supply a vehicle which will carry this experience of sleep. He has the same sort of justification for making the beings in Earwicker's dream speak Russian in fighting the siege of Sebastopol (which has got in by way of a picture hanging in Earwicker's house) as Thomas Hardy has, for example, to describe in his own literary vocabulary a landscape seen by an ignorant person. If it is objected that in *Finnegans Wake* the author is supposed to be not *describing*, but presenting the hero's consciousness directly, Joyce might reply that his procedure had precedent not only in poetry, but also in pre-naturalistic fiction: even the characters of Dickens were allowed to make speeches in blank verse, even the characters of Meredith were allowed to converse in apothegms. Why shouldn't H. C. Earwicker be allowed to dream in a language which draws flexibility and variety from the author's enormous reservoir of colloquial and literary speech, of technical jargons and foreign tongues?

Yet here is where the reader's trouble begins, because here, in spite of the defense just suggested, a convention that seems indispensable has been disconcertingly violated. What Joyce is trying to do is to break out of the Flaubertian naturalism into something that moves more at ease and that commands a wider horizon, something that is not narrowly tied down to the data about a certain man living in a certain year on a certain street of a certain city; and the reaction is of course quite natural: it was inevitable that the symbol and the myth, the traditional material of poetry, should have asserted themselves again against the formulas of scientific precision which had begun to prove so cramping. But here the act of escaping from them shocks, just as it sometimes did in Proust. Proust argues in an impressive way, in the final section of his novel, the case against nineteenth-century naturalism; yet who has not been made uncomfortable at finding that Proust's personal manias have been allowed to affect the structure of his book: that a story which has been presented as happening to real people should not maintain a consistent chronology, that it should never be clear whether the narrator of the story is the same person as the author of the book, and that the author, who ought to know everything, should in some cases leave us in doubt as to the facts about his hero? One had felt, in reading *Ulysses*, a touch of the same uneasiness when the phantasmagoria imagined by Bloom in the drunken Night Town scene was enriched by learned fancies which would seem to be more appropriate to Dedalus. And now in *Finnegans Wake* the balloon of this new kind of poetry pulls harder at its naturalistic anchor. We are in the first place asked to believe that a man like H. C. Earwicker would seize every possible pretext provided by his house and its location to include in a single night's dream a large number of historical and legendary characters. And is it not pretty far-fetched to assume that Earwicker's awareness of the life of Swift or the Crimean War is really to be accurately conveyed in terms of the awareness of Joyce, who has acquired a special knowledge of these subjects? Also, what about the references to the literary life in Paris and to the book itself as Work in Progress, which takes us right out of the mind of Earwicker and into the mind of Joyce?

There are not, to be sure, very many such winks and nudges as this, though the shadow of Joyce at his thankless task seems sometimes to fall between Earwicker and us. Joyce has evidently set himself limits as to how far he can go in this direction; and he may urge that since Earwicker is universal man, he must contain the implications of Joyce's destiny as he does those of Swift's and Napoleon's, though he has never heard of him as he has of them, and that to give these implications a personal accent is only to sign his canvas. Yet, even granting all this and recognizing the difficulty of the task and accepting without reservation the method Joyce has chosen for his purpose, the result still seems unsatisfactory, the thing has not quite come out right. Instead of the myths' growing out of Earwicker, Earwicker seems swamped in the myths. His personality is certainly created: we get to know him and feel sympathy for him. But he is not so convincing as Bloom was: there has been too much literature poured into him. He has exfoliated into too many arabesques, become hypertrophied by too many elements. And not merely has he to carry this load of myths; he has also been all wound round by what seems Joyce's growing self-indulgence in an impulse to pure verbal play.

Here another kind of difficulty confronts us. There is actually a special kind of language which people speak in dreams and in which they sometimes even compose poetry. This language consists of words and sentences which, though they seem to be gibberish or nonsense from the rational point of view, betray by their telescopings of words, their combinations of incongruous ideas, the involuntary preoccupations of the sleeper. Lewis Carroll exploited this dream language in *Jabberwocky*, and it has been studied by Freud and his followers, from whom Joyce seems to have got the idea of its literary possibilities. At any rate, *Finnegans Wake* is almost entirely written in it.

The idea was brilliant in itself, and Joyce has in many cases carried it out brilliantly. He has created a whole new poetry, a whole new humor and pathos, of sentences and words that go wrong. The special kind of equivocal and prismatic effects aimed at by the symbolist poets have here been achieved by a new method and on psychological principles which give them a new basis in humanity. But the trouble is, it seems to me, that Joyce has somewhat overdone it. His method of giving words multiple meanings allows him to go on indefinitely introducing new ideas; and he has spent no less than seventeen years embroidering *Finnegans Wake* in this way.

What has happened may be shown by the following examples.

First, a relatively simple one from a passage about the Tree: "Amengst menlike trees walking or trees like angels weeping nobirdy aviar soar anywing to eagle it!" It is quite clear in the last seven words how an ornithological turn has been given to "nobody ever saw anything to equal it." Here is a more complex one: Earwicker, picturing himself in the chapter in which he partially wakes up, is made to designate his hair with the phrase "beer wig." This has as its basis *bar wig*, which has rushed into the breach as *beer wig* under the pressure of Earwicker's profession as a dispenser of drinks in his pub, of the fact that his hair is yellow, and of his tendency to imagine that his queer last name is being caricatured by his neighbors as "Earwigger"—a tendency which has led to his dream being impishly haunted by earwigs. There are thus four different ideas compressed in these two words. But let us examine—with the aid of the hints provided by the *Exagmination*—an even more complicated passage. Here is Earwicker-Joyce's depiction of the madness and eclipse of Swift: "Unslow, malswift, pro mean, proh noblesse, Atrahore, melancolores, nears; whose glauque eyes glitt bedimmed to imm; whose fingrings creep o'er skull: till quench., asterr mist calls estarr and graw, honath Jon raves homes glowcoma." This passage, besides the more or less obvious ones, contains apparently the following ideas: Laracor, Swift's living in Ireland, combined with the *atra cura, black care*, that rides behind the horseman in the first poem of Book Three of Horace's *Odes*; the Horatian idea that death comes to the mean and the noble alike; *proh*, the Latin interjection of regret, and *pro*, perhaps referring to Swift's championship of the impoverished Irish; *melancolores, melancholy* plus *black-colored; glauque*, French *gray-blue*, plus Greek *glaux, owl*—gray evening plus Swift's blue eyes, which also had an owlish appearance; in *glitt bedimmed to imm*, the doubled consonants evidently represent a deadening of the senses; *creep o'er skull*, French *crépuscule, twilight; asterr*, Greek *aster, star*, Swift's Stella, whose real name was Esther; Vanessa's real name was Hester—so Stella calls Hester a (q)wench; perhaps German *mist, dung, trash*, plays some part here, too—as well as German *starr, rigid; graw* evidently contains German *grau*, gray; *honath Jon* is *honest John* and *Jonathan; glowcoma* is *glaucoma*, a kind of blindness, plus the idea of a pale glow of life persisting in a coma. This passage has some beauty and power; but isn't it overingenious? Would anyone naturally think of Horace when he was confronted with "Atrahore"? And, even admitting that it may be appropriate to associate Latin with Swift, how does the German get in? Swift did not know German nor had he any German associations.[2]

In some cases, this overlaying of meanings has had the result of rendering quite opaque passages which at an earlier stage—as we can see by comparing the finished text with some of the sections as they first appeared—were no less convincingly dreamlike for being more easily comprehensible. You will find three versions of a passage in *Anna*

Livia Plurabelle on page 164 of the *Exagmination*; and on page 213 of the book you will see that Joyce has worked up still a fourth. My feeling is that he ought to have stopped somewhere between the second and the third. Here is Version 1 of 1925: "Look, look, the dusk is growing. What time is it? It must be late. It's ages now since I or anyone last saw Waterhouse's clock. They took it asunder, I heard them say. When will they reassemble it?" And here is Version 4 of 1939: "Look, look, the dusk is growing. My branches lofty are taking root. And my cold cher's gone ashley. Fieluhr? Filou! What age is at? It saon is late. 'Tis endless now senne eye or erewone last saw Waterhouse's clogh. They took it asunder, I hurd thum sigh. When will they reassemble it?" There is a gain in poetry, certainly; but in the meantime the question and the answer have almost disappeared. Has it really made Anna Livia any more riverlike to introduce the names of several hundred rivers (*saon* is *Saône* doing duty as *soon*, and *cher* is the *Cher* for French *chair*)—as he also introduces in other sections the names of cities, insects, trees? And why drag in *Erewhon*? In the same way, the talk of the Old Men, which, when it first came out in *Navire d'Argent*, seemed almost equal in beauty to the Anna Livia Plurabelle chapter, has now been so crammed with other things that the voices of the actual speakers have in places been nearly obliterated.

Joyce has always been rather deficient in dramatic and narrative sense. *Ulysses* already dragged; one got lost in it. The moments of critical importance were so run in with the rest that one was likely to miss them on first reading. One had to think about the book, read chapters of it over, in order to see the pattern and to realize how deep the insight went. And *Finnegans Wake* is much worse in this respect. The main outlines of the book are discernible, once we have been tipped off as to what it is all about. It is a help that, in forming our hypothesis, the principle of Occam's razor applies; for it is Joyce's whole design and point that the immense foaming-up of symbols should be reducible to a few simple facts. And it must also be conceded by a foreigner that a good deal which may appear to him mysterious would be plain enough to anyone who knew Dublin and something about Irish history, and that what Joyce has done here is as legitimate as it would be for an American writer to lay the scene of a similar fantasy somewhere on Riverside Drive in New York and to assume that his readers would be able to recognize Grant's Tomb, green buses, Columbia University and the figure of Hendrik Hudson. A foreign reader of *Finnegans Wake* should consult a map of Dublin, and look up the articles on Dublin and Ireland in the *Encyclopedia Britannica*.

Yet it seems to me a serious defect that we do not really understand what is happening till we have almost finished the book. *Then* we can look back and understand the significance of Earwicker's stuttering over the word *father* on page 45; we can see that "Peder the Greste, altipaltar" on page 344 combines, along with Peter the Great and *agreste, pederast* and *pater;* we can conclude that the allusion on page 373 about "begetting a wife which begame his niece by pouring her young-things into skintighs" refers back to the little story on pages 21–23, and that this whole theme is a device of the "dream-work" to get over the incest barrier by disguising Earwicker's own children as the children of a niece.

But in the meantime we have had to make our way through five hundred and fifty-four pages; and there is much that is evidently important that we still do not understand. How, for example, is the story of the "prankquean" just mentioned related to the motif of the letter scratched up by the chicken from the dump heap; and what is the point about this letter? The theme is developed at prodigious length in the chapter beginning on page 104; and it flickers all through the book. It turns up near the end—pages 623–24—with new emotional connotations. The idea of letters and postmen plays a prominent part all through. Little Kevin is represented as giving the postman's knock; and Earwicker—though he here seems to be identifying himself with the other son, Jerry—is caught up into a long flight of fantasy in which he imagines himself a postman. The letter comes from Boston, Massachusetts, and seems to have been written by some female relation, perhaps the niece mentioned above. One feels that there is a third woman in the story, and that something important depends on this. Yet a considerable amount of rereading has failed, in the case of the present writer, to clear the matter up.

Finnegans Wake, in the actual reading, seems to me for two thirds of its length not really to bring off what it attempts. Nor do I think it possible to defend the procedure of Joyce on the basis of an analogy with music. It is true that there is a good deal of the musician in Joyce: his phonograph record of *Anna Livia* is as beautiful as a fine tenor solo. But nobody would listen for half an hour to a composer of operas or symphonic poems who went on and on in one mood as monotonously as Joyce has done in parts of *Finnegans Wake,* who scrambled so many motifs in one passage, or who returned to picked up a theme a couple of hours after it had first been stated, when the listeners would inevitably have forgotten it.[3]

I believe that the miscarriage of *Finnegans Wake,* in so far as it does miscarry, is due primarily to two tendencies of Joyce's which were already in evidence in *Ulysses*: the impulse, in the absence of dramatic power, to work up an epic impressiveness by multiplying and complicating detail, by filling in abstract diagrams and laying on intellectual conceits, till the organic effort at which he aims has been spoiled by too much that is synthetic; and a curious shrinking solicitude to conceal from the reader his real subjects. These subjects are always awkward and distressing: they have to do with the kind of feelings which people themselves conceal and which it takes courage in the artist to handle. And the more daring Joyce's subjects become, the more he tends to swathe them about with the fancywork of his literary virtuosity. It is as if it were not merely Earwicker who was frightened by the state of his emotions but as if Joyce were embarrassed, too.

Yet, with all this, *Finnegans Wake* has achieved certain amazing successes. Joyce has caught the psychology of sleep as no one else has ever caught it, laying hold on states of mind which it is difficult for the waking intellect to re-create, and distinguishing with marvelous delicacy between the different levels of dormant consciousness. There are the relative vividness of events reflected from the day before; the nightmare viscidity and stammering of the heavy slumbers of midnight; the buoyance and self-assertive vitality which gradually emerge from this; the half-waking of the early morning, which lapses back into the rigmaroles of dreams; the awareness, later, of the light outside, with its effect as of the curtain of the eyelids standing between the mind and the day. Through all this, the falling of twilight, the striking of the hours by the clock, the morning fog and its clearing, the bell for early mass, and the rising sun at the window, make themselves felt by the sleeper. With what brilliance they are rendered by Joyce! And the voices that echo in Earwicker's dream—the beings that seize upon him and speak through him: the Tree and the River, the eloquence of Shaun, the mumbling and running-on of the Old Men; the fluttery girl sweetheart, the resigned elderly wife; the nagging and jeering gibberish—close to madness and recalling the apparition of Virag in the Walpurgisnacht scene of *Ulysses*, but here identified with the Devil—which comes like an incubus with the darkness and through which the thickened voices of the Earwicker household occasionally announce themselves startlingly: "Mawmaw, luk, your beeftay's fizzin' over" or "Now a muss wash the little face." Joyce has only to strike the rhythm and the timbre, and we know which of the spirits is with us.

Some of the episodes seem to me wholly successful: the Anna Livia chapter, for example, and at the end of *Haveth Childers Everywhere*, which has a splendor and a high-spirited movement of a kind not matched elsewhere in Joyce. The passage in a minor key which precedes this major *crescendo* and describes Earwicker's real habitations—"most respectable...thoroughly respectable...partly respectable," and so forth—is a masterpiece of humorous sordidity (especially "copious holes emitting mice"); and so is the inventory—on pages 183–84—of all the useless and rubbishy objects in the house where Shem the Penman lives. The *Ballad of Persse O'Reilly* (*perce-oreille*, earwig)—which blazons the shame of Earwicker—is real dream literature and terribly funny; as is also the revelation—pages 572–73—of the guilty and intricate sex relationships supposed to prevail in the Earwicker family, under the guise of one of those unintelligible summaries of a saint's legend or a

Latin play. The waking-up chapter is charming in the passage—page 565—in which the mother comforts the restless boy and in the summing-up—page 579—of the married life of the Earwickers; and it is touchingly and thrillingly effective in throwing back on all that has gone before the shy impoverished family pathos which it is Joyce's special destiny to express.

Where he is least happy, I think, is in such episodes as the voyage, 311 ff., the football game, 373 ff., and the siege of Sebastopol, 338 ff. (all in the dense nightmarish part of the book, which to me is, in general, the dullest). Joyce is best when he is idyllic, nostalgic, or going insane in an introspective way; he is not good at energetic action. There is never any direct aggressive clash between the pairs of opponents in Joyce, and there is consequently no real violence (except Dedalus' smashing the chandelier in self-defense against the reproach of his dead mother). All that Joyce is able to do when he wants to represent a battle is to concoct an uncouth gush of language. In general one feels, also, in *Finnegans Wake* the narrow limitations of Joyce's interests. He has tried to make it universal by having Earwicker take part in his dream in as many human activities as possible: but Joyce himself has not the key either to politics, to sport or to fighting. The departments of activity that come out best are such quiet ones as teaching and preaching.

The finest thing in the book, and one of the finest things Joyce has done, is the passage at the end where Ann, the wife, is for the first time allowed to speak with her full and mature voice. I have noted that Joyce's fiction usually deals with the tacit readjustment in the relationships between members of a family, the almost imperceptible moment which marks the beginning of a phase. In *Finnegans Wake*, the turning-point fixed is the moment when the husband and wife know definitely—they will wake up knowing it—that their own creative sexual partnership is over. That current no longer holds them polarized—as man and woman—toward one another; a new polarization takes place: the father is pulled back toward the children. "Illas! I wisht I had better glances," he thinks he hears Ann-Anna saying (page 626) "to peer to you through this baylight's growing. But you're changing, acoolsha, you're changing from me, I can feel. Or is it me is? I'm getting mixed. Brightening up and tightening down. Yes, you're changing, sonhusband, and you're turning, I can feel you, for a daughterwife from the hills again. Imlamaya. And she is coming. Swimming in my hindmoist. Diveltaking on me tail. Just a whisk brisk sly spry spink spank sprint of a thing theresomere, saultering. Saltarella come to her own. I pity your oldself I was used to. Now a younger's there." It is the "young thin pale soft shy slim slip of a thing, sauntering by silvamoonlake" (page 202 in the Anna Livia Plurabelle section) that she herself used to be, who now seems to her awkward and pert, and the wife herself is now the lower river running into the sea. The water is wider here; the pace of the stream is calmer: the broad day of experience has opened. "I thought you were all glittering with the noblest of carriage. You're only a bumpkin. I thought you the great in all things, in guilt and in glory. You're but a puny. Home!" She sees him clearly now: he is neither Sir Tristram nor Lucifer; and he is done with her and she with him. "I'm loothing them that's here and all I lothe. Loonely in me loneness. For all their faults. I am passing out. O bitter ending! I'll slip away before they're up. They'll never see me. Nor know. Nor miss me. And it's old and old it's sad and old it's sad and weary I go back to you, my cold father, my cold mad father, my cold mad feary father." . . . The helpless and heartbreaking voices of the Earwicker children recur: "Carry me along, taddy, like you done through the toy fair"—for now she is herself the child entrusting herself to the sea, flowing out into the daylight that is to be her annihilation . . ." "a way a lone at last a loved a long the". . . .

The Viconian cycle of existence has come full circle again. The unfinished sentence which ends the book is to find its continuation in the sentence without a beginning with which it opens. The river which runs into the sea must commence as a cloud again; the woman must give up life to the child. The Earwickers will wake to another day, but the night has made them older: the very release of the daylight brings a weariness that looks back to life's source.

In these wonderful closing pages, Joyce has put over all he means with poetry of an originality, a purity and an emotional power, such as to raise *Finnegans Wake*, for all its excesses, to the rank of a great work of literature.

Notes

1. *Our Exagmination Round His Factification for Incamination of Work in Progress*, published by New Directions at Norfolk, Connecticut. This is a collection of papers from *Transition*, the Paris magazine in which *Finnegans Wake* first appeared. The writers have taken their cues from Joyce himself, and he seems to have chosen this way of providing the public with a key. It is, in fact, rather doubtful whether without the work done by *Transition* it would be possible to get the hang of the book at all. See also Max Eastman's account of an interview with Joyce on the subject in Part III, Chapter III, of *The Literary Mind*.

2. I chose this passage because a partial exposition of it, which I take to be more or less authoritative, had appeared in the *Exagmination* (in the paper by Mr. Robert McAlmon). I did not remember to have read it in its place in *Finnegans Wake*, and was unable to find it when I looked for it. Since then I have been told by another reader who has been over and over the book that this sentence about Swift is not included. This is interesting because it indicates the operation of a principle of selection. Joyce suffered himself from glaucoma, and it may be that he eliminated the reference because he felt that it was too specifically personal.

3. This essay was written in the summer of 1939, just after *Finnegans Wake* came out, and I have reprinted it substantially as it first appeared. Since then an

article by Mr. John Peale Bishop in *The Southern Review* of summer 1939, and studies by Mr. Harry Levin in *The Kenyon Review* of Autumn, 1939, and in *New Directions* of 1939, have thrown further light on the subject; and I have also had the advantage of discussions with Mr. Thornton Wilder, who has explored the book more thoroughly than anyone else I have heard of. It is to be hoped that Mr. Wilder will some day publish about *Finnegans Wake*; and in the meantime those interested in the book should consult the essays mentioned, upon which I have sometimes drawn in revising the present study.

One suggestion of Mr. Bishop's should certainly be noted here. He believes that the riddle of the letter is the riddle of life itself. This letter has been scratched up from a dung-heap and yet it has come from another world; it includes in its very brief length marriage, children and death, and things to eat and drink—all the primary features of life, beyond which the ideas of the illiterate writer evidently do not extend; and Earwicker can never really read it, though the text seems exceedingly simple and though he confronts it again and again.

I ought to amend what I said in this essay on the basis of a first reading by adding that *Finnegans Wake*, like *Ulysses*, gets better the more you go back to it. I do not know of any other books of which it is true as it is of Joyce's that, though parts of them may leave us blank or repel us when we try them the first time, they gradually build themselves up for us as we return to them and think about them. That this should be true is due probably to some special defect of *rapport* between Joyce and the audience he is addressing, to some disease of his architectural faculty; but he compensates us partly for this by giving us more in the long run than we had realized at first was there, and he eventually produces the illusion that his fiction has a reality like life's, because, behind all the antics, the pedantry, the artificial patterns, something organic and independent of these is always revealing itself; and we end by recomposing a world in our mind as we do from the phenomena of experience. Mr. Max Eastman reports that Joyce once said to him, during a conversation on *Finnegans Wake*, when Mr. Eastman had suggested to Joyce that the demands made on the reader were too heavy and that he perhaps ought to provide a key: "The demand that I make of my reader is that he should devote his whole life to reading my works." It is in any case probably true that they will last you a whole lifetime.

COTERIE AND PIONEERS

Dante . . . Bruno. Vico . . Joyce　　　　　**Samuel Beckett***

The danger is in the neatness of identifications. The conception of Philosophy and Philology as a pair of nigger minstrels out of the Teatro dei Piccoli is soothing, like the contemplation of a carefully folded ham-sandwich. Giambattista Vico himself could not resist the attractiveness of such coincidence of gesture. He insisted on complete identification between the philosophical abstraction and the empirical illustration, thereby annulling the absolutism of each conception—hoisting the real unjustifiably clear of its dimensional limits, temporalising that which is extratemporal. And now here am I, with my handful of abstractions, among which notably: a mountain, the coincidence of contraries, the inevitability of cyclic evolution, a system of Poetics, and the prospect of self-extension in the world of Mr. Joyce's "Work in Progress." There is the temptation to treat every concept like "a bass dropt neck fust in till a bung crate," and make a really tidy job of it. Unfortunately such an exactitude of application would imply distortion in one of two directions. Must we wring the neck of a certain system in order to stuff it into a contemporary pigeon-hole, or modify the dimensions of that pigeon-hole for the satisfaction of the analogymongers? Literary criticism is not book-keeping.

. . . .

Giambattista Vico was a practical roundheaded Neapolitan. It pleases Croce to consider him as a mystic, essentially speculative *"disdegnoso dell' empirismo."* It is a surprising interpretation, seeing that more than three-fifths of his *Scienza Nuova* is concerned with empirical investigation. Croce opposes him to the reformative materialistic school of Ugo Grozio, and absolves him from the utilitarian preoccupations of Hobbes, Spinoza, Locke, Bayle and Machiavelli. All this cannot be swallowed without

*This essay first appeared in *Our Exagmination Round His Factification for Incamination of Work in Progress* (Paris: Shakespeare & Co., 1929), and is reprinted with permission of Grove Press, Inc.

protest. Vico defines Providence as: *"una mente spesso diversa ed alle volte tutta contraria e sempre superiore ad essi fini particolari che essi uomini si avevano proposti; dei quali fini ristretti fatti mezzi per servire a fini più ampi, gli ha sempre adoperati per conservare l'umana generazione in questa terra."* What could be more definitely utilitarianism? His treatment of the origin and functions of poetry, language and myth, as will appear later, is as far removed from the mystical as it is possible to imagine. For our immediate purpose, however, it matters little whether we consider him as a mystic or as a scientific investigator; but there are no two ways about considering him as an *innovator*. His division of the development of human society into three ages: Theocratic, Heroic, Human (civilized), with a corresponding classification of language: Hieroglyphic (sacred), Metaphorical (poetic), Philosophical (capable of abstraction and generalisation), was by no means new, although it must have appeared so to his contemporaries. He derived this convenient classification from the Egyptians, via Herodotus. At the same time it is impossible to deny the originality with which he applied and developed its implications. His exposition of the ineluctable circular progression of Society was completely new, although the germ of it was contained in Giordano Bruno's treatment of identified contraries. But it is in Book 2., described by himself as *"tutto il corpo . . . la chiave maestra . . . dell' opera,"* that appears the unqualified originality of his mind; here he evolved a theory of the origins of poetry and language, the significance of myth, and the nature of barbaric civilization that must have appeared nothing less than an impertinent outrage against tradition. These two aspects of Vico have their reverberations, their reapplications—without however, receiving the faintest explicit illustration—in *"Work in Progress."*

It is first necessary to condense the thesis of Vico, the scientific historian. In the beginning was the thunder: the thunder set free Religion, in its most objective and unphilosophical form—idolatrous animism: Religion produced Society, and the first social men were the cavedwellers, taking refuge from a passionate Nature: this primitive family life receives its first impulse towards development from the arrival of terrified vagabonds: admitted, they are the first slaves: growing stronger, they exact agrarian concessions, and a despotism has evolved into a primitive feudalism: the cave becomes a city, and the feudal system a democracy: then an anarchy: this is corrected by a return to a monarchy: the last stage is a tendency towards interdestruction: the nations are dispersed, and the Phoenix of Society arises out of their ashes. To this six-termed social progression corresponds a six-termed progression of human motives: necessity, utility, convenience, pleasure, luxury, abuse of luxury: and their incarnate manifestations: Polyphemus, Achilles, Caesar and Alexander, Tiberius, Caligula and Nero. At this point Vico applies Bruno—though he takes very good care not to say so—and proceeds from rather arbitrary data to philosophical abstraction. There is no difference, says Bruno, between the smallest possible chord and the smallest possible arc, no difference between the infinite circle and the straight line. The maxima and minima of particular contraries are one and indifferent. Minimal heat equals minimal cold. Consequently transmutations are circular. The principle (minimum) of one contrary takes its movement from the principle (maximum) of another. Therefore not only do the minima coincide with the minima, the maxima with the maxima, but the minima with the maxima in the succession of transmutations. Maximal speed is a state of rest. The maximum of corruption and the minimum of generation are identical: in principle, corruption is generation. And all things are ultimately identified with God, the universal monad, Monad of monads. From these considerations Vico evolved a Science and Philosophy of History. It may be an amusing exercise to take an historical figure, such as Scipio, and label him No. 3; it is of no ultimate importance. What is of ultimate importance is the recognition that the passage from Scipio to Caesar is as inevitable as the passage from Caesar to Tiberius, since the flowers of corruption in Scipio and Caesar are the seeds of vitality in Caesar and Tiberius. Thus we have the spectacle of a human progression that depends for its movement on individuals, and which at the same time is independent of individuals in virtue of what appears to be a preordained cyclicism. It follows that History is neither to be considered as a formless structure, due exclusively to the achievements of individual agents, nor as possessing reality apart from and independent of them, accomplished behind their backs in spite of them, the work of some superior force, variously known as Fate, Chance, Fortune, God. Both these views, the materialistic and the transcendental, Vico rejects in favour of the rational. Individuality is the concretion of universality, and every individual action is at the same time superindividual. The individual and the universal cannot be considered as distinct from each other. History, then, is not the result of Fate or Chance—in both cases the individual would be separated from his product—but the result of a Necessity that is not Fate, of a Liberty that is not Chance (compare Dante's "yoke of liberty"). This force he called Divine Providence, with his tongue, one feels, very much in his cheek. And it is to this Providence that we must trace the three institutions common to every society: Church, Marriage, Burial. This is not Bossuet's Providence, transcendental and miraculous, but immanent and the stuff itself of human life, working by natural means. Humanity is its work in itself. God acts on her, but by means of her. Humanity is divine, but no man is divine. This social and historical classification is clearly adapted by Mr. Joyce as a structural convenience—or inconvenience. His position is in no way a philosophical one. It is the detached attitude of Stephen Dedalus in "Portrait of the Artist..." who describes Epictetus to the Master of Studies as "an old gentleman who said that the soul is very like a bucketful of water." The lamp is more important than the lamp-lighter. By structural I do not only mean a bold outward division, a bare skeleton for the housing of material. I mean the endless substantial variations on these three beats, and interior intertwining of these three themes into a decoration of arabesques—decoration and more than decoration. Part I. is a mass of past shadow, corresponding therefore to Vico's first human institution, Religion, or to his Theocratic age, or simply to an abstraction—Birth. Part 2 is the lovegame of the children, corresponding to the second institution, Marriage, or to the Heroic age, or to an abstraction—Maturity. Part 3 is passed in sleep, corresponding to the third institution, Burial, or to the Human age, or to an abstraction —Corruption. Part 4 is the day beginning again, and corresponds to Vico's Providence, or to the transition from the Human to the Theocratic, or to an abstraction—Generation. Mr. Joyce does not take birth for granted, as Vico seems to have done. So much for the dry bones. The consciousness that there is a great deal of the unborn infant in the lifeless octogenarian, and a great deal of both in the man at the apogee of his life's curve, removes all the stiff interexclusiveness that is often the danger in neat construction. Corruption is not excluded from Part 1. nor maturity from Part 3. The four "lovedroyd curdinals' are presented on the same plane—'his element curdinal numen and his enement curdinal marrying and his epulent curdinal weisswasch and his eminent curdinal Kay o' Kay!" There are numerous references to Vico's four human institutions—Providence counting as one! "A good clap, a fore wedding, a bad wake, tell hell's well": "their weatherings and their marryings and their buryings and their natural selections": "the lightning look, the birding cry, awe from the grave, everflowing on our times": "by four hands of forethought the first babe of reconcilement is laid in its last cradle of hume sweet hume."

Apart from this emphasis on the tangible conveniences common to Humanity, we find frequent expressions of Vico's insistence on the inevitable character of every progression—or retrogression: "The Vico road goes round and round to meet where terms begin. Still onappealed to by the cycles and onappalled by the recoursers, we feel all serene, never you fret, as regards our dutyful cask. . . . before there was a man at all in Ireland there was a lord at Lucan. We only wish everyone was as sure ot anything in this watery world as we are of everything in the newlywet fellow that's bound to follow. . . ." "The efferfreshpainted livy in beautific repose upon the silence of the dead from Pharoph the next first down to ramescheckles the last bust thing." "In fact, under the close eyes of the inspectors the traits featuring the chiaroscuro coalesce, their contrarieties eliminated, in one stable somebody similarly as by the providential warring of heartshaker with housebreaker and of dramdrinker against freethinker of our social something bowls along bumpily, experiencing a jolting series of prearranged disappointments, down the long lane of (it's as semper as oxhousehumper) generations, more generations and still more generations"—this last a case of Mr. Joyce's rare subjectivism. In a word, here is all humanity circling with fatal monotony about the Providential fulcrum—the "convoy wheeling encirculing abound the gigantig's lifetree." Enough has been said, or at least enough has been suggested, to show how Vico is substantially present in the Work in Progress. Passing to the Vico of the Poetics we hope to establish an even more striking, if less direct, relationship.

Vico rejected the three popular interpretations of the poetic spirit, which considered poetry as either an ingenious popular expression of philosophical conceptions, or an amusing social diversion, or an exact science within the reach of everyone in possession of the recipe. Poetry, he says, was born of curiosity, daughter of ignorance. The first men had to create matter by the force of their imagination, and "poet" means "creator." Poetry was the first operation of the human mind, and without it thought could not exist. Barbarians, incapable of analysis and abstraction, must use their fantasy to explain what their reason cannot comprehend. Before articulation comes song; before abstract terms, metaphors. The figurative character of the oldest poetry must be regarded, not as sophisticated confectionery, but as evidence of a poverty-stricken vocabulary and of a disability to achieve abstraction. Poetry is essentially the antithesis of Metaphysics: Metaphysics purge the mind of the senses and cultivate the disembodiment of the spiritual; Poetry is all passion and feeling and animates the inanimate; Metaphysics are most perfect when most concerned with universals; Poetry, when most concerned with particulars. Poets are the sense, philosophers the intelligence of humanity. Considering the Scholastics' axiom: "*niente è nell'intelleto che prima non sia nel senso*," it follows that poetry is a prime condition of philosophy and civilization. The primitive animistic movement was a manifestation of the "*forma poetica dello spirito*."

His treatment of the origin of language proceeds along similar lines. Here again he rejected the materialistic and transcendental views: the one declaring that language was nothing but a polite and conventional symbolism; the other, in desperation, describing it as a gift from the Gods. As before, Vico is the rationalist, aware of the natural and inevitable growth of language. In its first dumb form, language was gesture. If a man wanted to say "sea," he pointed to the sea. With the spread of animism this gesture was replaced by the word: "Neptune." He directs our attention to the fact that every need of life, natural, moral and economic, has its verbal expression in one or other of the 30,000 Greek divinities. This is Homer's "language of the Gods." Its evolution through poetry to a highly civilized vehicle, rich in abstract and technical terms, was as little fortuitous as the evolution of society itself. Words have their progressions as well as social phases. "Forest-cabin-village-city-academy" is one rough progression. Another: "mountain-plain-riverbank." And every word expands with psychological inevitability. Take the Latin word: "Lex."

1.   Lex = Crop of acorns.
2.   Ilex = Tree that produces acorns.
3.   Legere = To gather.
4.   Aquilex = He that gathers the waters.
5.   Lex = Gathering together of peoples, public assembly.
6.   Lex = Law.
7.   Legere = To gather together letters into a word, to read.

The root of any word whatsoever can be traced back to some pre-lingual symbol. This early inability to abstract the general from the particular produced the Type-names. It is the child's mind over again. The child extends the names of the first familiar objects to other strange objects in which he is conscious of some analogy. The first men, unable to conceive the abstract idea of "poet" or "hero," named every hero after the first hero, every poet after the first poet. Recognizing this custom of designating a number of individuals by the names of their prototypes, we can explain various classical and mythological mysteries. Hermes is the prototype of the Egyptian inventor: so for Romulus, the great law-giver, and Hercules, the Greek hero: so for Homer. Thus Vico asserts the spontaneity of language and denies the dualism of poetry and language. Similarly, poetry is the foundation of writing. When language consisted of gesture, the spoken and the written were identical. Hiero-glyphics, or sacred language, as he calls it, were not the invention of philosophers for the mysterious expression of profound thought, but the common necessity of primitive peoples. Convenience only begins to assert itself at a far more advanced stage of civilization, in the form of alphabetism. Here Vico, implicitly at least, distinguishes between writing and direct expression. In such direct expression, form and content are inseparable. Examples are the medals of the Middle Ages, which bore no inscription and were a mute testimony to the feebleness of conven-tional alphabetic writing: and the flags of our own day. As with Poetry and Language, so with Myth. Myth, according to Vico, is neither an allegorical expression of general philosophical axioms (Conti, Bacon), nor a derivative from particular peoples, as for instance the Hebrews or Egyptians, nor yet the work of isolated poets, but an historical state-ment of fact, of actual contemporary phenomena, actual in the sense that they were created out of necessity by primitive minds, and firmly believed. Allegory implies a threefold intellectual operation: the con-struction of a message of general significance, the preparation of a fabulous form, and an exercise of considerable technical difficulty in uniting the two, an operation totally beyond the reach of the primitive mind. Moreover, if we consider the myth as being essentially allegorical, we are not obliged to accept the form in which it is cast as a statement of fact. But we know that the actual creators of these myths gave full credence to their face-value. Jove was no symbol: he was terribly real. It was precisely their superficial metaphorical character that made them intelligible to people incapable of receiving anything more abstract than the plain record of objectivity.

Such is a painful exposition of Vico's dynamic treatment of Language, Poetry and Myth. He may still appear as a mystic to some: if so, a mystic that rejects the transcendental in every shape and form as a factor in human development, and whose Providence is not divine enough to do without the cooperation of Humanity.

On turning to the *"Works in Progress"* we find that the mirror is not so convex. Here is direct expression—pages and pages of it. And if you don't understand it, Ladies and Gentlemen, it is because you are too decadent to receive it. You are not satisfied unless form is so strictly divorced from content that you can comprehend the one almost without bothering to read the other. This rapid skimming and absorption of the scant cream of sense is made possible by what I may call a continuous process of copious intellectual salivation. The form that is an arbitrary and independent phenomenon can fulfil no higher function than that of stimulus for a tertiary or quartary conditioned reflex of dribbling comprehension. When Miss Rebecca West clears her decks for a sorrowful deprecation of the Narcisstic element in Mr. Joyce by the purchase of 3 hats, one feels that she might very well wear her bib at all her intellectual banquets, or alternatively, assert a more noteworthy control over her salivary glands than is possible for Monsieur Pavlov's unfortunate dogs. The title of this book is a good example of a form carrying a strict inner determination. It should be proof against the usual volley of cerebral sniggers: and it may suggest to some a dozen incredulous Joshuas prowling around the Queen's Hall, springing their tuning-forks lightly against finger-nails that have not yet been refined out of existence. Mr. Joyce has a word to say to you on the subject: "Yet to concentrate solely on the literal sense or even the psychological content of any document to the sore neglect of the enveloping facts themselves circumstantiating it is just as harmful; etc." And another: "Who in his hearts doubts either that the facts of feminine clothiering are there all the time or that the feminine fiction, stranger than the facts, is there also at the same time, only a little to the rere? Or that one may be separated from the orther? Or that both may be contemplated simultaneously? Or that each may be taken up in turn and considered apart from the other?"

Here form *is* content, content *is* form. You complain that this stuff is not written in English. It is not written at all. It is not to be read—or rather it is not only to be read. It is to be looked at and listened to. His writing is not *about* something; *it is that something itself*. (A fact that has been grasped by an eminent English novelist and historian whose work is in complete opposition to Mr. Joyce's). When the sense is sleep, the words go to sleep. (See the end of *"Anna Livia."*) When the sense is dancing, the words dance. Take the passage at the end of Shaun's pastoral: "To stirr up love's young fizz I tilt with this bridle's cup champagne, dimming douce from her peepair of hideseeks tight squeezed on my snowy-breasted and while my pearlies in their sparkling wisdom are nippling her bubblets I swear (and let you swear) by the bumper round of my poor old snaggletooth's solidbowel I ne'er will prove I'm untrue to (theare!) you liking so long as my hole looks. Down." The language is drunk. The very words are tilted and effervescent. How can we qualify this general esthetic vigilance without which we cannot hope to snare the sense which is for ever rising to the surface of the form and becoming the form itself? St. Augustine puts us on the track of a word with his *"intendere"*; Dante has: *"Donne ch'avete intelletto d'amore,"* and *"Voi che, intendendo, il terzo ciel movete"*; but his *"intendere"* suggests a strictly intellectual operation. When an Italian says to-day *"Ho inteso,"* he means something between *"Ho udito"* and *"Ho capito,"* a sensuous untidy art of intellection. Perhaps "apprehension" is the most satisfactory English word. Stephen says to Lynch: "Temporal or spatial, the esthetic image is first luminously apprehended as selfbounded and self-contained upon the immeasurable background of space or time which is not it . . . . You apprehend its wholeness." There is one point to make clear: the Beauty of *"Work in Progress"* is not presented in space alone, since its adequate apprehension depends as much on its visibility as on its audibility. There is a temporal as well as a spatial unity to be apprehended. Substitute "and" for "or" in the quotation and it becomes obvious why it is as inadequate to speak of "reading" *"Work in Progress"* as it would be extravagant to speak of "apprehending" the work of the late Mr. Nat Gould. Mr. Joyce has desophisticated language. And it is worth while remarking that no language is so sophisticated as English. It is abstracted to death. Take the word "doubt": it gives us hardly any sensuous suggestion of hesitancy of the necessity for choice, of static irresolution. Whereas the German "Zweifel" does, and, in lesser degree, the Italian "dubitare." Mr. Joyce recognises how inadequate "doubt" is to express a state of extreme uncertainty, and replaces it by "in twosome twiminds." Nor is he by any means the first to recognize the importance of treating words as something more than mere polite symbols. Shakespeare uses fat, greasy words to express corruption: "Duller shouldst thou be than the fat weed that rots itself in death on Lethe wharf." We hear the ooze squelching all through Dickens's description of the Thames in *"Great Expectations."* This writing that you find so obscure is a quintessential extraction of language and painting and gesture, with all the inevitable clarity of the old inarticulation. Here is the savage economy of hieroglyphics. Here words are not the polite contortions of 20th century printer's ink. They are alive. They elbow their way on to the page, and glow and blaze and fade and disappear. "Brawn is my name and broad is my nature and I've breit on my brow and all's right with every feature and I'll brune this bird or Brown Bess's bung's gone bandy." This is Brawn blowing with a light gust through the trees or Brawn passing with the sunset. Because the wind in the trees means as little to you as the evening prospect from the Piazzale Michelangiolo—though you accept them both because your non-acceptance would be of no significance, this little adventure of Brawn means nothing to you—and you do not accept it, even though here also your non-acceptance is of no significance. H. C. Earwigger, too, is not content to be mentioned like a shilling-shocker villain, and then dropped until the exigencies of the narrative require that he be again referred to. He continues to suggest himself for a couple of pages, by means of repeated permutations on his "normative letters," as if to say: "This is all about me, H. C. Earwigger: don't forget this is all about me!" This inner elemental vitality and corruption of expression imparts a furious restlessness to the form, which is admirably suited to the purgatorial aspect of the work. There is an endless verbal germination, maturation, putrefaction, the cyclic dynamism of the intermediate. This reduction of various expressive media to their primitive economic directness, and the fusion of these primal essences into an assimilated medium for the exteriorisation of thought, is pure Vico, and Vico, applied to the problem of style. But Vico is reflected more explicitly than by a distillation of disparate poetic ingredients into a synthetical syrup. We notice that there is little or no attempt a subjectivism or abstraction, no attempt at metaphysical generalisation. We are presented with a statement of the particular. It is the old myth: the girl on the dirt track, the two washerwomen on the banks of the river. And there is considerable animism: the mountain "abhearing," the river puffing her old doudheen. (See the beautiful passage beginning: "First she let her hair fall and down it flussed.") We have Type-names: Isolde—any beautiful girl: Earwigger—Guinness's Brewery, the Wellington monument, the Phoenix Park, anything that occupies an extremely comfortable position between the two stools. Anna Livia herself, mother of Dublin, but no more the only mother than Zoroaster was the only oriental stargazer. "Teems of times and happy returns. The same anew. Ordovico or viricordo. Anna was, Livia is, Plurabelle's to be. Northmen's thing made Southfolk's place, but howmultyplurators made eachone in person." Basta! Vico and Bruno are here, and more substantially than would appear from this swift survey of the question. For the benefit of those who enjoy a parenthetical sneer, we would draw attention to the fact that when Mr. Joyce's early pamphlet *"The Day of the Rabblement"* appeared, the local philosophers were thrown into a state of some bewilderment by a reference in the first line to "The Nolan." They finally succeeded in identifying this mysterious indi-

vidual with one of the obscurer ancient Irish kings. In the present work
he appears frequently as "Browne & Nolan" the name of a very remarkable
Dublin Bookseller and Stationer.

To justify our title, we must move North, *"Sovra'l bel fiume d'Arno
alla gran villa"* . . . Between *"colui per lo cui verso—il meonio cantor non
è più solo"* and the "still to-day insufficiently malestimated notesnatcher,
Shem the Penman," there exists considerable circumstantial similarity.
They both saw how worn out and threadbare was the conventional language of cunning literary artificers, both rejected an approximation to
a universal language. If English is not yet so definitely a polite necessity
as Latin was in the Middle Ages, at least one is justified in declaring
that its position in relation to other European langauges is to a great
extent that of mediaeval Latin to the Italian dialects. Dante did not
adopt the vulgar out of any kind of local jingoism nor out of any determination to assert the superiority of Tuscan to all its rivals as a form
of spoken Italian. On reading his *"De Vulgari Eloquentia"* we are struck
by his complete freedom from civic intolerance. He attacks the world's
Portadownians: *"Nam quicumque tam obscenae rationis est, ut locum
suae nationis delitosissium credat esse sub sole, huic etiam prœ cunctis
propriam volgare licetur, id est maternam locutionem. Nos autem, cui
mundus est patria . . .* etc." When he comes to examine the dialects he
finds Tuscan: *"turpissimum . . . fere omnes Tusci in suo turpiloquio
obtusi . . . non restat in dubio quin aliud sit vulgare quod quaerimus
quam quod attingit populus Tuscanorum."* His conclusion is that the
corruption common to all the dialects makes it impossible to select one
rather than another as an adequate literary form, and that he who
would write in the vulgar must assemble the purest elements from each
dialect and construct a synthetic language that would at least possess
more than a circumscribed local interest: which is precisely what he
did. He did not write in Florentine any more than in Neapolitan. He
wrote a vulgar that *could* have been spoken by an ideal Italian who
had assimilated what was best in all the dialects of his country, but
which in fact was certainly not spoken nor ever had been. Which
disposes of the capital objection that might be made against this at-
tractive parallel between Dante and Mr. Joyce in the question of language, i.e that at least Dante wrote what was being spoken in the
streets of his own town, whereas no creature in heaven or earth ever
spoke the language of *"Work in Progress."* It is reasonable to admit that
an international phenomenon might be capable of speaking it, just as in
1300 none but an inter-regional phenomenon could have spoken the
language of the Divine Comedy. We are inclined to forget that Dante's
literary public was Latin, that the form of his Poem was to be judged
by Latin eyes and ears, by a Latin Esthetic intolerant of innovation,
and which could hardly fail to be irritated by the substitution of *"Nel
mezzo del cammin di nostra vita"* with its 'barbarous' directness for the

suave elegance of: "*Ultima regna canam, fluido contermina mundo*,"
just as English eyes and ears prefer: "Smoking his favourite pipe in the
sacred presence of ladies" to: "Rauking his flavourite turfco in the
smukking precincts of lydias." Boccaccio did not jeer at the "*piedi
sozzi*" of the peacock that Signora Alighieri dreamed about.

I find two well made caps in the "*Convivio*," one to fit the collective
noodle of the monodialectical arcadians whose fury is precipitated by
a failure to discover "innocefree" in the Concise Oxford Dictionary and
who qualify as the "ravings of a Bedlamite" the formal structure raised
by Mr. Joyce after years of patient and inspired labour: "*Questi sono
da chiamare pecore e non uomini; chè se una pecora si gittasse da una
ripa di mille passi, tutte l'altre le andrebbono dietro; e se una pecora
per alcuna cagione al passare d'una strada salta, tutte le altre saltano,
eziando nulla veggendo da saltare. E io ne vidi già molte in un pozzo
saltare, per una che dentro vi salto, forse credendo di saltare un muro*."
And the other for Mr. Joyce, biologist in words: "*Questo* (formal innovation) *sarà luce nuova, sole nuovo, il quale sorgerà ore l'usato tra-
monterà e darà luce a coloro che sono in tenebre e in oscurità per lo
usato sole che a loro non luce*." And, lest he should pull it down over
his eyes and laugh behind the peak, I translate "*in tenebre e in oscurità*"
by "bored to extinction." (Dante makes a curious mistake speaking of
the origin of language, when he rejects the authority of Genesis that
Eve was the first to speak, when she addressed the Serpent. His in-
credulity is amusing: "*inconvenienter pulatur tam egregium humani
generis actum, vel prius quam a viro, foemina profluisse*." But before
Eve was born, the animals were given names by Adam, the man who
"first said goo to a goose." Moreover it is explicitly stated that the
choice of names was left entirely to Adam, so that there is not the slight-
est Biblical authority for the conception of language as a direct gift of
God, any more than there is any intellectual authority for conceiving
that we are indebted for the "Concert" to the individual who used to
buy paint for Giorgione).

We know very little about the immediate reception accorded to
Dante's mighty vindication of the "vulgar," but we can form our own
opinions when, two centuries later, we find Castiglione splitting more
than a few hairs concerning the respective advantages of Latin and
Italian, and Poliziano writing the dullest of dull Latin Elegies to justify
his existence as the author of "*Orfeo*" and the "*Stanze*." We may also compare, if we think it worth while, the storm of ecclesiastical abuse raised
by Mr. Joyce's work, and the treatment that the Divine Comedy must
certainly have received from the same source. His Contemporary Holi-
ness might have swallowed the crucifixion of "*lo sommo Giove*," and all
it stood for, but he could scarcely have looked with favour on the
spectacle of three of his immediate predecessors plunged head-foremost
in the fiery stone of Malebolge, nor yet the identification of the Papacy

in the mystical procession of Terrestial Paradise with a *"puttana sciolta."*
The *"De Monarchia"* was burnt publicly under Pope Giovanni XXII
at the instigation of Cardinal Beltrando and the bones of its author
would have suffered the same fate but for the interference of an influential man of letters, Pino della Tosa. Another point of comparison is
the preoccupation with the significance of numbers. The death of Beatrice
inspired nothing less than a highly complicated poem dealing with
the importance of the number 3. in her life. Dante never ceased to be
obsessed by this number. Thus the Poem is divided into three Cantiche,
each composed of 33 Canti, and written in terza rima. Why, Mr. Joyce
seems to say, should there be four legs to a table, and four to a horse,
and four seasons and four Gospels and four Provinces in Ireland? Why
twelve Tables of the Law, and twelve Apostles and twelve months and
twelve Napoleonic marshals and twelve men in Florence called Otto-
lenghi? Why should the Armistice be celebrated at the eleventh hour
of the eleventh day of the eleventh month? He cannot tell you because
he is not God Almighty, but in a thousand years he will tell you, and in
the meantime must be content to know why horses have not five legs,
nor three. He is conscious that things with a common numerical characteristic tend towards a very significant interrelationship. This preoccupation is freely translated in his present work: see the "Question and
Answer" chapter, and the Four speaking through the child's brain. They
are the four winds as much as the four Provinces, and the four Episco-
pal Sees as much as either.

A last word about the Purgatories. Dante's is conical and consequently implies culmination. Mr. Joyce's is spherical and excludes culmination.
In the one there is an ascent from real vegetation—Ante-Purgatory, to ideal
vegetation—Terrestial Paradise: in the other there is no ascent and no ideal
vegetation. In the one, absolute progression and a guaranteed consummation: in the other, flux—progression or retrogression, and an apparent
consummation. In the one movement is unidirectional, and a step forward
represents a net advance: in the other movement is non-directional—
or multi-directional, and a step forward is, by definition, a step back.
Dante's Terrestial Paradise is the carriage entrance to a Paradise that
is not terrestial: Mr. Joyce's Terrestial Paradise is the tradesmen's entrance to the sea-shore. Sin is an impediment to movement up the cone,
and a condition of movement round the sphere. In what sense, then, is
Mr. Joyce's work purgatorial? In the absolute absence of the Absolute.
Hell is the static lifelessness of unrelieved viciousness. Paradise the
static lifelessness of unrelieved immaculation. Purgatory a flood of movement and vitality released by the conjunction of these two elements.
There is a continuous purgatorial process at work, in the sense that
the vicious circle of humanity is being achieved, and this achievement
depends on the recurrent predomination of one of two broad qualities.
No resistance, no eruption, and it is only in Hell and Paradise that there

are no eruptions, that there can be none, need be none. On this earth that is Purgatory, Vice and Virtue—which you may take to mean any pair of large contrary human factors—must in turn be purged down to spirits of rebelliousness. Then the dominant crust of the Vicious or Virtuous sets, resistance is provided, the explosion duly takes place and the machine proceeds. And no more than this; neither prize nor penalty; simply a series of stimulants to enable the kitten to catch its tail. And the partially purgatorial agent? The partially purged.

The Rhythm of *Ulysses*   Stuart Gilbert*

In his earlier, autobiographic novel, *A Portrait of the Artist as a Young Man*, James Joyce, through the mouth of Stephen Dedalus, defines the qualities which, in his view, gives æsthetic beauty to a work of art.

> ' "It awakens, or ought to awaken, or induces, or ought to induce, an æsthetic stasis, an ideal pity or an ideal terror, a stasis called forth, prolonged and at last dissolved by what I call the rhythm of beauty."
> "What is that exactly?" asked Lynch.
> "Rhythm", said Stephen, "is the first formal æsthetic relation of part to part in any æsthetic whole or of an æsthetic whole to its part or parts or of any part to the æsthetic whole of which it is a part." '

Ulysses is a complex of such relations; at a first and casual reading these are perceived vaguely, as a misty nebula of light; in the course of a more attentive perusal their number and permeance will gradually become apparent, "as," to quote the admirable metaphor of M. Valery Larbaud, "at night, after one has been contemplating the sky for a little while, the number of stars seems to have increased."

One of the simpler aspects of this technique—a device which, for all its apparent artificiality, exactly resembles Nature's method—is the presentation of fragments of a theme or allusion in different parts of the work; these fragments have to be assimilated in the reader's mind for him to arrive at complete understanding. "It is a truth perpetually," as Herbert Spencer remarked, "that accumulated facts, lying in disorder, begin to assume some order when an hypothesis is thrown among them." Several such hypotheses are not so much "thrown" as disposed with artfully concealed art amid the welter of accumulated facts in *Ulysses*. Moreover, again following Nature's method, Joyce depicts only the

*This essay first appeared in *James Joyce's Ulysses: A Study* (London: Faber and Faber, 1930) and is reprinted with permission of Faber and Faber.

present time and place of the times and places that are passing, a rapid flux of images. "Hold to the now, the here, through which all future plunges into the past."[1] It is for the reader to assemble the fragments and join the images into a band.

Sometimes the thought of the moment, rising to the surface of the mind under the impact of some external stimulus, is merely the echo of a name or fragment of a phrase. That, then, is all Joyce sets down. But, sooner or later, the reader will come upon a circumstance or thought which will explain the allusion implicit in the name or broken sentence.

Thus, before setting out on his day's wanderings, Mr Bloom examines his hat.[2]

"The sweated legend in the crown of his hat told him mutely: Plasto's high grade ha. He peeped quickly inside the leather headband. White slip of paper. Quite safe.

On the doorstep he felt in his hip pocket for the latchkey. Not there. In the trousers I left off. Must get it. Potato I have."

The explanation of "the white slip of paper" comes only in a subsequent episode. "His right hand came down into the bowl of his hat. His fingers found quickly a card behind the headband and transferred it to his waistcoat pocket." Presently Mr Bloom visits a post office.

"He handed the card through the brass grill.

'Are there any letters for me?' he asked."

The card, we learn, is inscribed *Henry Flower*, the name adopted by Mr Bloom for his correspondence with Martha Clifford. In a later episode[3] Mr Bloom is taking leave of Richie Goulding: "Well, so long. High grade. Card inside, yes." These fragments could seem meaningless to a reader who had forgotten the earlier passages; the broken phrases assume an order only when "an hypothesis is thrown among them." In the same way the allusion in "Potato I have" becomes clear only when the reader arrives at the *Circe* episode and learns that it is "a relic of poor mamma," a "Potato Preservative against Plague and Pestilence," a talisman, in fact.

Similarly, after lunch,[4] Mr Bloom thinks: "That wonder-worker if I had." This cryptic regret is explained many pages later[5] where we find the *Wonderworker* is a "thaumaturgic remedy" designed to "insure instant relief" from postprandial disorders.

But, besides such small isolated correspondences, there are a number of themes, generally stated in the early episodes (those dealing with the morning hours of Stephen and Mr Bloom), which recur more or less frequently throughout *Ulysses*. Some of these relate to esoteric theories, which will be dealt with later; a few are shared by both Stephen and Mr Bloom (several instances of this persistent, though unconscious, exchange of thoughts and impressions between them will be commented on in the course of this study); the majority are concerned with their personal experiences, remarks or events which have left an impress on the mind of each. Thereafter, a chance word, the glimpse of some apparently irrelevant object, a sudden eddy of the stream of consciousness, will suffice to evoke the associated memory. The occasional obscurities in passages recording the silent monologue of Stephen and Mr. Bloom are partly due to the brusqueness and brevity of such allusions. Thus in the episode (constructed on a musical pattern and dominated from beginning to end by musical forms and rhythms) which describes Mr Bloom's belated lunch at the Ormond Restaurant, we find a fragment of silent monologue which, to a reader who has forgotten or "skipped" the relevant passages in earlier episodes, may well seem almost meaningless. While Mr Bloom is having his meal in the restaurant, Mr Dedalus (Stephen's father) is singing at the hotel piano the operatic ballad, *When first I saw that form endearing.*

> "Tenors get women by the score. Increase their flow. Throw flower at his feet when will we meet? My head it simply. Jingle all delighted. He can't sing for tall hats. Your head it simply swurls. Perfumed for him. What perfume does your wife? I want to know. Jing. Stop. Knock. Last look at mirror always before she answers the door. The hall. There? How do you? I do well. There? What? Or? Phila of cachous, kissing comfits, in her satchel. Yes? Hands felt for the opulent."

In the broken phrases of this monologue of Mr Bloom there are several indirect allusions to Blazes Boylan, Mrs Bloom's lover, who has an appointment with her for four o'clock. Mr Bloom, as usual, refrains from mentioning the name of Boylan, his *bête noire*. It is a little past four o'clock and the latter, after some badinage with the bar-sirens ("Has he forgotten?" Mr Bloom asks himself) has just driven off in a jingling jaunting-car to his *rendez-vous*. The jingle of the car continues to echo in Mr Bloom's brain, mingled with the voice of the singer warbling *amoroso* "Full of hope and all delighted." Mr Bloom thinks of the *bonnes fortunes* of tenors (the Dubliners' remarkable cult of the operatic singer is discussed in the opening passage of my commentary on the *Sirens*); Boylan is by way of being a singer as well as an impresario, though "he can't sing for tall hats." They get women *by the score* (the musical word-play is characteristically Joycean). A singer, Bartell d'Arcy, was, it happens, one of Mrs Bloom's earliest admirers; "he commenced kissing me on the choir stairs."[6] *My head it simply.* Mr Bloom has received by the morning post a letter from his young daughter Milly. "There is a young student comes here...he sings Boylan's (I was on the pop of writing Blazes Boylan's) song about those seaside girls." After reading the letter Mr Bloom hums the refrain of "Boylan's song."

> *"All dimpled cheeks and curls,*
> *Your head it simply swirls.*

Seaside girls. Torn envelope. Hands stuck in his trousers' pockets, jarvey off for the day, singing. Friend of the family. Swurls, he says . . .

> *Those girls, those girls,*
> *Those lovely seaside girls.*"[7]

His thought of women's infatuation for tenors has evoked Mr Bloom's bugbear—*via* Milly's allusion and a memory of the torn envelope on the bed (Boylan's letter). *Jingle all delighted.* The words Mr Dedalus is singing blend with the vision of an elate don Juan on his jingling car. *Your head it simply swurls* ("swurls, he says"). *Perfumed for him.* In the course of the morning Mr Bloom has procured for his wife, who likes that kind of literature, an erotic work entitled: *Sweets of Sin.* Glancing at its contents he has read: "All the dollarbills her husband gave her were spent in the stores on wondrous gowns and costliest frillies. For him! For Raoul! . . . Her mouth glued on his in a luscious voluptuous kiss while his hands felt for the opulent curves. . . ." The "for him" of Mr Bloom's soliloquy is a recall of this masterpiece of the luscious-voluptuous. *Perfumed* (a reference to Mrs Bloom's philaromatic disposition: her husband, too, has a keen nose for odours) evokes another train of thought—his own mild counterpart of Marion's infidelity, a letter he has received from the typist, Martha Clifford. (Moreover, the song Mr Dedalus is singing is from the opera *Martha.* "Martha it is. Coincidence. Just going to write.") She wrote: "Do tell me what kind of perfume does your wife use. I want to know." Mr Bloom recalls her letter almost verbatim. *What perfume does your wife? I want to know.* The car stops with a jingling jerk before Mr Bloom's house. *Jing. Stop. Knock.* Here, as elsewhere, a *martellato* rhythm emphasizes Boylan's masterful hammering on the lady's door. In imagination, irrepressible now, Bloom visualizes his wife's reception of Boylan, and his evocation of their eager greeting in the hall ends, appropriately enough, on an afterclang of the *Sweets of Sin.*

Hundreds of other instances of the manner in which the eighteen episodes of *Ulysses* are interlocked, how a knowledge of each part is necessary for the understanding of the whole, will be found in the course of this study, and other reasons which led the author to adopt this unusual method of exposition will, it is hoped, become manifest. For the purposes of the present chapter a brief description of the formal symmetry of the work may suffice, stating but not discussing the Homeric correspondences.

Each episode of *Ulysses* has its Scene and Hour of the Day, is (with the exception of the first three episodes) associated with a given Organ of the human body,[8] relates to a certain Art, has its appropriate Symbol and a specific Technic. Each episode has also a title, corresponding to a personage or episode of the Odyssey. Certain episodes have also their appropriate colour (a reference, as M. Larbaud has pointed out, to Catholic liturgy). The references are given in the following table of the episodes.

Title	Scene	Hour	Organ	Art	Colour	Symbol	Technic
1. Telemachus	The Tower	8 a.m.		Theology	White, gold	Heir	Narrative (young)
2. Nestor	The School	10 a.m.		History	Brown	Horse	Catechism (personal)
3. Proteus	The Strand	11 a.m.		Philology	Green	Tide	Monologue (male)
4. Calypso	The House	8 a.m.	Kidney	Economics	Orange	Nymph	Narrative (mature)
5. Lotus-eaters	The Bath	10 a.m.	Genitals	Botany, Chemistry		Eucharist	Narcissism
6. Hades	The Graveyard	11 a.m.	Heart	Religion	White, black	Caretaker	Incubism
7. Aeolus	The Newspaper	12 noon	Lungs	Rhetoric	Red	Editor	Enthymemic
8. Lestrygonians	The Lunch	1 p.m.	Esophagus	Architecture		Constables	Peristaltic
9. Scylla and Charybdis	The Library	2 p.m.	Brain	Literature		Stratford, London	Dialectic
10. Wandering Rocks	The Streets	3 p.m.	Blood	Mechanics		Citizens	Labyrinth
11. Sirens	The Concert Room	4 p.m.	Ear	Music		Barmaids	Fuga per canonem
12. Cyclops	The Tavern	5 p.m.	Muscle	Politics		Fenian	Gigantism
13. Nausicaa	The Rocks	8 p.m.	Eye, Nose	Painting	Grey, blue	Virgin	Tumescence, detumescence
14. Oxen of the Sun	The Hospital	10 p.m.	Womb	Medicine	White	Mothers	Embryonic development
15. Circe	The Brothel	12 midnight	Locomotor Apparatus	Magic		Whore	Hallucination
16. Eumaeus	The Shelter	1 a.m.	Nerves	Navigation		Sailors	Narrative (old)
17. Ithaca	The House	2 a.m.	Skeleton	Science		Comets	Catechism (impersonal)
18. Penelope	The Bed		Flesh			Earth	Monologue (female)

It will be observed that there is no corresponding "Organ of the Body" for the first three episodes. The explanation of this is probably that these episodes deal exclusively with the acts and thoughts of Stephen Dedalus, who, of the trinity of major personages appearing in *Ulysses* (Mr. Bloom, his wife and Stephen), represents the spiritual element; in the same way, for the last episode, which is wholly devoted to the meditation of Marion Bloom (whose symbol is the Earth), there is no corresponding Art for she is a manifestation of Nature herself, the antithesis of art. The manner in which the appropriate symbols, arts, etc., are associated with the subject and technic of the episodes will be apparent when I come to discuss each episode individually. For the present it is sufficient to point out the symmetry of the technical structure: a prelude (corresponding to the *Telemachia* of the Odyssey) of three episodes—(1) Narrative (young), (2) Catechism (personal), (3) Monologue (male); a central section (the Odyssey proper) of thematic development ending in the brothel scene, written in the dramatic form, the climax of the work, and a finale (the *Nostos* or *Return*) in three episodes balancing the prelude—(1) Narrative (old), (2) Catechism (impersonal), (3) Monologue (female). The central episode (the *Wandering Rocks*) is itself divided into eighteen short parts differing in theme and treatment, all interlocked by a curious technical device; thus reproducing in miniature the structure of the whole.

Each episode, taken independently, has its internal rhythm; in one of the most remarkable in this respect, the episode of the *Sirens*, there is a specific musical analogy, the *fugue*; in the episode of the *Oxen of the Sun*, where the style is a linguistic counterpart of the development of the embryo, there is a continuously increasing flow of vitality which ends in a word-dance of clipped phrases, *argot*, oaths and ejaculations; a veritable *locus classicus* of Impolite Conversation, which would have delighted the Dean of St Patrick's.

There could be no greater error than to confuse the work of James Joyce with that of the "harum-scarum" school or the *surrealiste* group (to which some of the most brilliant of the younger French writers belong, or once belonged) whose particular *trouvaille* is a sort of automatic writing, no revision being allowed. To suppose that the subconscious can best be portrayed by direct action of the subconscious—that well and truly to depict the state of drunkenness one should oneself be drunk— is mere *naïveté*. It is your thin young man who best can drive fat oxen along the rocky road to Dublin, and the "subconscious," elusive as an Indian snipe (but often far less appetising), will fall only to the clean-sighted aim of an expert *shikari*. As for "free verse"—surely the words are incompatibles, like the juvenile slogan of "free love"—at its best it is no less artificial and intricate in its rhythms than an ode of Pindar, at its worst a mere spate of undigested verbiage. With the work of the "modernist" school may be contrasted one of Joyce's poems of the *Ulysses* period.[9]

Alone

The moon's greygolden meshes make
All night a veil,
The shorelamps in the sleeping lake
Laburnum tendrils trail.

The sly reeds whisper to the night
A name—her name—
And all my soul is a delight,
A swoon of shame.

Zurich, 1916

The touch of irony in the second stanza, the allusion to an ancient myth (the "sly reeds" which betrayed Midas' shame to the world), is characteristic.

James Joyce is, in fact, in the line of classical tradition which begins with Homer; like his precursors he subjects his work, for all its wild vitality and seeming disorder, to a rule of formal discipline as severe as that of the Greek dramatists; indeed, the "unities" of *Ulysses* go far beyond the classic triad, they are as manifold and withal symmetrical as the dædal network of nerves and blood-streams which pervade the living organism.

Notes

1. *Ulysses*, page 178.
2. Page 55.
3. Page 274.
4. Page 277.
5. Page 678.
6. Page 701.
7. Page 64.
8. Together these compose the whole body, which is thus a symbol of the structure of *Ulysses*, a living organism, and of the natural interdependence of the parts between themselves. Blake uses a like symbolism in *Jerusalem*, where (as Mr Foster Damon points out) "Judah, Issachar and Zebulin represent the head, heart and loins of Luvah" and Great Britain is similarly divided.
9. *Pomes Penyeach* (Shakespeare & Co., Paris).

Joyce's Chapters of Going Forth by Day   Frank Budgen*

It is important to keep clear of labels. Joyce's esthetic creed was made by himself for himself, and it will be hard to see him as a follower or hail him as a leader of any school. If any device lay handy in the free-for-all communal workshop, he was quite willing to make use of it with thanks to the inventor (as in the case of the *parole intérieure*) but always as the *larron impénitent*. If you saw Joyce in the company of any doctrinaire you might be sure the association would end at the next crossroads. It is truer of Joyce than of most writers to say that his books grew out of his own life, and it follows that their origins lie in the vital circumstances out of which they arose. Looking for these is like looking for the source of a river and finding a tangle of a dozen springs and rills which have to serve our practical purpose, for if we looked any farther we should come to the sky and sea, source of all rivers.

Leopold Bloom in *Ulysses* has several dozy moments in the course of his day's wandering, and Joyce presents these with uncanny skill. A dream of the night before haunts him throughout the day till he drops to sleep, leaving his bigger and better half to her famous monologue which "turns slowly, evenly, though with variations, capriciously but surely like the huge earthball round and round spinning." After that day whose presentation had taken him the greater part of a decade Joyce must have found himself staring questioningly at the mysterious night.

For about half the time that it took to compose *Ulysses* Joyce lived in Zürich, at that time the second capital of psychoanalysis. Joyce preferred butter as a subject of conversation, and talk about dreams and the subconscious was likely to drive him to a bored silence or to a *Ma che!* of impatience. But there it was. You might call the subject a nightmare or a mare's nest, love it or detest it; it was like the foehn wind: you couldn't escape it.

Einstein's theory of the universe was becoming common property, and to another group of explorers the atom was yielding up its secrets. The airplane was flying over national frontiers with messages of all kinds. Wireless waves were carrying nimble thought at its own proper speed over land and sea, while contrary agencies were intensifying national consciousness and bringing into being national self-sufficiencies. The forward and outward drive was matched by a passionate nostalgia which led us backward and inward to legends and to all other evidences of our beginnings.

During my stay in Switzerland I kept for my own amusement a record of my dreams. I showed this to Joyce, together with a poem I

*This essay first appeared in *Horizon*, 4 (Sept. 1941) and is reprinted with permission from The Vanguard Press.

called "At the Gates of Sleep," and, at the same time, discussed with him my difficulties in recording dreams. I had cultivated the memory necessary for the dream happenings, but in setting them down on paper the whole atmosphere—the essential experience—was lost. I found this atmosphere to be incommunicable with any means I knew. If these conversations were remembered (and Joyce was not a man who forgot a great deal), it is possible that they arose later as a provocation to the master craftsman in Joyce.

Joyce was a cosmopolitan wanderer, sensitive to the intellectual climate of the places and times he lived in. He refused the servitude implicit in the acceptance of any one influence, but in the acceptance of many he could remain free. There's safety in numbers. I indicate but a few of these. Every reader of *Finnegans Wake* will perceive as many more. Joyce himself can hardly have known them all, whence they came, or how he assigned them their place and function. But, when the lightning flash of inspiration showed him the night mind of man as his province, there lay all the material of life, of his own and past ages, awaiting only to be baptized in the Liffey to be made suitable for his creative purpose.

Finnegans Wake is a resurrection myth. A river is a symbol of life and of that perpetual resurrection which is life. She is just as old as she is young, and just as young as she is old. While she is being born of her mother, the sky, in the Wicklow hills, she is being received in the arms of her father ocean in Dublin Bay. She renews herself constantly by a "commodious vicus of recirculation." The human race does the same whether regarded as a whole or in its parts as tribes, cities, or nations. The resurrection motive is announced on the first page of *Finnegans Wake* and is repeated with variations throughout the book.

> The oaks of ald now they lie in peat yet elms leap where askes lay. Phall if you but will, rise you must: and none so soon either shall the pharce for the nunce come to a setdown secular phoenish.

> The house of Atreox is fallen indeedust (Ilyam, Ilyum! Maeromor Mournomates!) averging on blight like the mundibanks of Fennyana, but deeds bounds going arise again. Life, he himself said once, (his biografiend, in fact, kills him verysoon, if yet not, after) is a wake, livit or krikit, and on the bunk of our breadwinning lies the cropse of our seedfather, a phrase which the establisher of the world by law might pretinately write across the chestfront of all manorwombanborn.

> And then. Be old. The next thing is. We are once amore as babes awondering in a wold made fresh where with the hen in the storyaboot we start from scratch.

> Yet is no body present here which was not there before. Only is order othered. Nought is nulled. *Fuitfiat!*

...receives through a portal vein the dialytically separated elements of precedent decomposition for the verypetpurpose of subsequent recombination. . . .

"Bygmester Finnegan, of the Stuttering Hand," was a builder who liked a drop of drink, and while he was working on a wall "of a trying thirstay mournin" he didn't feel quite himself. "His howd feeled heavy, his hoddit did shake." He slipped and fell from his ladder, and they found him dead on the ground. They took him home, wrapped him in a nice clean sheet, put him on the bed, and called all the neighbors and a whole lot of his fellow tradesmen in to the wake. "And the all gianed in with the shoutmost shoviality. Agog and Magog and the round of them agrog." The drinks were going round, there was dancing on the floor and altogether "grand funferall," but a row started, a bottle was thrown, and some of the spirits fell on the sleeping giant, who, at the smell, taste, and touch of the lifewater he loved, becomes Finnegan again, sits up, casts off his grave clothes, and joins in the fun.

> Whack. Huroo. Take your partners.
> On the floor your ankles shake.
> Isn't it the truth I've told you,
> Lots of fun at Finnegan's wake?

"There are plenty of other versions of the resurrection story," said Joyce, "but this was the most suitable to my purpose." The music-hall ditty serves as leitmotiv and signature tune introducing the giant city-founder Finn MacCool. The cosmic viewpoint and the comic muse are old associates, but the presence of lyric inspiration in the alliance is rarer, perhaps unique, yet here they are in organic union in *Finnegans Wake*. I believe it was Joyce's aim to include every genre of poetic composition in this book. I well remember him telling me with pleasure that his friend, James Stephens, had found all poetic elements blended in what at that time was called *Work in Progress*. Comic the book certainly is, and certainly serious though never solemn. "Loud heap miseries upon us but entwine our arts with laughters low." If you laughed at the comic in *Finnegans Wake* Joyce was pleased, but if you missed the hidden serious he was apt to be reproachful as he was, mildly, when I failed to see more than the fun of the thing in the dialogue in pidgin English and Nippon English between the archdruid and St. Patrick in Part IV.

Much more is intended in the colloquy between Berkely the archdruid and his pidgin speech and Patrick in answer and his Nippon English. It is also the defence and indictment of the book itself, B's theory of colour and Patrick's practical solution of the problem. Hence the phrase in the preceding Mutt and Jeff banter "Dies is Dorminus master," = Deus et Dominus noster plus the day is lord over sleep, i.e., when it days.

But nobody is likely to deny the seriousness of *Finnegans Wake* (for what claims to be universal cannot be less), and it shall be left to others to define the poetic territory it covers. But what of life? I felt as I was reading through *Finnegans Wake* in its final form for the first time that for all its universality an essential element of life had been left out of it—the element of pain and death, nor does this element appear until the final pages. But the reason soon appears. "From lighting up o'clock sharp" till sunrise, Finn and his family live as timeless phantoms in a world where life and death, youth and age, birth and corruption, and all extremes meet, that middle kingdom, that limbo of sleep and dreams, where Death's brother entertains his subjects with the pageant of history without tears—all ambiguities, anachronisms, and incongruities—presented by his pageant masters, "Messrs. Thud and Blunder." The story of the pageant is the founding and perpetual re-creation of the city of Dublin—the city of Finn MacCool.

The worst of writing about *Finnegans Wake* is that all our words are wrong. Story is wrong, of course, for a story is one thing happening after another along a one-way time street, coming from and going to some place, whereas *Finnegans Wake* is going nowhere in all directions on an every-way roundabout with infiltrations from above and below. On every page Joyce insists on this all-time dream-time by every device of suggestion and allusion and by a continual modification and cancellation of all-time words. For example: "It stays in book of that which is. I have heard anyone tell it jesterday (master currier with brassard was't) how one should come on morrow here but it is never here that one today. Well but to remind to think, you where yestoday Ys Morganas war and that it is always tomorrow in toth's tother's place. Amen."

And sometimes a confidential voice seems to talk "straight turkey" to us with all the air of imparting historical information, but so numerous are the asides, and so tightly packed the ghostly narrative with parentheses, that when the confidential narrator comes to a full stop we find ourselves in possession of a multitude of hints and suggestions but of no story at all. Instead of a story of happenings, a contour or an accent is added to the picture of one or other of his personages, or the place in which they live is lit with a new light. If we go back to where we started and try to unravel the phantom tissue clause by clause, the whole fabric falls to pieces. The effort is like trying to put salt on birds' tails or juggle with live eels. Here and there a "Fuit" or "Fiat" or "Fiatfuit" warns us that we are in a world of essences where there is constant change but no growth and no development, no time sequence, and consequently no story. Nevertheless, far from that calm storm center where the people of *Finnegans Wake* lie asleep, the world is spinning toward another sunrise.

We find ourselves obliged to leave that one-way route which compels us to think of a giant Finn who lived once upon a time, founded a city, and then died, and was succeeded by a lot of different people until the story begins when he is represented by the burly publican of an inn on the road to Mullingar. As an aid to adapting my own mind to the pattern or plot of *Finnegans Wake*, I have found it useful to look on the book rather as a picture. A painter friend of mine owns one painted by a Flemish artist representing the war in heaven, the creation, temptation, fall, expulsion, and first murder lying side by side in one composition. The one or other of the many actions may be looked at apart or taken in forward or backward sequence, or all may be seen together as one simultaneous whole. But Joyce with his own material can do what no painter can do within the limits of color and a flat surface. The Futurists tried it and failed. He can build up his picture out of many superimposed planes of time, so that any one of his persons can give any number of impersonations. It is as if we looked at a picture of, say, Gog and Magog, master builders, and without changing their identity or position they became Dr. Magog laying down the law to his friend Mr. Gog, or young Gog and his clever Mog, or Prime Minister Magog receiving his union ticket from Bricklayers' President Gog and being told to get hold of some tools and finish the job.

Bound up with the dream time of Joyce's book is the dream language. I have already quoted a saying of Joyce's (evidently a practiced hand-off for a straight tackler), "Yes, there are enough words in the Oxford Dictionary, but they are not the right ones." Why are they not the right ones? Because they are words forged for the purpose of communicating thoughts and synchronizing activities in our waking and working hours and inapt (as I found them) to communicate the experiences of a dream or the myth of our race presented as a dream.

This brings us very near to the question of comprehensibility, which has quite a number of angles. Some writers are obscure because their thought is too deep or too high or too tenuous, others because they write of things in themselves comprehensible but which we knew nothing about, as, for example, in my own case, golf, bridge, music, or quantum theory, and still others because they have a religious experience peculiar to themselves which they may express but can never communicate. One writer may be too universal, another too local, and very few writers who are any good at all are wholly clear to all of us—or wholly incomprehensible, provided we consider the effort necessary to understand their material worth while. It is not the fundamental idea of *Finnegans Wake* that makes it difficult to understand and not the nature of the persons represented, for the idea of resurrection and recurrence is a popular idea and the figures of myth are popular figures. It is not even the verbal devices employed, which are, in the main, popular inventions. The material is difficult because of the breadth of Joyce's erudition and the narrowness of his locality. He puns in half a dozen languages, and all his local allusions are to the highways, byways, waterways, back streets, and backchat of Dublin. I am quite sure that *Finnegans Wake* is no stylistic experiment for its own sake. The innovations in form and material grew out of the matter and are a natural organic part of it. Where there is no snobbery of originality philistine resentment should be disarmed in advance. In connection with the verbal material of *Finnegans Wake* only one question seems to be worth considering: is that third element of the beautiful in Joyce's esthetic doctrine, that *"claritas,"* which Stephen Dedalus translates as "radiance" or "whatness," and which a painter might, perhaps, call "the essential character" of his subject apprehended in life and embodied in his material? The best available way of answering this question is to quote a couple of passages from the book and let the reader try to substitute Oxford Dictionary words for those used by Joyce without loss of essential character.

The first passage describes the ghostly unsubstantial meal at Finnegan's Wake: "Whase on the joint of a desh? Finfoefom the Fush. Whase be his baken head? A loaf of Singpantry's Kennedy bread. And whase hitched to the hop in his tayle? A glass of Danu O'Dunnell's foamous olde Dobbelin ayle. But, lo, as you would quaffoff his fraudstuff and sink teeth through that pythe of a flowerwhite bodey behold of him as behemoth for he is noewhemoe. Finiche! Only a fadograph of a yestern scene."

And here the wish of her womanhood observed passing through the soul of a sleeping girl: "Add lightest knot unto tiptition. O Charis! O Charissima! A more intriguant bambolina could one not colour up out of Boccucia's Enameron. Would one but to do apart a lilybit her virginelles and, so, to breath, so, therebetween, behold, she had instantt with her handmade as to graps the myth inmid the air. Mother of moth! I will to show herword in flesh. Approach not for ghost sake! It is dormition!"

However, let the reader grapple with Joyce's dream time and dream words as best he may, always remembering that, although it may be a good principle to act so that our conduct may serve as a rule of life to others, a writer need not write with the same circumspection—the reason being, no doubt, that English literature is a much tougher plant than social behavior. And let us be thankful that there is no puzzle at all about the dream place. It is the valley of the Liffey from Lucan to the sea and beyond to Howth Head, but the center of it, the focus of the picture, is the little village of Chapelizod which lies athwart the river on the southwest corner of Phoenix Park. More particularly the place is a little inn facing the bridge where the publican, his family, and servants lie asleep.

As the name implies—Chapelle d'Iseult—it is the place to which Tristan came to fetch his master's bride. Alfred Harmsworth was born there; Arthur Guinness built his house on a neighboring hill. In another direction an imposing monument in stone perpetuates the memory of

Arthur Wellesley, Duke of Wellington. Phoenix Park, at once the scene and the symbol of Finn's constant resurrection, links Chapelizod with Dublin, "a phantom city phaked of philim pholk," and the giant himself lies partly in Phoenix Park, where his feet are buried under the Magazine Mound, though his head is as far away as Howth. Here he "calmly extensolies" while the "shortlegged bergins . . . are all there scraping along to squeeze out a likelihood that will salve and solve life's robulous rebus, hopping round his middle like kippers on a griddle, O, as he lays dormont from the macroborg of Holdhard to the microbirg of Pied de Poudre." Chapelizod is the scene of Sheridan Lefanu's delightful novel, *The House by the Churchyard*. His Dangerfield, Devereux, Lilian, Sturk, and Ezekiel Irons flit like shades across the pages of Joyce's book. Joyce's father worked in the massive distillery, now redundant, derelict, and to let, formerly the barracks of Lefanu's loyal artillerymen. Commenting on a précis of Lefanu's book I made for him in 1937, Joyce wrote, referring to that spot in Phoenix Park where the fierce Dangerfield struck down Sturk: "The encounter between my father and a tramp (the basis of my book) actually took place at that part of the park." And Lefanu's elm, "the loftleaved elm Lefanunian," together with a mossy stone, tell the story of Anna Livia.

Ulysses is almost barren of descriptive passages. The Dublin of Bloomsday has to be constructed out of the words of Bloom and his fellow wanderers. But in *Finnegans Wake* are many memorable passages of landscape evocation. And that is an understatement, for it seems to me that the evening and night landscape in English literature has never been more magically realized than in *Finnegans Wake*. The potency of this realization is due largely, I think, to the fact that Joyce builds up his scene out of the memory of all senses, even that of touch. The passage at the end of the old wives' gossip about the life of Anna Livia Plurabelle is too well known to quote, but here is a fragment of one of equal beauty from the chapter called *The Mime of Mick Nick and the Maggies*. It describes the coming on of night and the animals in the Zoo going to rest:

"The trail of Gill not yet is to be seen, rocksdrops, up benn, down dell, a craggy road for rambling. Nor yet through starland that silver sash. What era's o'ering? Lang gone late. Say long, scielo! Sillume, see lo! Selene, sail O! Amune! Ark!? Noh?! Nought stirs in spinney. The swayful pathways of the dragonfly spider stay still in reedery. Quiet takes back her folded fields. Tranquille thanks. Adew. In deerhaven, imbraced, alleged, injoynted and unlatched, the birds, tommelise too, quail silent. . . . Was avond ere a while. Now conticinium. As Lord the Laohun is sheutseuyes. The time of lying together will come and the wildering of the nicht till cockeedoodle aubens Aurore. Panther monster. Send leabarrow loads amorrow. While loevdom shleeps. Elenfant has siang his triump, *Great is Eliphas Magistrodontos* and after kneeprayer pious for behemuth and mahamoth will rest him from tusker toils. Salamsalaim. Rhinohorn isnoutso pigfellow but him ist gonz wurst. Kikikuki. Hopopodorme. Sobeast! No chare of beagles, frantling of peacocks, no muzzing of the camel, smuttering of apes. Lights, pageboy, lights! Brights we'll be brights. With help of Hanoukan's lamp. When otter leaps in outer parts then Yul remembers Mei. Her hung maid mohns are bluming, look, to greet those loes on coast of amethyst; arcglow's seafire siemens lure and wextward warnerforth's hookercrookers."

And apart from the extended passages such as these there are on every page evocative words that call up an instant vision of a hillside bestrewn with boulders, a tree at a riverside, a white column, red earth, a rippling brown river.

But the landscape is not only background and ambient for the persons. It *is* the persons. Finn is Howth, and he is the landlord of an inn on the road to Mullingar. Shem and Shaun are the *rive gauche* and the *rive droite* of mother Liffey, and they are the rival brothers whose struggles are the history of the family and city of Finn. And so on. And here, perhaps, it may be said that Joyce looked upon Dublin, which, with its environs, formed the ancient kingdom of Dyffinarsky, as predominantly a Scandinavian city. Objective historical grounds apart, he was no doubt the more confirmed in this viewpoint through his hostility to that petit-bourgeois parochialism of Irish nationalism which loves to cloak itself in Celtic myth. The Nordic element in Ireland in any case is a bridge to Europe, and Joyce was a European as well as a Dubliner.

The population of *Finnegans Wake* is small compared with that of *Ulysses*. There are seven persons in it—one family including servants, and to these may be added three group personalities. The city is built out of these essences as the multitudinous shapes and substances of the world are built out of a small number of atoms.

First comes Finn himself, who died of a fall and was reborn at his wake. In remote totem shape he is the swift salmon of the river, the tough goat of the hill. His human origins are numerous. As Ur-father Adam he "lived in the broadest way immarginable . . . before joshuan judges had given us numbers of Helveticus committed deuteronomy." And there is a hint of a later oriental origin when he comes sailing "in the bark of life . . . the gran Phenician rover," but the two main sources that give him his local shape and character are Scandinavian and Celtic, the two branches of the family of fair strangers. As Scandinavian he is Humphrey Chimpden Earwicker; as Celt he is Persse O'Reilly; and O'Reilly and Earwicker become one when Persse O'Reilly becomes Pierce Oreille. This hero of many origins is called for short H.C.E., his own initials or those of Here Comes Everybody, a nickname applied to a more than usually pompous member of one of the Victorian administrations, Harold Childers Erskine. The unity of personality in Joyce's Adamite-Nordic-Celtic hero is not less complete because of a chronic and in-

curable dualism which manifests itself in a stammer of "HeCitEncy"—
his "tribalbalbutience." Earwicker wants Sunday closing and Sunday
clothing, but the O'Reilly wants seven days' license and shirtsleeves all
the week. He built a beautiful city and let it decay into a slum. He is a
"big cleanliving giant," happily married and enjoying the highest social
position, but he was caught in a most compromising situation with a
couple of nursemaids in the park. He supports religious reform and
family sanctity but sells contraceptives to the populace. And so the
duality of his mixed origin keeps him precariously balanced throughout
the whole of a master-builder's, Lord Mayor's, and publican's existence.

The invention of names for his characters is one of Joyce's favorite
methods of delineation. I haven't counted the names given to Earwicker
but should not be surprised if they ran into hundreds. This character-
defining by the giving of names is a device often used in "eddas and
oddes bokes of tomb."

This crookbacked hill, silvery fish, many-named human patriarch,
burly publican is never dressed twice alike. As gardener Adam he has-
tens to meet his overlord dressed in "topee, surcingle, solascarf and
plaid, plus fours, puttees and bulldog boots, ruddled cinnabar with flag-
rant marl," while as Kersse (Persse is as often spelt Kersse on account
of the Irish tendency to supplant the sound P with the sound K) he
sails into Dublin Bay "unwalloped in an unusuable suite of clouds."
Nevertheless, he is always "as modern as tomorrow afternoon and in
appearance up to the minute."

It is as Kersse that he woos, wins, and weds Anna Livia. And she?
Was she a dewdrop in a Wicklow vale? And did he find her while he
was looking for wild flowers? Was she the tailor's daughter? and did
he first see her lurking about her father's shop when he came in asking
"in his translatentic norjankeltian: Hwere can a ketch or hook alive
a soot an sowterkins?" This is not so clear and so it is probably both.
Her smallness at all ages is always insisted on. "She was just a young
thin pale soft shy slim slip of a thing then, sauntering by silvamoonlake
and he was a heavy trudging lurching lieabroad of a Curraghman...."
As tailor's daughter she was so small that, when he rang up about his
suit, she had to stand on a pile of samples to answer the phone, and
Kersse-Humphrey, anxious about her lack of bulk, followed her around
the dinner table trying to persuade her to eat a forkful of fat.

As an immortal river she is the daughter of Father Ocean and
Mother Sky, and she was born at some mysterious spot in the Wicklow
hills. Her partner, the male principle, came from a far place, but she
was always there. He has no youth and no age except the age of the
father and the hero, and no death, but inasmuch as Anna Livia represents the life of the body she shares the fate and goes the way of flesh.
Three children—twin boys and one girl—are not a big family. However,
in a wider sense she is mother of all Dublin. From three to a third of

a million is simple if unusual arithmetic. She writes the number of her children down one, one, one, as she might write the customers' credit drinks on the bar slate, and that makes a hundred and eleven. She adds them together and puts the three in place of the third one. Then she adds H.C.E. and herself to make the constantly recurring 1132. So is the city made.

All the houses and public documents of Dublin, all its civic glories, its laws, its liberties, learning, and amenities are the work of Bygmester Finn. He himself declares it in a broadcast he is called upon to give by the four masters. He grandly proclaims all the civilizing work he has done for the City of the Ford of Hurdles until his frustrating other self, in what appears to be a charity organization broadcast, steals his air and describes in detail the rotting misery of Poolblack's highly respectable slums. There are few correspondences between *Finnegans Wake* and *Ulysses*, but we seem to hear in the brave stammer of Finn more than a hint of the indomitable Simon Dedalus. Anna Livia has no parallel in *Ulysses*. She represents, as does the woman always in Joyce's work, the mortal body of the race, but there is none of the heavy fleshiness of Molly Bloom in her make-up. She is the active, cheerful, never-done-working wife and mother, bearing children, running the home, scrubbing the twins after their constant combats, comforting them when they wake squalling in the night, giving gifts to all her "daughter-sons," spreading the gossip, gratefully drinking the black ale brewed for her by Finn, sitting on Sunday in the church he built for her, but worshiping mainly at home, for "washup" is one of her forms of worship.

The twins, Shem and Shaun, are opposites, poles asunder and inseparable, hostile and complementary, held together and apart by the river of life that bore them. The inevitable self-portrait is Shem the Penman, called also Glugg and Jerry, the Gripes and the Gracehoper, while his brother, Shaun the Post, called also Chuff and Kevin, the Mookse and the Ondt, is all or any of Joyce's contemporaries. Shaun has to deliver a letter written by Shem, but the letter is never written and therefore never delivered (just as "that royal one has not yet drunk a gouttelette from his consummation . . . and all that has been done has yet to be done and done again. . . ."). With his twin rivals Joyce is giving poetic form to the constant human experience that the world maintains its balance through a conflict of opposites. Families are founded on it, societies grow out of it, parliaments flourish on it, and the human individual finds his refreshing opposite and complement in club and pub. If no sinner or saint or rebel or tyrant faced us we should have to split ourselves to find one. *Finnegans Wake* provides for this lonely contingency with the constantly recurring dual personality Browne and Nolan, at once the well-known firm of Dublin booksellers and Giordano Bruno of Nola, whose dualistic philosophy turns the bookselling unity, Browne and Nolan, into the hostile duality, Browne versus Nolan. Michael and Lucifer were the original heavenly pattern for this brotherly strife, and Cain and Abel, Jacob and Esau, Willingdone and Boomapart, and millions of other pairs have given and will forever give the earthly repetition.

Joyce's self-caricature as Shem is a tour de force in the comic grotesque, a genre in which Joyce excels. The likeness is unmistakable for all the posturing and grimacing in the distorting mirror. Joyce was no satirist, but he was a master of mimicry and caricature. He was rather a Rowlandson than a Daumier. He loved the spectacle of life too well to condemn any part of it. The comment implicit in caricature was enough. A step further might involve him in moral judgments forbidden by his individualistic rule of life and by his esthetic creed.

Shem is a sham, and a low sham. He lives on tinned food and likes it, and instead of getting drunk on good honest booze "he sobbed himself wheywhiningly sick of life on some sort of a rhubarbarous maundarin yellagreen funkleblue windigut diodying applejack squeezed from sour grapefruice." He believes in nothing and agrees with everybody, boasts about his people and their social position, stinks the place out, "lives on loans and is furtivefree yours of age." As a patriot he is a washout, for he "became a farsoonerite, saying he would far sooner muddle through the hash of lentils in Europe than meddle with Irrland's split little pea," and as a writer he bores everybody stiff with talking about his "usylessly unreadable Blue Book of Eccles." He ducks all duties and dodges all obligations, and while all the world was at war for great causes he "kuskykorked himself up tight in his inkbattle house, badly the worse for boosegas, there to stay in afar for the life. . . ." Browne in the person of Justius rises up against this Nayman of Noland, and there is little left of him after his dressing down till he is saved and restored by remembering his mother river and the contemplation of her inexhaustible treasure of life flowing past.

There is no trace of father and son conflict in *Finnegans Wake*, and therefore no reconciliation. The big man is master of his house and city. By way of rebirth he manifests himself through all the generations of his sons when they become of man's estate. All strife is of brother with brother, but even these fraternal wars are bloodless combats. Their hostility is a static hostility, for they are living on the plain of Shinar in that tower built into the sky in a unity that will last till day overcomes and scatters them. Joyce accepted the tower of Babel as a symbol of sleep. "Behold the people is one, and they have all one language." And he thought it strange that he should have been working several years on his book before the correspondence occurred to him.

Shem and Shaun never appear except in opposition, but whereas Shem is a clear-cut personality—an unmistakable caricature-portrait of the author—Shaun is by comparison a shadowy figure. The reason for this, perhaps, is that many models sat for Shaun, and only one for Shem. Most painters will agree that the use of many models for one figure is apt to lead to the abstract and away from the organic. One feels that a type or a race is being examined by the four masters rather than an individual person. What is clear about the shadowy Shaun is that he is a true believer, a gourmand, a sensualist, a persuasive talker (as witness his sermon to the twenty-nine daughters of February), an arriviste with his face turned toward the west where the money is, a favored of the gods, and a great success with the girls.

There are twenty-nine girls representing each a day of February fill-dyke, but only the twenty-ninth is the twins' sister and one of Anna Livia's hundred and eleven. Who begat and who bore the other twenty-eight need not concern us in this "semitary of Somnionia." Iseult's birthday comes once in four years so that she will be still a desirable beauty of twenty-five when her sisters are scored with a century of crowsfeet. She is the colorful cloud overhanging mother river, overhearing brother rivals mudslinging wordily about words and things, such as space and time. She reminds them that, for her, space is contracting and time flying, and she uses all the arts allowed a leap-year daughter to win them from their useless conflict for her useful purpose, but when she falls it is for mountain father Finn, whose eyes are ever fixed on his river's fresh youth in which he is overseen. "Yes, you're changing, sonhusband, and you're turning, I can feel you, for a daughterwife from the hills again."

All members of the Finn family have a side on which they merge with their opposite, as Earwicker takes on the character of a river and Anna Livia (A.L.P.) reflects the image of a mountain, Shem becomes Shaunesque and Shaun Shemesque, and daughter-mother Iseult hovers between sky and riverend. Even potman Joe borrows some of Earwicker's publican authority, and maidservant Kate rivalizes with her mistress while ironing the guvnor's lumbago on the kitchen table. She reminds him of the days when she was principal boy in the pantomime, and for his benefit (as he can't move) she repeats the performance: ". . . when I started so hobmop ladlelike, highty tighty, to kick the time off the cluckclock lucklock quamquam camcam potapot panapan kickakickkack. Hairhorehounds, shake up pfortner. Fuddling fun for Fullacan's sake."

Because of their ancient earthiness I associate this pair with the gossiping elm and stone washerwomen who tell the story of Anna Livia, with the Mutt and Jute stick and stone on the field of Clontarf who discuss that "law of isthmon" by which cities arise and are doomed to their "Finishthere Punct," and who, as Muta and Juva, observe the dawn lighting up the stained-glass windows of the village church and talk of the Eurasian outsider come to convert the high king of all Ireland to the true faith.

A group personality of twelve functions as customers at the big man's bar, as a jury charged with the examination of Earwicker's conduct, as loungers staring at a river, and their right-minded comment is delivered always with long words ending in "ation." But more difficult to understand and more important in their relation to the principal persons in the book are the four masters, analysts, waves, winds, provinces, evangelists, or institutions and their accompanying gray ass. They are the guardians of tradition, keepers of records, male sibyls, seekers after higher truths, lecherous admirers of male and female flesh. Their records, however, are lost, their memories confused, and their virility diluted to neutrality with femininity, yet they achieve an immortality of decrepitude as if the life in them were constantly renewed with injections of some secret all-glandular preparation. A Doctor Walker and a pretty nurse attend to their infirmities. They flounder blindly and deafly around in the dream space of the inn, "in all fathom of space" mumbling of the "good old days not worth remembering," sucking at bottles and urging each other to "pass the push for craw's sake," with senile amorousness fondling the hands of their nurse, trying to count up the mother-of-pearl buttons on her glove. It appears that nobody wants them in the house, but their power of infiltration is equal to that of dryrot, draughts, smells, dust, or circulars. Boneless, bloodless, toothless, covered with bedsores, "dolled up in their blankets," they manage somehow to be present at all family celebrations, even peeping through the salt-encrusted portholes at Tristan and Iseult on their honeymoon in a "lovely steamadory built by Fumadory." They are most in evidence when night is darkest and sleep deepest, and therefore they may be taken to represent the point of identity of the contraries, corruption and birth, but whatever its philosophic significance this fearsome foursome of disintegration is certainly one of the most astonishing of all Joyce's grotesque inventions.

I have never been able to see much racial difference between the Irish and the rest of us. If the bottle is well shaken it looks like the mixture as before. But there is a difference between the Irish and English imagination. The Irish imagination is continuous and expresses itself in a constant play of wit and fancy on the immediate material of life. It embroiders on the facts until the original fabric is hardly visible. In its popular aspect it is a thing of exaggerations, legpulls, backbites, sly digs, winks, thumb jerks, and talking through a lattice of fingers, all enjoyed by a lot of cheerful people in their shirtsleeves sitting in a draughty kitchen. All Persse O'Reilly, in fact, and at its creative best a Book of Kells or a Tristram Shandy. The English imagination is discontinuous. It functions only on high days, holy days, and Sundays, and because it is something apart it occasionally looks like a suburban parlor with a harmonium in it, but when it has functioned creatively it has imposed its offspring and its order on whole provinces of the mind. It is, in fact, all Earwicker. Finnegans Wake, like its hero, is a product of both. It is a fusion of Earwicker imagination and O'Reilly fancy, of plastic vision and graphic wit. The figures are of mythical proportions, but they are built up out of the commonest material, out of puns and slang, hurdy-gurdy tunes and music hall catchwords, and all the instruments of popular humor.

Joyce worked with the material of the market place, and if he is not understood there, it is certainly not on account of any preciosity in himself. His figures, for their forthrightness, belong there like Rodin's burgesses, for Joyce wrote out of the center of his consciousness where his own experience was at one with that of his fellow men. All the more strange that he should be sometimes regarded as a dweller in an ivory tower. Ivory tower! You don't get an Earwicker, sailor, publican, city builder, and city father; an Anna Livia, lover, mother, and house drudge; or a Bloom, with his associated Dubliners, to say nothing of Molly Bloom, out of an ivory tower.

And as this borders on politics I must confess that I was once guilty of helping to create the impression that Joyce was nonpolitical. He was certainly non-party, but no man can be nonpolitical who spends the greater part of his life in celebrating his native city. His first book was a series of studies showing the virtues and vices of his fellow Dubliners. He went on to paint a portrait of himself against the moral and physical background of Dublin. He recorded a lengthy day in the life of his mother city as seen and felt for the greater part by a stranger within her gates. His last work glorifies the spirit that founded and maintained the city of the Ford of Hurdles and affirms his belief in the persistence of that spirit through all changing circumstances. Joyce was certainly skeptical of all political parties and all political creeds, but he believed in the city and rejoiced in its life. He refused only to take part in the struggle as to who should govern it. The political novelist of the notebook or classbook order may at any moment descend on us (we are a beleaguered city, and the danger is very real), and when he does we shall know how to appreciate the artist who saw and felt and gave shape to that which is durable in life.

Many philosophies flit mothlike with characteristic words across the pages of *Finnegans Wake*, and ancient ritual books and compilations, particulary the Norse *Edda* and the Egyptian *Book of the Dead*, are more constantly recurring themes, but the two Italians, Vico and Bruno, provide Joyce with the philosophic motive and to some extent with the patterns of his book. Vico's theory of cyclic evolution, which allows for identity of personality in change and for recurrence in progression, might well appeal to the poet who dressed up the archer king of Ithaca in a black suit and bowler hat and sent him out on a quest for advertisements, or whose H.C.E. rules the city whatever party is in power. And Bruno's theory of duality and identity of contraries must have needed little demonstration to the individualist who refused to serve and become his own taskmaster, to the exile who took his city into exile with him.

There is a passage in Part IV of *Finnegans Wake* (in the language of somebody rolling over for the last doze before waking up) which seems to me to be a statement of the philosophy of the book: "The untireties of livesliving being the one substrance of a streamsbecoming. Totalled in toldteld and teldtold in tittletell tattle. Why? Because, graced be Gad and all giddy gadgets, in whose words were the beginnings, there are two signs to turn to, the yest and the ist, the wright side and the wronged side, feeling aslip and wauking up, so an, so farth. Why? On the sourdsite we have the Moskiosk Djinpalast with its twin adjacencies, the bathouse and the bazaar, allahallahallah, and on the sponthesite it is the alcovan and the rosegarden, boony noughty, all puraputhry. Why? One's apurr apuss a story about brid and breakfedes and parricombating and coushcouch but others is of tholes and oubworn buyings, dolings and chafferings in heat, contest and enmity. Why? Every talk has his stay, vidnis Shavarsanjivana, and all-a-dreams perhapsing under lucksloop at last are through. Why? It is a sot of a swigswag, systomy dystomy, which everabody you ever anywhere at all doze. Why? Such me."

Thus if you say that life is being you are right; equally right if you say that life is becoming; doubly right if you say that life is both being and becoming. If you say that life is a two-sided affair of perpetual conflict you affirm what is evident to every true body; if you declare that life is one and indivisible you echo that which the mind in its salmon leap of inspiration has been able to perceive. And characteristically the dreamer's final answer to the insistent "Why?" is the personal "Such me," which I take to mean, "You can search me, but that is how I feel about it."

Many a man is the battleground of his virtues, as Nietzsche said, and it seems to me to follow that many an artist may be the battleground of his talents. Joyce, I believe, kept peace within himself by choosing a motif upon which all his many selves might co-operate. Hence the rich and varied freights of *Ulysses* and *Finnegans Wake*. But did he manage to stow all the precious cargo in one hold? Was nothing left on the quayside for a later voyage? What became of the master of the short story, and of the severe yet pitiful regard for the stunted souls and thwarted destinies of weak human beings in *Dubliners?* Are there any other short stories in English that are neither de Maupassant curtains nor Chekhov fade-outs?

I have heard Joyce express disdain for "telling a story" and years later (on rereading Flaubert's *Contes*) say that that was just the thing he would most love to do. It is possible, however, to have done with a technical medium and to put it away altogether as a painter may give up portrait painting and take to wall painting, and so it is likely that, having found a way of making people and things speak for themselves, Joyce would never have returned to speaking about them. What is not possible is that an artist shall suppress any part of his humanity. The key of *Ulysses* is too bright, its movement too rapid, for that pity and reconciliation which provide the magical end of the story, "The Dead," to have any part in it, but that same human element expressed with yet greater artistry does return in the last pages of *Finnegans Wake*, when Anna Livia goes forth by day, as a woman (wife and mother, representative of all flesh) to join the countless generations of the dead, as a river to become one with the god, her father Ocean. She tells her human agony with the voice and gesture of the river. A leaf is floating with her, a prize from the woods of Lucan, and the city is asleep, but the sun is rising in her mother's house. She is full of memories, and she lisps them to the mind, her mate, whom she sees over the bay in his mountain form, whose gulls wheel over her. There is no answer from Finn. Her words are softly spoken, sometimes half articulate, so that we feel we have to bend to hear them as we bend to hear precious words on the lips of the dying. Memories fail her. Dreams of past grandeur fade. Her children she thought so fine disgust her. Her human fear of loss of personality overcomes her as her sweet waters are fouled by the brackish water of the estuary which is like a foretaste of death. She tides herself over her fears with illusions of grandeurs to come, how she will be received by her mighty sisters, wild Amazia and haughty Niluna. With a last thought of Finn and a wish to live again, as if a wish had in itself a force of fulfillment, she passes over the bar into her father's home.

> Carry me along, taddy, like you done through the toy fair! If I seen him bearing down on me now under whitespread wings like he'd come from Arkangels, I sink I'd die down over his feet, humbly, dumbly, only to washup. Yes, tid. There's where. First. We pass through grass behush the bush to. Whish! A gull. Gulls. Far calls. Coming, far! End here. Us then. Finn, again! Take. Bussoftlhee, mememormee! Till thousendsthee. Lps. The keys to. Given! A way a lone at last a loved a long the . . .

The last work of Joyce ends, as did his first, in the contemplation of the mystery of death. In both cases the rebellious pity of the human heart finds in the beauty of a constant element of nature—in the one falling snow, in the other smooth-gliding water—the symbol and the instrument of reconciliation with human destiny. We had hoped for further years and other labors. We cannot imagine a fitter swan song.

MAINSTREAM

Talking About Injustice:
James Joyce in the Modern World   Richard M. Kain*

> —*Are you talking about the new Jerusalem?* says the citizen.
> —*I'm talking about injustice,* says Bloom.

"Filthy in word, filthy in thought, furious, raging, obscene"—how often these and similar charges have been leveled at Joyce's *Ulysses!* But it is not a modern critic from whom these words are quoted, nor is it Joyce who is being attacked; it is Thackeray misjudging the greatest satirist in the annals of English literature—Jonathan Swift.

The earnestness and honesty of satirists, their clear-eyed vision of evil, their moral horror, have ever been subject to misinterpretation by tender-minded readers. The weapons of irony and indirection are double edged and often return to wound the assailant as well as the victim. Since most twentieth-century authors use these weapons, it is not surprising to find that misguided zealots have accused modern literature of the very evils it attacks. Licentiousness, social irresponsibility, perversion—from these sins it is a short step to attributing to recent writing the decline of patriotism, the lowering of the birth rate, or the rise of Hitler. For the last it may be said that literature has no place in the discussion of fascism; the burning of the books was eloquent testimony to the power the Nazis feared most.

But it is hardly necessary to prove *Ulysses* a masterpiece of modern literature. It stands, an immense dolmen, towering above the barren wasteland of twentieth-century culture. It has been savagely attacked, and perhaps just as extravagantly admired. It cannot be overlooked or by-passed.

In *Finnegans Wake* Joyce begs the indulgence of the "ideal reader suffering from an ideal insomnia"; and, indeed, that work requires an

*This essay first appeared in *Fabulous Voyager: James Joyce's Ulysses* (Chicago: University of Chicago Press, 1947) and is reprinted with permission from The University of Chicago Press.

encyclopedic knowledge of philology, folklore, history, and metaphysics. No such extensive demands are made by *Ulysses*. The work can be understood by the literate reader. It requires patience and intelligence— above all, sympathy and insight. The elucidation of minor points, tracing of literary echoes, and other methods of scholastic exegesis bid fair to discourage the public who should read *Ulysses*. Just as Shakespeare has often been ruined for schoolboys, so Joyce's brilliant insights into the dilemmas of modern civilization are too often smothered under a moraine of footnotes.

It is unfortunate, too, that Joyce is chiefly known as a technician, a bewildering experimentalist. This kind of fame is sterile; it creates of one of the most vital and provocative novels a preserve for graduate courses in literature. It makes *Ulysses* a monument of art for art's sake. The fascination of seeing a genuinely original and creative mind at work upon the factors of our culture is lost. Joyce is prophetic, as all great writers have been prophetic. His is the clearest and most incisive voice of our age, and we should do well to heed him.

For *Ulysses* is a world book. The "Divine Comedy" of our age, it brings an uncompromising intelligence to bear upon the moral failures of modern civilization. The dislocations of society, as well as the diseases of the soul, are dissected with searing brilliance by one who was in a rare position to observe them, who possessed rare skill in analyzing them and rare courage in revealing them. Not for nothing were Joyce's heroes Swift and Ibsen. Like them he had the intelligence to see and the intrepidity to utter what he saw. The words of the young Joyce, in *Stephen Hero*, are pertinent: "Civilisation may be said indeed to be the creation of its outlaws." As Swift mercilessly demolished the eighteenth-century idols of the tribe and Ibsen those of the nineteenth century, so Joyce has done for our day. We are all in his debt.

Nor is *Ulysses* as grim as this introduction might seem to make it. Joyce's humor is infectious, his gusto irrepressible. He has much of the "joyicity" of the grasshopper of *Finnegans Wake*. Moralists who point to his "message" and moralists who lament his apparent lack of a "message" both fall into one misinterpretation. They forget that Joyce is a satirist, and a satirist without a sense of humor is as much an anomaly as a Dublin without pubs. *Ulysses* is fun to read.

The time is ripe for a reconsideration of this important monument of modern culture. Joyce's brilliant and unpredictable career has been brought to a close, and his last novel, *Finnegans Wake*, surveyed and annotated. One should be able to judge *Ulysses* more fully and justly than before.

Finnegans Wake, that strange nightmare epic, appeared in September, 1939, at a time when the attention of the Western world was directed to other than literary matters. It aroused a brief flurry of excitement upon publication and a rebirth of interest in the summer of

1944, caused by Campbell and Robinson's *Skeleton Key*. At neither time, however, was more than a passing glance directed to the acknowledged masterpiece of twenty years' standing—and this despite the fact that *Ulysses* can be understood much more clearly in relation to the later work, for in *Finnegans Wake* appear the two basic themes of *Ulysses*— social criticism and philosophical relativity—the first somewhat submerged, the second considerably magnified.

The brief handbook, *James Joyce*, by Harry Levin, published in 1941, is not only an excellent guide to the entire career of Joyce but a masterpiece of judicial and perceptive criticism. His study of *Ulysses* is sound and challenging, though, of necessity, limited in scope. The indebtedness of the present study to the work of Levin will be apparent, as will be the modifications of his conclusions, particularly his charges that Joyce is deficient in human sympathy and in philosophical outlook.

Of earlier criticisms, Edmund Wilson's treatment of *Ulysses* in *Axel's Castle* remains an unsurpassable introduction. Important pioneer work was done by Valéry Larbaud, T. S. Eliot, and S. Foster Damon. Stuart Gilbert's elaborate commentary is more likely to terrify the general reader than to enlighten him, not to speak of providing a somewhat misleading perspective. His work suffers from two shortcomings: first, and less important, that the publication of the study before the novel was generally available necessitated extensive paraphrase (and expurgation) of the text. Of greater consequences is his exclusive preoccupation with esoteric symbolism, leading him to overlook many basic artistic and philosophical values. It will be necessary in this study to evaluate Gilbert's findings and to assess their aesthetic significance.

Readers of Joyce need not be told of the importance of the word in his style. No writer has used repetition, modulation, and permutation of single words so extensively or with such felicity. Hence the concordance to *Ulysses*, published in 1937 by Miles L. Hanley, is an invaluable aid to the fullest analysis of the novel.

Joyce has been the most bitterly attacked and grossly misunderstood of modern writers. The charges against him are numerous—that he is indefensibly obscure and indecent, that he lacks human sympathy, that his work is a formless and meaningless chaos, that he has no philosophy but cynical nihilism. Sometimes these opinions may be condoned, when they arise from a lack of understanding or sympathy on the part of the reader; but, more often, attacks are based upon deliberate misreading, misinterpretation, prejudice, or lack of literary and social perspective.

Joyce alludes to these charges in *Finnegans Wake*. His tone is one of irony, tinged with amusement, without concealing a justified contempt for the unappreciative public: "Sniffer of carrion, premature gravedigger, seeker of the nest of evil in the bosom of a good word, you, who sleep at our vigil and fast for our feast, you with your dislocated reason, have cutely foretold . . . . the reducing of records to ashes, the levelling of all customs by blazes." And when he refers to his "usylessly unreadable" novel, "an epical forged cheque on the public for his own private profit," it is impossible not to feel his suppressed disappointment.

One cannot answer these attacks in a few words; indeed, the intention of this study is to provide a critical method by which the unique quality of the book may be appreciated and understood. Yet it is well to establish some basic principles of aesthetics as a preparation for the detailed analyses which follow.

First, as to motives of artistic creation. The imputation of sordid motives to the artist has long been one of the weapons of prejudiced criticism. Allegations of insincerity or incompetence follow as obvious corollaries. Hence we may never expect to see the end of such charges as that the artist is striving for notoriety, seeking money, or merely indulging in specious originality or exhibitionism at the expense of a gullible public.

Such amateur psychologizing is as difficult to prove as it is to disprove. But the nature of society, its innate conservatism and fear of change, makes it seem to the public that the burden of proof rests upon the defense rather than upon the prosecution. It was so in the days of Socrates; the charge then was the corruption of youth. Regrettably one must assume that it will be so in the future, no matter what form of government or social organization is adopted.

The root of the trouble lies in a misunderstanding of the function of art in society. So long as art is regarded primarily as a source of innocent entertainment or as a medium of escape, any artist who turns his attention to social criticism or personal analysis will be misunderstood. He will be labeled neurotic, scatological, nihilistic.

Yet no one acquainted with the history of culture can afford to make so naïve an interpretation of the nature of art. Whether or not the public knows it, even without the awareness of the artist himself, all art implies a certain standard of values. These standards may be taken for granted, but they are nevertheless present. Even Hollywood cannot escape acceptance or rejection of the mores of society.

There remain several attitudes possible for the practitioner of the arts. He may pander deliberately to the lowest level of taste in his potential audience, confirming their prejudices and accepting without question the demands made upon him. Such is the readiest way to financial success; it must be conceded that the advance guard of modern letters has failed miserably if the box-office is their goal.

The artist may sincerely be able to assume the basic rightness of the social pattern, seeing in it a compromise that is working more or less satisfactorily and which he feels no burning need to analyze or attack. This attitude can generally be adopted more readily in a society that is relatively stable, or one which is in the ascendant, rising confidently to its zenith; it may also be treasured sincerely by an individual who is jealously guarding the values of a society in decline. Of the first condition one can cite the example of Fielding or, with qualification, of Dickens; of the second, Doctor Johnson or Edith Wharton.

It is indeed difficult for the serious artist today to adopt this creed of wholehearted acceptance. The economic, political, and philosophical dislocations of the twentieth century are so great that a perceptive observer can scarcely ignore them. He may, indeed, proffer a positive solution, if he is happy enough to have faith in any panacea; but such solutions are difficult to find or accept. The more usual tone of modern art is therefore one of scrutiny and self-examination, turning many times upon the artistic process itself. This way lies skepticism, to be sure, but it may also provoke a reorientation of basic values. Society, clinging fearfully to its standards, finds it hard to accept or understand such an outlook; it fears what it does not know.

One of the fundamental axioms of artistic appreciation is, in Coleridge's phrase, the willing suspension of disbelief. In the present context the notion might be better rendered as a willing suspension of distrust. Adopt for a moment the frame of reference, the tone, the code of values, which the artist implies; read with an open mind, being sure that these intentions are as well understood as possible. Then, and then only, can one pose as a fair judge.

Let us turn for a moment to a brief survey of the conditions of modern society. The entire world is today witnessing the convulsive death throes of the political and economic beliefs of the last century. The future of capitalism and of liberal democracy seems now to be at stake; and again the student of cultural history is amazed by the uncanny prescience of writers who long ago sensed the imminence of the present catastrophic changes in society. Ignoring the revolutionary spokesmen of the nineteenth century, as early as 1900 Thomas Mann had examined with diligence the decline of bourgeois standards of value in *Buddenbrooks*. In 1912 an obscure German scholar, Oswald Spengler, penned the title of his philosophical masterpiece, *The Decline of the West*, published in the momentous month of July, 1918. From 1912 to 1924 Thomas Mann probed with increased powers of poetic sensitivity the problems of a young man of the prewar generation, Hans Castorp of *The Magic Mountain*. During these years a similar task was undertaken on a colosssal scale by Marcel Proust in France; and during these years Joyce wrote his panoramic *Ulysses*, depicting the disintegration of moral and philosophical values.

The intellectual finds that the long-vaunted integrity of man, the keynote of humanism, has suffered from the depredations of evolutionary biology, of normal and abnormal psychology, and of materialist interpretations of history. Humanism has been discredited, so often has it been used to defend reactionary politics, authoritarianism, and the economic status quo, while a vigorous naturalism and relativism in philosophy and literature seek a new basis for humane values. Likewise has the neatly geometrical Newtonian universe—the world view of classical physics and astronomy—been shattered by concepts of relativity, the quantum theory, wave mechanics, and the principles of indeterminacy. Marx, Darwin, Freud, and Einstein have brought into question bourgeois standards of value.

In his penetrating Introduction to the volume, *Books That Changed Our Minds*, Malcolm Cowley finds that the works selected by contributors as the most significant of recent years have one trait in common. Though ostensibly on diverse and seemingly unrelated subjects—logic, metaphysics, cultural history, psychology, economics, and sociology—the works of Darwin, Marx, Veblen, Freud, Bergson, and others agree in refuting the accepted faith in rationalism. Nineteenth-century liberalism was based on the supremacy of human reason, and its freedom from economic, national, or racial prejudices. From it stemmed the hopes for continuous social and economic progress, the belief in popular education, reform, democracy. It is a matter not of cynicism but of clear-eyed observation to remark that these hopes are open to widespread qualification today.

Of the three major writers of the twentieth century—Marcel Proust in French, Thomas Mann in German, and James Joyce in English literature—Joyce appears to be the one who faced most unflinchingly the decadence of bourgeois society. Marcel Proust retired to the nostalgic dreams of a social pattern from which he had been exiled by ill-health— a society which was itself rapidly passing away—and labored to render the aesthetic impressions left upon his memory. Thomas Mann grappled courageously with the data of science and society, hoping to retrieve from destruction some of the values of a world that was passing, and closed his masterpiece with a pious hope that his faith in the brotherhood of man might somehow be realized. James Joyce alone felt the searing brilliance of "time's livid final flame," on which Stephen reflected throughout *Ulysses*. With microscopic exactitude Joyce revealed the inherent contradictions and short-comings of modern civilization. It is my purpose to analyze and explain in detail his findings and the skill with which they are rendered.

In many ways Joyce was unusually qualified by temperament and circumstance to proceed with this necessary task of social analysis, necessary in the sense that no satisfactory social order can be successfully reared upon the dry husks and hollow shells of outworn beliefs. Raised under the strict dogmas of Catholicism and subjected to the discipline of a Jesuit education, he was plunged from the metaphysics of the Middle Ages into the practical exigencies of modern life. Thus, comparatively insulated during his early years from the basic contradictions of modern society, he found them all the more glaring, once they were exposed to his eyes. The situation inherent in so much satiric literature of the past—the visitor from a foreign land examining the customs of an age—was exemplified in the biography of Joyce. The young author, emerging from his scholastic education in 1902, was indeed a modern Rasselas, leaving the Happy Valley to judge the world.

Jesuit education not only provided Joyce with this perspective but was a source of additional isolation. In Joyce's excellent study of his mental development, *A Portrait of the Artist*, Stephen feels that his education, so assiduously cultivated, was itself an object of indifference or contempt in modern society: "it wounded him to think that he would never be but a shy guest at the feast of the world's culture and that the monkish learning, in terms of which he was striving to forge out an esthetic philosophy, was held no higher by the age he lived in than the subtle and curious jargons of heraldry and falconry."

Another feature of Joyce's life deserves mention. One may question whether it is ever entirely possible to break away from the Catholic church. Readers of the *Portrait* will recall the urgent necessity to defend his position which obsessed the hero; an equally urgent necessity undoubtedly motivated the writing of the book. Stephen defends himself on the grounds of personal independence. The note occurs again and again. In refusing to sign the petition for the banning of Yeats's play, Stephen responds to his schoolmates quietly: "You are right to go your way. Leave me to go mine." "I shall express myself as I am," he answers another plea for conformity. And in rejoinder to Cranly's efforts to return him to the fold of religion:

Did you believe in it when you were at school? I bet you did.—
    —I did—Stephen answered.
    —And were you happier then?—Cranly asked softly—happier than you are now, for instance?—
    —Often happy—Stephen said—and often unhappy. I was someone else then.—
    —How someone else? What do you mean by that statement?—
    —I mean—said Stephen—that I was not myself as I am now, as I had to become.—

Levin says wittily that Joyce lost his religion but kept his categories, but the matter is not quite so simple. Cranly remarks to Stephen in the *Portrait* that "your mind is supersaturated with the religion in which you say you disbelieve," and in the same discussion Stephen confirms this interpretation:

    —I imagine—Stephen said—that there is a malevolent reality behind those things I say I fear.—

Now to renounce one's faith with misgivings such as these is to create within one's self a constant tension, a tension out of which a forceful art will be wrested. Far removed from a complacent acceptance of belief, Joyce, like Dostoevski before him, will be acutely aware of the ambivalence of the human mind, of the drawing-power of the forces which he wishes to reject or escape. Joyce's view of life will be that of an unhappy and homesick exile.

An exile in fact, too. In addition to the strains of uncertain disbelief will be those of loss of faith in his country. It has often been remarked that, though Joyce removed himself physically from Ireland, all his artistic work was devoted to the country he rejected. Again one finds the condition of aloofness and distance, so necessary to vital social analysis.

Ireland was in other respects a happy accident of Joyce's birth, for there the inconsistencies of modern economic and political practice were aggravated by a hated imperialism, centuries old. A revealing passage in the *Portrait*, apropos of a British teacher at University College, clearly shows this instinctive revolt from all things connected with the master-country:

> —The language in which we are speaking is his before it is mine. How different are the words *home, Christ, ale, master*, on his lips and on mine! I cannot speak or write these words without unrest of spirit. . . . . My soul frets in the shadow of his language.—

A national humiliation so long ingrained is bound to confirm one's innate tendencies to revolt and to sharpen one's eyes to injustice, chicanery, and hypocrisy wherever they are found. Nor was the rising Irish nationalism any more to the young Joyce's liking. He could never forgive the betrayal of Parnell. Whether it was attributable to provincial morality or to cowardice, it was unforgettable. Tim Healy, the politician who succeeded Parnell, was to Joyce little better than a traitor. It is said that he was the subject of a youthful polemic—"Et Tu Healy?"—written by Joyce at the age of nine. He appears in *Ulysses* as one of the hue and cry who pursue Bloom in a nightmare. In *Finnegans Wake*, in a characteristic triple pun, Dublin becomes Healiopolis, Egyptian home of the embalmed phoenix (Phoenix Park in Dublin was the scene of terroristic murders in Joyce's youth), as well as the city of the careerist politician.

Strict religious discipline, rejection of faith, geographical exile, and a strong sense of economic exploitation and political tyranny—add to these the natural independence and sensitivity of the artist. The conventional slogans of society were to Stephen merely wooden swords. But they had a malignant power, too—an unseen, but nonetheless effective, ability to suppress and censor self-development. Conformity itself was dangerous. Stephen speaks of his fear of "the chemical action which would be set up in my soul by a false homage to a symbol." Injustice can never be condoned. A diary entry at the end of the *Portrait* is as passionate as it is brief—"He said Bruno was a terrible heretic. I said he was terribly burned."

The cost of such an attitude is loneliness, but there is also an ardent faith, a consciousness of mission. Stephen realizes this fully. Conversing with a college friend, he says: "When the soul of a man is born in this country there are nets flung at it to hold it back from flight. You talk to me of nationality, language, religion. I shall try to fly by those nets.—" In an eloquent, yet uneasily self-conscious, statement of his artistic creed, the young Stephen asserts: "I will tell you what I will do and what I will not do. I will not serve that in which I no longer believe, whether it call itself my home, my fatherland or my church: and I will try to express myself in some mode of life or art as freely as I can."

When the *Portrait* was written, it was still possible for Joyce to be optimistic about the reception of his work and the message he might bear to mankind. Grandiloquently, Stephen concludes his diary of the birth of the artist with the words: "I go to encounter for the millionth time the reality of experience and to forge in the smithy of my soul the uncreated conscience of my race." Yet other disillusionments were to follow. The lengthy haggling over the publication of his relatively inoffensive volume of short stories, *Dubliners*, took its toll of his patience. Herbert Gorman's biography of Joyce recounts the tedious details of this process. All the author's delicacy of style, insight, and sympathy were overlooked; a few questionable phrases and political allusions were all that mattered to the publishers. The novelist was certainly justified in regarding it as one more sign of the impossible stupidity of the *bourgeoisie*.

Joyce never returned to Dublin after 1912, when he tried in vain to have his publishers release the volume. His books have been banned in Ireland; his native land has exiled him more fully than he was ever comfortable in exiling himself from it. Then, in 1914, when he was ready to start on *Ulysses*, the first World War began. Here was the cataclysm which revealed on an immense scale the inequities and inconsistencies of modern civilization. Here, indeed, was "the ruin of all space, shattered glass and toppling masonry, and time one livid final flame." Isolated in neutral Switzerland, Joyce consumed himself in the writing of an encyclopedic novel of modern life.

The complex personality of Joyce awaits a definitive biographer. To his friends he seemed jocose and flippant, little given to introspection, yet all his work is confessional. To what degree does it reflect subconscious motivations as well as the external causations here cited? The prurience may well be a form of inverted puritanism, the cynical acceptance of commercial values (as when Stephen demands payment for his writings in *Stephen Hero*, the *Portrait*, and *Ulysses*) a painful sham, the scorn for country and church a desperate gesture. Like D. H. Lawrence, Joyce seems to have been fascinated by what he hated and repelled by what he loved. Is his psychological fiction, like Lawrence's, a series of psychological fictions, in the Freudian sense of the word, the disguised manifestation of latent personal tensions and desires? Or, to draw a closer analogy, the Joyce who embraces "silence, exile, and cunning" as his weapons and who builds his theory of static art seems more akin in spirit to Flaubert, whose artistic discipline was a bastion against a world he despised. Between the poles of Lawrence and Flaubert, between confession and repression, lies *Ulysses*.

Alienated from homeland, church, bourgeois society, local politics, and Empire allegiance, Joyce centered his masterpiece in the story of two homesick wanderers. The satiric imaginary travels of Gulliver, Candide, and Rasselas have here their modern counterpart, just as Bloom finds his ancient prototype in Odysseus, legendary voyager of the past. Indeed, as we shall see, one day in Dublin, June 16, 1904, is but a brief segment of that journey of man we call "life." The path of Everyman through space and time to infinity is the ultimate mystery. Man, finally, is the fabulous voyager.

The Backgrounds of "The Dead"   Richard Ellmann*

The silent cock shall crow at last. The west shall shake the east awake.
Walk while ye have the night for morn, lightbreakfastbringer. . . .
    —*Finnegans Wake* (473)

The stay in Rome [from July 1906 until March 1907] had seemed purposeless, but during it Joyce became aware of the change in his attitude toward Ireland and so toward the world. He embodied his new perceptions in "The Dead." The story, which was the culmination of a long waiting history, began to take shape in Rome, but was not set down until he left the city. The pressure of hints, sudden insights, and old memories rose in his mind until, like King Midas's barber, he was compelled to speech.

Although the story dealt mainly with three generations of his family in Dublin, it drew also upon an incident in Galway in 1903. There Michael ("Sonny") Bodkin courted Nora Barnacle; but he contracted tuberculosis and had to be confined to bed. Shortly afterwards Nora resolved to go to Dublin, and Bodkin stole out of his sickroom, in spite of the rainy weather, to sing to her under an apple tree and bid her goodbye. In Dublin Nora soon learned that Bodkin was dead, and when she met Joyce she was first attracted to him, as she told a sister, because he resembled Sonny Bodkin.[1]

Joyce's habit of ferreting out details had made him conduct minute

*This essay first appeared in *James Joyce* (New York: Oxford University Press, 1959) and is reprinted with premission from the Oxford University Press.

interrogations of Nora even before their departure from Dublin. He was disconcerted by the fact that young men before him had interested her. He did not much like to know that her heart was still moved, even in pity, by the recollection of the boy who had loved her. The notion of being in some sense in rivalry with a dead man buried in the little cemetery at Oughterard was one that came easily, and gallingly, to a man of Joyce's jealous disposition. It was one source of his complaint to his Aunt Josephine Murray that Nora persisted in regarding him as quite similar to other men she had known.[2]

A few months after expressing this annoyance, while Joyce and Nora Barnacle were living in Trieste in 1905, Joyce received another impulsion toward "The Dead." In a letter Stanislaus happened to mention attending a concert of Plunket Greene, the Irish baritone, which included one of Thomas Moore's *Irish Melodies* called "O, Ye Dead!"[3] The song, a dialogue of living and dead, was eerie enough, but what impressed Stanislaus was that Greene rendered the second stanza, in which the dead answer the living, as if they were whimpering for the bodied existence they could no longer enjoy:

> It is true, it is true, we are shadows cold and wan;
> And the fair and the brave whom we loved on earth are gone;
>> But still thus ev'n in death,
>> So sweet the living breath
> Of the fields and the flow'rs in our youth we wandered o'er,
>> That ere, condemn'd, we go
>> To freeze, 'mid Hecla's snow,
> We would taste it awhile, and think we live once more!

James was interested and asked Stanislaus to send the words, which he learned to sing himself. His feelings about his wife's dead lover found a dramatic counterpart in the jealousy of the dead for the living in Moore's song: it would seem that the living and the dead are jealous of each other. Another aspect of the rivalry is suggested in *Ulysses*, where Stephen cries out to his mother's ghost, whose "glazing eyes, staring out of death, to shake and bend my soul, . . . to strike me down," he cannot put out of mind: "No, mother. Let me be and let me live."[4] That the dead do not stay buried is, in fact, a theme of Joyce from the beginning to the end of his work; Finnegan is not the only corpse to be resurrected.

In Rome the obtrusiveness of the dead affected what he thought of Dublin, the equally Catholic city he had abandoned, a city as prehensile of its ruins, visible and invisible. His head was filled with a sense of the too successful encroachment of the dead upon the living city; there was a disrupting parallel in the way that Dublin, buried behind him, was haunting his thoughts. In *Ulysses* the theme was to be reconstituted, in more horrid form, in the mind of Stephen, who sees corpses rising from their graves like vampires to deprive the living of joy. The bridebed, the childbed, and the bed of death are bound together, and death "comes, pale vampire, through storm his eyes, his bat sails bloodying the sea, mouth to her mouth's kiss."[5] We can be at the same time in death as well as in life.[6]

By February 11, 1907, after six months in Rome, Joyce knew in general what story he must write. Some of his difficulty in beginning it was due, as he said himself,[7] to the riot in Dublin over *The Playboy of the Western World*. Synge had followed the advice of Yeats that Joyce had rejected, to find his inspiration in the Irish folk, and had gone to the Aran Islands. This old issue finds small echoes in the story. The nationalistic Miss Ivors tries to persuade Gabriel to go to Aran (where Synge's *Riders to the Sea* is set), and when he refuses twits him for his lack of patriotic feeling. Though Gabriel thinks of defending the autonomy of art and its indifference to politics, he knows such a defense would be pretentious, and only musters up the remark that he is sick of his own country. But the issue is far from settled for him.

"The Dead" begins with a party and ends with a corpse, so entwining "funferal" and "funeral" as in the wake of Finnegan. That he began with a party was due, at least in part, to Joyce's feeling that the rest of the stories in *Dubliners* had not completed his picture of the city. In a letter of September 25, 1906,[8] he had written his brother from Rome to say that some elements of Dublin had been left out of his stories: "I have not reproduced its ingenuous insularity and its hospitality, the latter 'virtue' so far as I can see does not exist elsewhere in Europe." He allowed a little of this warmth to enter "The Dead." In his speech at the Christmas party Gabriel Conroy explicitly commends Ireland for this very virtue of hospitality, though his expression of the idea is distinctly after-dinner: "I feel more strongly with every recurring year that our country has no tradition which does it so much honour and which it should guard so jealously as that of its hospitality. It is a tradition that is unique as far as my experience goes (and I have visited not a few places abroad) among the modern nations." This was Joyce's oblique way, in language that mocked his own, of beginning the task of making amends.

The selection of details for "The Dead" shows Joyce making those choices which, while masterly, suggest the preoccupations that mastered him. Once he had determined to represent an Irish party, the choice of the Misses Morkans' as its location was easy enough. He had already reserved for *Stephen Hero* a Christmas party at his own house, a party which was also to be clouded by a discussion of a dead man. The other festive occasions of his childhood were associated with his hospitable great-aunts Mrs Callanan and Mrs Lyons, and Mrs Callanan's daughter Mary Ellen, at their house at 15 Usher's Island, which was also known as the "Misses Flynn school."[9] There every year the Joyces who were old enough would go, and John Joyce carved the goose and made the speech. Stanislaus Joyce says that the speech of Gabriel Conroy in "The Dead" is a good imitation of his father's oratorical style.[10]

In Joyce's story Mrs Callanan and Mrs Lyons, the Misses Flynn, become the spinster ladies, the Misses Morkan, and Mary Ellen Callanan becomes Mary Jane. Most of the other party guests were also reconstituted from Joyce's recollections. Mrs Lyons had a son Freddy, who kept a Christmas card shop in Grafton Street.[11] Joyce introduces him as Freddy Malins, and situates his shop in the less fashionable Henry Street, perhaps to make him need that sovereign Gabriel lent him. Another relative of Joyce's mother, a first cousin, married a Protestant named Mervyn Archdale Browne, who combined the profession of music teacher with that of agent for a burglary insurance company. Joyce keeps him in "The Dead" under his own name. Bartell d'Arcy, the hoarse singer in the story, was based upon Barton M'Guckin, the leading tenor in the Carl Rosa Opera Company. There were other tenors, such as John McCormack, whom Joyce might have used, but he needed one who was unsuccessful and uneasy about himself; and his father's often-told anecdote about M'Guckin's lack of confidence[12] furnished him with just such a singer as he intended Bartell d'Arcy to be.

The making of his hero, Gabriel Conroy, was more complicated. The root situation, of jealousy for his wife's dead lover, was of course Joyce's. The man who is murdered, D. H. Lawrence has one of his characters say, desires to be murdered;[13] some temperaments demand the feeling that their friends and sweethearts will deceive them. Joyce's conversation often returned to the word "betrayal,"[14] and the entangled innocents whom he uses for his heroes are all aspects of his conception of himself. Though Gabriel is less impressive than Joyce's other heroes, Stephen, Bloom, Richard Rowan, or Earwicker, he belongs to their distinguished, put-upon company.

There are several specific points at which Joyce attributes his own experiences to Gabriel. The letter which Gabriel remembers having written to Gretta Conroy early in their courtship is one of these; from it Gabriel quotes to himself the sentiment, "Why is it that words like these seem to me so dull and cold? Is it because there is no word tender enough to be your name?" These sentences are taken almost directly from a letter Joyce wrote to Nora in 1904.[15] It was also Joyce, of course, who wrote book reviews, just as Gabriel Conroy does, for the *Daily Express*. Since the *Daily Express* was pro-English, he had probably been teased for writing for it during his frequent visits to the house of David Sheehy, M.P. One of the Sheehy daughters, Kathleen, may well have been the model for Miss Ivors, for she wore that austere bodice and sported the same patriotic pin.[16] In Gretta's old sweetheart, in Gabriel's letter, in the book reviews and the discussion of them, as well as in the physical image

of Gabriel with hair parted in the middle and rimmed glasses, Joyce
drew directly upon his own life.

His father was also deeply involved in the story. Stanislaus Joyce
recalls that when the Joyce children were too young to bring along to
the Misses Flynns' party, their father and mother sometimes left them
with a governess and stayed at a Dublin hotel overnight instead of returning to their house in Bray.[17] Gabriel and Gretta do this too. Gabriel's
quarrels with his mother also suggest John Joyce's quarrels with his
mother, who never accepted his son's marriage to a woman of lower
station.[18] But John Joyce's personality was not like Gabriel's; he had no
doubts of himself, in the midst of many failures he was full of self-esteem.
He had the same unshakable confidence as his son James. For Gabriel's
personality there is among Joyce's friends another model.[19] This was
Constantine Curran, sometimes nicknamed "Cautious Con." He is a more
distinguished man than Joyce allows, but Joyce was building upon, and
no doubt distorting, his memories of Curran as a very young man. That
he has Curran partly in mind is suggested by the fact that he calls
Gabriel's brother by Curran's first name Constantine, and makes Gabriel's
brother, like Curran's, a priest.[20] Curran has the same high color and
nervous, disquieted manner[21] as Gabriel, and like Gabriel he has traveled
to the continent and has cultivated cosmopolitan interests. Curran, like
Conroy, married a woman who was not a Dubliner, though she came
from only as far west as Limerick. In other respects he is quite different.
Gabriel was made mostly out of Curran, Joyce's father, and Joyce himself. Probably Joyce knew there was a publican in Howth named Gabriel
Conroy; or, as Gerhard Friedrich has proposed,[22] he may have borrowed
the name from the title of a Bret Harte novel. But the character, if not
the name, was of his own compounding.[23]

Joyce now had his people, his party, and something of its development. In the festive setting, upon which the snow keeps offering a different perspective until, as W. Y. Tindall suggests,[24] the snow itself
changes, he develops Gabriel's private tremors, his sense of inadequacy,
his uncomfortable insistence on his small pretensions. From the beginning he is vulnerable; his well-meant and even generous overtures are
regularly checked. The servant girl punctures his blithe assumption that
everyone is happily in love and on the way to the altar. He is not sure
enough of himself to put out of his head the slurs he has received long
ago; so in spite of his uxorious attitude towards Gretta he is a little
ashamed of her having come from the west of Ireland. He cannot bear
to think of his dead mother's remark that Gretta was "country cute," and
when Miss Ivors says of Gretta, "She's from Connacht, isn't she?" Gabriel
answers shortly, "Her people are." He has rescued her from that bog.
Miss Ivor's suggestion, a true Gaelic Leaguer's, that he spend his holiday
in the Irish-speaking Aran Islands (in the west) upsets him; it is the
element in his wife's past that he wishes to forget. During most of the

story, the west of Ireland is connected in Gabriel's mind with a dark and rather painful primitivism, an aspect of his country which he has steadily abjured by going off to the continent. The west is savagery; to the east and south lie people who drink wine and wear galoshes.

Gabriel has been made uneasy about his attitude, but he clings to it defiantly until the ending. Unknown to him, it is being challenged by the song, "The Lass of Aughrim." Aughrim is a little village in the west not far from Galway. The song has a special relevance; in it a woman who has been seduced and abandoned by Lord Gregory comes with her baby in the rain to beg for admission to his house. It brings together the peasant mother and the civilized seducer, but Gabriel does not listen to the words; he only watches his wife listening. Joyce had heard this ballad from Nora; perhaps he considered also using Tom Moore's "O, Ye Dead" in the story, but if so he must have seen that "The Lass of Aughrim" would connect more subtly with the west and with Michael Furey's visit in the rain to Gretta. But the notion of using a song at all may well have come to him as the result of the excitement generated in him by Moore's song.

And now Gabriel and Gretta go to the Hotel Gresham, Gabriel fired by his living wife and Gretta drained by the memory of her dead lover. He learns for the first time of the young man in Galway, whose name Joyce has deftly altered from Sonny or Michael Bodkin to Michael Furey. The new name suggests, like the contrast of the militant Michael and the amiable Gabriel, that violent passion is in her Galway past, not in her Dublin present. Gabriel tries to cut Michael Furey down. "What was he?" he asks, confident that his own profession of language teacher (which of course he shared with Joyce) is superior; but she replies, "He was in the gasworks," as if this profession was as good as any other. Then Gabriel tries again, "And what did he die of so young, Gretta? Consumption, was it?" He hopes to register the usual expressions of pity, but Gretta silences and terrifies him by her answer, "I think he died for me."[25] Since Joyce has already made clear that Michael Furey was tubercular, this answer of Gretta has a fine ambiguity. It asserts the egoism of passion, and unconsciously defies Gabriel's reasonable question.

Now Gabriel begins to succumb to his wife's dead lover, and becomes a pilgrim to emotional intensities outside of his own experience. From a biographical point of view, these final pages compose one of Joyce's several tributes to his wife's artless integrity. Nora Barnacle, in spite of her defects of education, was independent, unself-conscious, instinctively right. Gabriel acknowledges the same coherence in his own wife, and he recognizes in the west of Ireland, in Michael Furey, a passion he has himself always lacked. "Better pass boldly into that other world, in the full glory of some passion, than fade and wither dismally with age," Joyce makes Gabriel think. Then comes that strange sentence in the final paragraph: "The time had come for him to set out on his journey westward." The cliché runs that journeys westward are towards death, but the west has taken on a special meaning in the story. Gretta Conroy's west is the place where life had been lived simply and passionately. The context and phrasing of the sentence suggest that Gabriel is on the edge of sleep, and half-consciously accepts what he has hitherto scorned, the possibility of an actual trip to Connaught. What the sentence affirms, at last, on the level of feeling, is the west, the primitive, untutored, impulsive country from which Gabriel had felt himself alienated before; in the story, the west is paradoxically linked also with the past and the dead. It is like Aunt Julia Morkan who, though ignorant, old, grey-skinned, and stupefied, seizes in her song at the party "the excitement of swift and secure flight."

The tone of the sentence, "The time had come for him to set out on his journey westward," is somewhat resigned. It suggests a concession, a relinquishment, and Gabriel is conceding and relinquishing a good deal —his sense of the importance of civilized thinking, of continental tastes, of all those tepid but nice distinctions on which he has prided himself. The bubble of his self-possession is pricked; he no longer possesses himself, and not to possess oneself is in a way a kind of death. It is a self-abandonment not unlike Furey's, and through Gabriel's mind runs the imagery of Calvary. He imagines the snow on the cemetery at Oughterard, lying "thickly drifted on the crooked crossed crosses and headstones, on the spears of the little gate, on the barren thorns." He thinks of Michael Furey who, Gretta has said, died for her, and envies him his sacrifice for another kind of love than Christ's. To some extent Gabriel too is dying for her, in giving up what he has most valued in himself, all that holds him apart from the simpler people at the party. He feels close to Gretta through sympathy if not through love; now they are both past youth, beauty, and passion; he feels close also to her dead lover, another lamb burnt on her altar, though she too is burnt now; he feels no resentment, only pity. In his own sacrifice of himself he is conscious of a melancholy unity between the living and the dead.

Gabriel, who has been sick of his own country, finds himself drawn inevitably into a silent tribute to it of much more consequence than his spoken tribute to the party. He has had illusions of the rightness of a way of life that should be outside of Ireland; but through this experience with his wife he grants a kind of bondage, of acceptance, even of admiration to a part of the country and a way of life that are most Irish. Ireland is shown to be stronger, more intense than he. At the end of A *Portrait of the Artist*, too, Stephen Dedalus, who has been so resolutely opposed to nationalism, makes a similar concession when he interprets his departure from Ireland as an attempt to forge a conscience for his race.

Joyce did not invent the incidents that conclude his story, the second honeymoon of Gabriel and Gretta which ends so badly. His method of composition was very like T. S. Eliot's, the imaginative absorption of stray material. The method did not please Joyce very much because he considered it not imaginative enough, but it was the only way he could work. He borrowed the ending for "The Dead" from another book. In that book a bridal couple receive, on their wedding night, a message that a young woman whom the husband jilted has just committed suicide. The news holds them apart, she asks him not to kiss her, and both are tormented by remorse. The wife, her marriage unconsummated, falls at last to sleep, and her husband goes to the window and looks out at "the melancholy greyness of the dawn." For the first time he recognizes, with the force of a revelation, that his life is a failure, and that his wife lacks the passion of the girl who has killed herself. He resolves that, since he is not worthy of any more momentous career, he will try at least to make her happy. Here surely is the situation that Joyce so adroitly recomposed. The dead lover who comes between the lovers, the sense of the husband's failure, the acceptance of mediocrity, the resolve to be at all events sympathetic, all come from the other book. But Joyce transforms them. For example, he allows Gretta to kiss her husband, but without desire, and rarefies the situation by having it arise not from a suicide but from a memory of young love. The book Joyce was borrowing from was one that nobody reads any more, George Moore's *Vain Fortune*; but Joyce read it,[26] and in his youthful essay, "The Day of the Rabblement," overpraised it as "fine original work."[27]

Moore said nothing about snow, however. No one can know how Joyce conceived the joining of Gabriel's final experience with the snow. But his fondness for a background of this kind is also illustrated by his use of the fireplace in "Ivy Day," of the streetlamps in "Two Gallants," and of the river in *Finnegans Wake*. It does not seem that the snow can be death, as so many have said, for it falls on living and dead alike, and for death to fall on the dead is a simple redundancy of which Joyce would not have been guilty. For snow to be "general all over Ireland" is of course unusual in that country. The fine description: "It was falling on every part of the dark central plain, on the treeless hills, falling softly upon the Bog of Allen and, farther westward, softly falling into the dark mutinous Shannon waves," is probably borrowed by Joyce from a famous simile in the twelfth book of the Iliad, which Thoreau translates:[28] "The snowflakes fall thick and fast on a winter's day. The winds are lulled, and the snow falls incessant, covering the tops of the mountains, and the hills, and the plains where the lotus-tree grows, and the cultivated fields, and they are falling by the inlets and shores of the foaming sea, but are silently dissolved by the waves." But Homer was simply describing the thickness of the arrows in the battle of the Greeks and Trojans; and while Joyce seems to copy his topographical details, he uses the image here chiefly for a similar sense of crowding and quiet pressure. Where Homer speaks of the waves silently dissolving the snow, Joyce adds the final detail of "the mutinous Shannon waves" which suggests the "Furey" quality of the west. The snow that falls upon Gabriel, Gretta, and Michael Furey, upon the Misses Morkan, upon the dead singers and the living, is mutuality, a sense of their connection with each other, a sense that none has his being alone. The party-goers prefer dead singers to living ones, the wife prefers a dead lover to a live lover.

The snow does not stand alone in the story. It is part of the complex imagery that includes heat and cold air, fire, and rain, as well as snow. The relations of these are not simple. During the party the living people, their festivities, and all human society seem contrasted with the cold outside, as in the warmth of Gabriel's hand on the cold pane. But this warmth is felt by Gabriel as stuffy and confining, and the cold outside is repeatedly connected with what is fragrant and fresh. The cold, in this sense of piercing intensity, culminates in the picture of Michael Furey in the rain and darkness of the Galway night.

Another warmth is involved in "The Dead." In Gabriel's memory of his own love for Gretta, he recalls incidents in his love's history as stars, burning with pure and distant intensity, and recalls moments of his passion for her as having the fire of stars. The irony of this image is that the sharp and beautiful experience was, though he has not known it until this night, incomplete. There is a telling metaphor: he remembers a moment of happiness, standing with Gretta in the cold, looking in through a window at a man making bottles in a roaring furnace, and suddenly calling out to the man, "Is the fire hot?" The question sums up his naïve deprivation; if the man at the furnace had heard the question, his answer, thinks Gabriel, might have been rude; so the revelation on this night is rude to Gabriel's whole being. On this night he acknowledges that love must be a feeling which he has never fully had.

Gabriel is not utterly deprived. Throughout the story there is affection for this man who, without the sharpest, most passionate perceptions, is yet generous and considerate. The intense and the moderate can meet; intensity bursts out and declines, and the moderated can admire and pity it, and share the fate that moves both types of mankind towards age and death. The furthest point of love of which Gabriel is capable is past. Furey's passion is past because of his sudden death. Gretta is perhaps the most pitiful, in that knowing Furey's passion, and being of his kind, she does not die but lives to wane in Gabriel's way; on this night she too is fatigued, not beautiful, her clothes lie crumpled beside her. The snow seems to share in this decline; viewed from inside at the party, it is desirable, unattainable, just as at his first knowledge of Michael Furey, Gabriel envies him. At the end as the partygoers walk to the cab the snow is slushy and in patches, and then, seen from the window of the hotel room, it belongs to all men, it is general, mutual. Under its canopy, all human beings, whatever their degrees of intensity, fall into union. The mutuality is that all men feel and lose feeling, all interact, all warrant the sympathy that Gabriel now extends to Furey, to Gretta, to himself, even to old Aunt Julia.

In its lyrical, melancholy acceptance of all that life and death offer, "The Dead" is a linchpin in Joyce's work. There is that basic situation of cuckoldry, real or putative, which is to be found throughout. There is the special Joycean collation of specific detail raised to rhythmical intensity. The final purport of the story, the mutual dependency of living and dead, is something that he meditated a good deal from his early youth. He had expressed it first in his essay on Mangan in 1902, when he spoke already of the union in the great memory of death along with life;[29] even then he had begun to learn like Gabriel that we are all Romes, our new edifices reared beside, and even joined with, ancient monuments. In *Dubliners* he developed this idea. The interrelationship of dead and living is the theme of the first story in *Dubliners* as well as of the last; it is also the theme of "A Painful Case," but an even closer parallel to "The Dead" is the story, "Ivy Day in the Committee Room." This was in one sense an answer to his university friends who mocked his remark that death is the most beautiful form of life by saying that absence is the highest form of presence. Joyce did not think either idea absurd. What binds "Ivy Day" to "The Dead" is that in both stories the central agitation derives from a character who never appears, who is dead, absent. Joyce wrote Stanislaus that Anatole France had given him the idea for both stories.[30] There may be other sources in France's works, but a possible one is "The Procurator of Judaea." In it Pontius Pilate reminisces with a friend about the days he was procurator in Judaea, and describes the events of his time with Roman reason, calm, and elegance. Never once does he, or his friend, mention the person we expect him to discuss, the founder of Christianity, until at the end the friend asks if Pontius Pilate happens to remember someone of the name of Jesus, from Nazareth, and the veteran administrator replies, "Jesus? Jesus of Nazareth? I cannot call him to mind." The story is overshadowed by the person whom Pilate does not recall; without him the story would not exist. Joyce uses a similar method in "Ivy Day" with Parnell and in "The Dead" with Michael Furey.

In *Ulysses* the climactic episode, *Circe*, whirls to a sepulchral close in the same juxtaposition of living and dead, the ghost of his mother confronting Stephen, and the ghost of his son confronting Bloom. But Joyce's greatest triumph in asserting the intimacy of living and dead was to be the close of *Finnegans Wake*. Here Anna Livia Plurabelle, the river of life, flows toward the sea, which is death; the fresh water passes into the salt, a bitter ending. Yet it is also a return to her father, the sea, that produces the cloud which makes the river, and her father is also her husband, to whom she gives herself as a bride to her groom. Anna Livia is going back to her father, as Gabriel journeys westward in feeling to the roots of his fatherland; like him, she is sad and weary. To him the Shannon waves are dark and mutinous, and to her the sea is cold and mad. In *Finnegans Wake* Anna Livia's union is not only with love but with death; like Gabriel she seems to swoon away.[31]

That Joyce at the age of twenty-five and -six should have written this story ought not to seem odd. Young writers reach their greatest eloquence in dwelling upon the horrors of middle age and what follows it. But beyond this proclivity which he shared with others, Joyce had a special reason for writing the story of "The Dead" in 1906 and 1907. In his own mind he had thoroughly justified his flight from Ireland, but he had not decided the question of where he would fly *to*. In Trieste and Rome he had learned what he had unlearned in Dublin, to be a Dubliner. As he had written his brother from Rome with some astonishment, he felt humiliated when anyone attacked his "impoverished country."[32] "The Dead" is his first song of exile.

Notes

1. Letter to me from Mrs Kathleen Barnacle Griffin.

2. See Richard Ellmann, *James Joyce* (New York, 1959) p. 222.

3. S. Joyce, "The Background to 'Dubliners,'" *Listener*, LI (25 March 1954) pp. 526–7.

4. *Ulysses* (Random House: 1942; Bodley Head: 1937) p. 12 (8).

5. Ibid. p. 48 (44).

6. The converse of this theme appears in *Ulysses* (p. 113 [107]), when Bloom, walking in Glasnevin, thinks, "They are not going to get me this innings. Warm beds: warm fullblooded life."

7. See *James Joyce* p. 248.

8. See ibid. p. 239.

9. Interview with Mrs May Joyce Monaghan, 1953.

10. He excepts the quotation from Browning, but even this was quite within the scope of the man who could quote Vergil when lending money to his son. (See *James Joyce* p. 316.)

11. Interview with Mrs Monaghan.

12. See *James Joyce* p. 14.

13. Birkin in *Women in Love*.

14. Information from Professor Joseph Prescott.

15. At Cornell.

16. Interview with Mrs Mary Sheehy Kettle, 1953.

17. *My Brother's Keeper* (Viking, 1958; Faber, 1958) p. 38 (58).

18. See *James Joyce* p. 17.

19. Interview with S. Joyce, 1953.

20. Suggested to me by Professor Vivian Mercier.

21. See Joyce's letter, *James Joyce* p. 234.

22. Gerhard Friedrich, "Bret Harte as a Source for James Joyce's 'The Dead,'" *Philological Quarterly*, XXXIII (Oct. 1954) pp. 442–4.

23. The name of Conroy's wife Gretta was borrowed from another friend, Gretta

(actually Margaret) Cousins, the wife of James H. Cousins. Since Joyce mentioned in a letter at the same time that he was meditating "The Dead" the danger of becoming "a patient Cousins" (Letter to S. Joyce, Feb. 1907), this family was evidently on his mind.

24. W. Y. Tindall, *The Literary Symbol* (New York, 1955) p. 227.

25. Adaline Glasheen has discovered here an echo of Yeats's nationalistic play, *Cathleen ni Houlihan* (1902), where the old woman who symbolizes Ireland sings a song of "yellow-haired Donough that was hanged in Galway." When she is asked, "What was it brought him to his death?" she replies, "He died for love of me; many a man has died for love of me." (I am indebted to Mrs Glasheen for pointing this out to me.)

26. He evidently refreshed his memory of it when writing "The Dead," for his copy of *Vain Fortune*, now at Yale, bears the date "March 1907."

27. *The Critical Writings of James Joyce*, ed. Ellsworth Mason and Richard Ellmann (Viking: 1959; Faber: 1959) p. 71.

28. Professor Walter B. Rideout kindly called my attention to the similarity of these passages.

29. *Critical Writings* p. 83.

30. Letter to S. Joyce, 11 February 1907.

31. See also *James Joyce* pp. 724–6.

32. Lettter to S. Joyce, 25 September 1906.

The Cubist *Portrait*   Hugh Kenner*

A *Portrait of the Artist*, the title says, *as a Young Man*. If we are to take this title at its face value, then it is unique among Joyce titles; even *Dubliners* varies according as we judge it general or partitive. And since it is too long a title—nine words!—to emboss legibly on the spine of a shortish novel, the sort of detail Joyce didn't overlook, he must have felt sure he needed all those words.

Those nine words do at least three things. First, they impose a pictorial and spatial analogy, an expectation of static repose, on a book in which nothing except the spiritual life of Dublin stands still, a book of fluid transitions in which the central figure is growing older by the page. The book is a becoming which the title tells us to apprehend as a being. Second, they have the same grammatical form as "A Portrait of the Merchant as a Young Man," or "A Portrait of the Blacksmith as a Young Man." The title does not wholly avow that the artist in question is the same being who painted the portrait. It permits us to suppose that we may be regarding the generic artist, the artistic type, the sort of person who sets up as an artist, or acts the artist, or is even described

*This essay first appeared in *Approaches to Joyce's Portrait* (Pittsburgh: University of Pittsburgh Press, 1977), and is reprinted with permission from The University of Pittsburgh Press.

by irreverent friends as The Artist, or as "bullockbefriending bard."[1] And a third thing the title says is that we have before us a portrait of the artist *as a young man.* Here there is a clear analogy with Rembrandt, who painted self-portraits nearly every year of his life beginning in his early twenties. Like most Joycean analogies it is an analogy with a tacit difference, because the painter of self-portraits looks in a mirror, but the writer of such a novel as we have before us must look in the mirror of memory.

A Rembrandt portrait of the artist at twenty-two shows the flesh of twenty-two and the features of twenty-two as portrayed by the hand of twenty-two and interpreted by the wisdom of twenty-two. Outlook and insight, subject and perception, feed one another in a little oscillating node of objectified introspection, all locked into an eternalized present moment. What that face knows, that painter knows, and no more. The canvas holds the mirror up to a mirror, and it is not surprising that this situation should have caught the attention of an Irish genius, since the mirror facing a mirror, the book that contains a book, the book (like Swift's *A Tale of a Tub*) which is about a book which is itself, or the book (like Beckett's *Malone Dies*) which is a history of the writing both of itself and of another book like itself, or the poem (like Yeats's "The Phases of the Moon") which is about people who are debating whether to tell the poet things he put into their heads when he created them, and moreover are debating this while he is in the very act of writing the poem about their debate; this theme, "mirror on mirror mirroring all the show," has been since at least Swift's time an inescapable mode of the Irish literary imagination, which is happiest when it can subsume ethical notions into an epistemological comedy.

So far so good; but Joyce has brooded on the theme more than is customary even in Ireland, and has not been arrested, like Swift or Beckett or Yeats, by the neatness of the logical antinomy. For it inheres in his application of Rembrandt's theme that the portrait of the artist as a young man must be painted, from memory, by an older man, if older only by the time it takes to write a book. Joyce was careful to inform us at the bottom of the last page that this book took ten years. So we have a portrait in which the subject ages from birth to twenty years within the picture space, while the artist lived through ten more years in the course of painting it.

There follows a conclusion of capital importance, that we shall look in vain for analogies to the two principal conventions of a normal portrait, the static subject and the static viewpoint, those data from which all Renaissance theories of painting derive. The one substantial revision I would want to make in the essay I wrote on this book in 1947 is its title. I titled it "The *Portrait* in Perspective" and I now think that the analogies of perspective are simply inapplicable.[2] The laws of perspective place painter and subject in a fixed geometrical relation to one another, in space and by analogy in time. Here both of them are moving, one twice as fast as the other. Joyce's *Portrait* may be the first piece of cubism in literary history.

When we open it, though, what do we discover? We discover, behind and around the central figure, what Wyndham Lewis described as a swept and tidied naturalism, and nowhere more completely than in the places, the accessory figures, the sights and sounds, the speeches and the names. The names. Joyce is famous for his care with fact: "He is a bold man," he once wrote, "who dares to alter . . . whatever he has seen and heard,"[3] and he used, in *Dubliners*, the unaltered names of real people, so often that their concerted determination to sue him the moment he should step off the boat became an implacable, efficient cause for his long exile from Ireland, which commenced virtually on the eve of the publication of *Dubliners*.

Not quite to digress, a Dubliner once told me a story. The BBC, he said, had had an unfortunate experience. They had broadcast in all Sassenach innocence a radio transcription of the funeral episode in *Ulysses*, with its story about the pawnbroker Reuben J. Dodd whose son underwent love's pangs and had to be fished out of the Liffey on the end of a boathook. His father rewarded the boatman with two shillings, and a party to Joyce's dialogue judged this "one and eightpence too much" (*U*, 95). These words emerged from United Kingdom and also from Irish loudspeakers; whereafter there arrived at Broadcasting House a letter signed "Reuben J. Dodd, Jr." Since one does not receive letters from fictional characters, the BBC dismissed it as a joke until, my man said, "they were persuaded, to their heavy cost, that it was no joke."

For Joyce authenticity of detail was of overriding moment. If actual names were artistically correct, he used them at whatever risk. If they were not, he supplied better ones, but always plausible ones. Yes. And what stares us in the face wherever we open the first book-length narrative of this ferocious and uncompromising realist? Why, a name like a huge smudged fingerprint: the most implausible name that could conceivably be devised for a denizen of lower-class Catholic Dublin: a name that no accident of immigration, no freak of etymology, no canon of naturalism however stretched can justify: the name of Stephen Dedalus.

It seems odd that we accept this name without protest; it is given to no eccentric accessory figure, but to the central character himself. Perhaps it has never had the effect Joyce counted on. For would he not have meant it to arrest speculation at the outset, detaching his central figure at a stroke from the conventions of quiet naturalism? Instead Joyce himself, the Satanic antinomian, attracted attention almost as soon as the book did, and the book was received as no more than thinly veiled autobiography. It was natural to scrutinize the name of Stephen Dedalus for a piece of indulgent symbolism, which (with Stephen's own help to be sure) it yielded quite readily. The strange name (Joyce's text says "strange") seemed a figure of "prophecy" (168), prophecy of light and escape, and of fabulous artifice.

"Fabulous artificer," we read in *Ulysses*, "the hawklike man" (*U*, 201). On the last page of *A Portrait* Stephen invokes him as his new saint, his name-saint, borrowed from an older religion than Catholic Dublin's. In Crete, Daedalus had made Pasiphaë's wooden cow, not by "hacking in fury at a block of wood" like the man who made the cow in Stephen's parable (214), but by disposing sensible matter for a kinetic end, the relief of the queen's monstrous lust. Then he made the labyrinth to contain her offspring; when Cretans sought to detain him with its secret, *ignotas animum dimittit in artes*, he set his mind to truly arcane arts and made wings to fly away. And in 1903, in December, only months before Joyce had commenced the first of the many drafts of the story of Stephen Dedalus, two brothers, sons of a bishop of the Church of the United Brethren in Christ, had flown on man-made wings at Kitty Hawk, North Carolina. Their feat was like Schliemann's validation of the story of Troy. Their motor developed 16 h.p., and the aeronaut lay prone.

If we think of Dedalus with the help of the Wrights, his triumph consists less in the Shelleyan flight than in the artifice. *Et ignotas animum dimittit in artes*. Orthodoxy's saints had, some of them, invoked God and been levitated. This one had contrived, using lore as arcane, no doubt, as aerodynamics and the new science of the wind tunnel. Insofar as the name of Dedalus carries some manifesto from Joyce, it would seem to be this, that intricate disciplines, *ignotae artes*, must henceforth supplant the enthusiast's *O Altitudo!*

But that does not explain the name's presence, not altogether. The man who could maneuver any Greek hero he liked into Bloom's Dublin without so much as mentioning Odyssean names could have exploited the Daedalus symbolism all he pleased without asking us to believe that Dublin at the drab end of the nineteenth century contained somebody named Stephen Dedalus. That name, simply looked at as the name of a character, is so odd it seems a pseudonym. And indeed it seems to have been modeled on a pseudonym. It combines a Christian martyr with a fabulous artificer, and was very likely based on another name constructed in the same way, a name adopted by a famous Irishman, in fact the most lurid Dubliner of them all. During the brief time of his continental exile, Oscar Wilde joined a Christian martyr's name with a fabulous wanderer's, and called himself Sebastian Melmoth.

Wilde built his pseudonym of exile deliberately. Saint Sebastian was the fashionable martyr of nineteenth-century aestheticism. Melmoth— *Melmoth the Wanderer*—was the hero of a novel that yet another Irish romancer, Charles Maturin, had written eighty years before. The two names joined the Christian and the pagan, the sufferer and the exile. In combination they vibrate with heavy exoticism, linking Wilde with the creed of beleaguered beauty and with the land of his ancestors, affirming at the same time something richer and stranger about this shuffling Celtic scapegoat than would seem possible (Wilde thought) to a countryman of people with names like Casey, Sullivan, and Moonan. It is a haunted, homeless name, crying for exegesis, deliberately assumed by a haunted, homeless man. He was a man, furthermore, in whom Joyce did not fail to see enacted one of his own preoccupations, the artist as scapegoat for middle-class rectitude. And if Joyce modeled, as seems likely, the name of the hero of his novel on the pseudonym of the fallen Oscar Wilde, then he was invoking a Wildean parallel for Dublin readers to recognize.

Once we recognize it, *A Portrait* acquires a new paradigm, quite as useful as the autobiographical paradigm that did service for so long. If it is probably in the long run no more sufficient (no map is the territory), that is no reason not to explore it. Different maps show different things.

We may state the new paradigm as follows. *A Portrait* is a sort of Euclidean demonstration, in five parts, of how a provincial capital—Dublin, though Toronto or Melbourne would do—goes about converting talent into rebellious bohemianism. Once converted, the talent exhausts its energies striking poses. This demonstration is completed in *Ulysses*, where the bourgeois misfit *par excellence* turns out to be the bohemian's spiritual father. Dublin, by the time Joyce came to look back on the process to which he had barely escaped falling victim, had already extruded the arch-bohemian of a generation, Oscar Wilde, who had completed the Icarian myth by falling forever. If we are going to be consistent about the symbolism of names, we should reflect that Stephen is the son of Daedalus-Joyce much as Hamlet is the son of Claudius-Shakespeare, and in the myth the son's role is to fall. It seems clear that Joyce sees Stephen as a lad who is going to fall, not as a chrysalis from which the author himself is about to wing forth. He remarked to Frank Budgen that Stephen had "a shape that can't be changed," which appears to mean that by Bloomsday his metamorphoses have ended.[4] He no longer says, "Welcome, O life" (252). He is "displeased and sleepy" in the morning (*U*, 3), a *bricoleur* of theories in the afternoon, and drunk in the evening: in short, a character about Dublin, the artist-fellow. That is Dublin's accomplishment, to have turned him into that.

How Dublin goes about manufacturing Dubliners is the theme of Joyce's first book of fiction. Character after character in *Dubliners* is shown us at a moment when we can guess how he is going to turn out, what he will be like when he finally acquires "a shape that can't be changed." (In *Ulysses*, as though to validate our foresight, we are shown how Bob Doran for one turned out, after Polly married him; he is a periodic drunk.) And a surprising number of the characters in *Dub-*

liners, caught by Joyce's stroboscope en route to immutability, resemble Joyce himself about as strikingly as Stephen Dedalus does.

Mr. James Duffy, for instance, in "A Painful Case," has been endowed with the author's Christian name and a surname with just as many letters in it as there are in Joyce. He has moved out of Dublin, but not far, only as far as suburban Chapelizod, which he elected because he judged the other suburbs "mean, modern and pretentious" (*D*, 107). Like his creator, who kept a notebook labeled "Epiphanies," he keeps on his desk a sheaf of papers labeled "Bile Beans." The woman with whom he attempts to strike up a relationship is named Mrs. Sinico, after a singing teacher Joyce frequented in Trieste. He has even translated *Michael Kramer*, as Joyce did in the summer of 1901. The manuscript of his translation is exceptionally tidy. And he listens, as did the author of *Exiles* and of the final pages of *Finnegans Wake*, to "the strange impersonal voice which he recognized as his own, insisting on the soul's incurable loneliness. We cannot give ourselves, it said: we are our own" (*D*, 111). "Ourselves, oursouls alone," echoes Anna Livia across thirty years (*FW*, 623). Mr. Duffy is "A Portrait of the Artist as Dublin Bank-clerk."

Or consider Jimmy Doyle, in "After the Race," whose name is Jimmy Joyce's with two letters altered. Jimmy Doyle, who becomes infatuated with continental swish and hangs around racing drivers, owes detail after detail of his taste for the anti-Dublin to the life of Jimmy Joyce, who even made a few shillings that first bleak Paris winter by interviewing a French motor-racing driver for the *Irish Times*. Or consider Little Chandler in "A Little Cloud," with his taste for Byron, his yearning after a literary career, his poverty, his fascination with escape from Dublin, his wife and baby. Almost every detail of his story has its source in the author's life. Or consider Gabriel Conroy in "The Dead."

Gabriel Conroy, who is sick of his own country and has "visited not a few places abroad" (*D*, 203), who writes book reviews, as did Joyce, for the *Daily Express*, teaches language, as did Joyce, parts his hair in the middle, as did Joyce, wears rimmed glasses, as did Joyce, has taken a west-country wife, as did Joyce, snubs people unexpectedly, as did Joyce, and is eternally preoccupied, as was Joyce, with the notion that his wife has had earlier lovers: Gabriel Conroy, attending a festivity in a house that belonged to Joyce's great-aunts, and restive in his patent-leather cosmopolitanism among the provincials of the capital by the Liffey, is pretty clearly modeled on his author by rather the same sort of process that was later to produce the Stephen Dedalus of the final *Portrait*.

These Dubliners who are modeled on the author can enlighten us in two ways. They can remind us that Stephen Dedalus is in that respect not privileged; Joyce's works contain many variations on himself. And they can help us see what Joycean shadow-selves are. They are not the author. They are potentialities contained within the author. They are what he has not become.

The sharpest exegetical instrument we can bring to the work of Joyce is Aristotle's great conception of potency and act. His awareness of it helps distinguish Joyce from every other writer who has used the conventions of naturalist fiction. Naturalism as it was developed in France was based on scientific positivism, which affirms that realities are bounded by phenomena, persons by behavior, that what seems is, that what is must be. But Joyce is always concerned with multiple possibilities. For a Zola, a Maupassant, a Flaubert, it is always meaningless to consider what might have been; since it was not, to say that it might have been is without meaning. But in the mind of Joyce there hung a radiant field of multiple possibilities, ways in which a man may go, and corresponding selves he may become, bounding him by one outward form or another while he remains the same person in the eye of God. The events of history, Stephen considers in *Ulysses*, are branded by time and hung fettered "in the room of the infinite possibilities they have ousted" (*U*, 25). Pathos, the subdominant Joycean emotion, inheres in the inspection of such limits: men longing to become what they can never be, though it lies in them to be it, simply because they have become something else.

All potentiality is bounded by alien and circumstantial limits. For the people in *Dubliners* it is bounded by the city. They sense this, all of them, and yearn to remove themselves, but in their yearning they reveal their subjection to the axiom that we cannot desire what we do not know. If they have notions of what it would be like to live another way, in another place, they confect these notions out of what Dublin makes available. Ignatius Gallaher, who is Little Chandler's image of liberation, is a walking anthology of Dublin's tavern gestures of rebellion. The sailor called Frank—"kind, manly, open-hearted" (*D*, 38)—is a sailor-doll Eveline's imagination has pieced together from a list supplied to her by Dublin escapism, and which she has projected onto the fellow who tries and fails to talk her onto the boat to Liverpool. The Frank with whom she fancies what she calls marriage is a chimera of her own mind, and when she refuses to flee she refuses herself. "Eveline" is another Irish mirror-story; it may help us understand Stephen's remark in *Ulysses*, that if Socrates step forth from his house today, it is to Socrates that his steps will tend (*U*, 213).

And so it is with Stephen, whom we are shown electing, by a hundred small acts of election, to become what Dublin will permit "the artist" to be: a wastrel, a heavy drinker, a sponger's victim, a bitterly incandescent talker. Joyce might have been that. Like anyone else in Dublin or anywhere else, Joyce was confronted every day of his life with decisions and choices, courses of conduct elected or not elected, each of which if he elects it branches into a branching family of further choices. If the nose on Cleopatra's face had been shorter, the destiny of the world would have altered. If the swan had not come to Leda, Troy would not have fallen nor Homer therefore educated Greece, nor Greece in turn Rome, and we should none of us perhaps exist. So there lies before a man an indefinitely large potentiality of events he may set in motion, ways he may go, or selves he may become. (For Joyce no self is immutable, it is a costume; hence the costume changes in "Circe.") But each way, each self, each branching from a branch, is supplied to Dubliners by Dublin. The field therefore, however large, is closed. In Dublin one can only become a Dubliner. As for a Dubliner in exile, since his exile was elected within Dublin and is situated along one of the many paths that lead out of Dublin and so are connected to Dublin, he is a Dubliner still.

Joyce contained, then, within him, multitudes. All the men in *Dubliners* are men he might have been, all imprisoned in devious ways by the city, all come to terms of some sort with it, all meeting or refusing shadow selves who taunt them with the specter of another course once possible but now possible no longer. *Dubliners* is a portrait of the artist as many terminated men. And it foreshadows the more famous *Portrait* in another way, having one subject who does not stay still in time. The boy in "The Sisters" does not become Gabriel Conroy, but he might. Eveline does not become the Maria of "Clay," but she might. Bob Doran does not become Little Chandler, but he might. And none of the men becomes James Joyce, nor none of the women Nora, but they contain those possibilities also. Joyce thought of his genius rather as patient persistence than as a divine gift; he even toyed with delegating to another man, James Stephens, the work of finishing *Finnegans Wake*.

Only by a series of accidents, such as checking into Mrs. Mooney's boarding house, does anyone become what he does become, and though he can be only what he is, he can look back along the way to what he is and test it for branching points now obsolete. So the subject of *Dubliners* is a single subject, metamorphosing along many lines of potentiality as the circle of light directed by the storyteller picks out, successively, a small boy (three small boys?) of the time when he was a small boy, or adolescents of the time when he was an adolescent. Each story lets us think that it obeys the pictorial convention of a fixed perspective, subject and viewer set in place until the work of portrayal is finished. But the book is a succession of such pictures, or the trace of a moving metamorphosing subject, seen from a viewpoint that is always very close to him.

This in turn yields the formula for *A Portrait of the Artist as a Young Man*: the moving point of view, product not only of a book ten years in the writing, but of a standpoint which remains close to the subject, as he moves; the moving subject, passing from infancy forward for twenty years; and the subject himself, like the characters in *Dubliners*, a potentiality drawn from within the author, the most fully developed of the alternative selves he projected during a long life with careful labor.

If the differences between Stephen and Joyce seem small, all differences are small, all decisive ones especially. One has only to accept or refuse some opportunity, and the curve of one's life commences a long slow bending away from what otherwise might have been. This line of argument is not only Aristotelian, but wholly familiar to a man brought up, like Joyce, amid clerical exhortations. From the time he could first remember hearing human words, he must have listened to hundreds of homilies, ruminations, admonitions, to the effect that little sins prepare the habit great sins will later gratify, or that the destiny of the soul is prepared in early youth because there is nothing that does not matter.

So Stephen Dedalus is a perfectly normal Joyce character, not the intimate image of what Joyce in fact was, but a figure he generated by his natural way of working. Stephen, unlike a character in *Dubliners*, is followed for twenty years instead of being caught in one posture on one day by stroboscope. But like the characters in *Dubliners*, who also do many things Joyce did, he leaves undone many others things Joyce did, and does many things Joyce did not. These are not trivial divergences. They are the many small points of decision that inhibit him from being Joyce.

Fascinated by Dublin's lifelong hold on its citizens, Joyce himself made no pretence of having escaped it except in body. To the last he kept in repair his knowledge of its shops and streets, pressing visitors for news of alterations, making note of the fact that a business had changed hands. Stephen's talk of flying by nets remains Stephen's talk. One does not fly by such nets, though the illusion that one may fly by them may be one variety of Dublin birdlime.

But Stephen Dedalus is a young man who imagines that he is going to put the city behind him. He is going to fly, like Shelley's skylark. (When Joyce flew, it was like Orville Wright). Stephen will fall into cold water, like Icarus or like Oscar Wilde. (That is one reason *Ulysses* describes him as "hydrophobe" [*U*, 673].)

Given this formula for his principal character, Joyce used everything he could find or remember that was relevant, all the time fabricating liberally—even the sermon, it is now well known, was fabricated—in order to simplify and heighten a being whose entire emotional life is an act of ruthless simplification. Considered as a genius, the finished Stephen is a tedious cliché, weary, disdainful, sterile. He writes one exceedingly conventional poem, not a *Chamber Music* kind of poem but a poem in the idiom of the empurpled nineties, a poem of which Wilde might perhaps have acknowledged the paternity, and a poem unlikely to outlive its decade. He has, as Joyce said, a shape that can't be changed.

Or has by the end of the book. The Stephen of most of the book is an interaction between that changing subject and that changing viewpoint. To *end* such a book is a difficulty. It is less difficult when the perspective is fixed. What we call "tone"—the writer's attitude to his subject—is the product of a fixed relationship between writer and subject. It is the exact analogy of perspective in painting. Its two familiar modes are sympathy and irony. Irony says, "I see very well what is going on here and know how to value it." But Joyce's view of Stephen is not ironic; it is not determined by a standpoint of immovable superiority. Sympathy says, "Withhold your judgment; if you undervalue this man you will offend *me*." Joyce's view of Stephen is not sympathetic either, not in that sense: not defensive, nor self-defensive. Like a Chinese or a medieval painter, he expects our viewpoint to move as the subject moves. We are to be detached from Stephen, however profoundly we comprehend; we are not to reject him nor defend him, nor feel a kind of embarrassment on the writer's behalf. We have not "irony," we have simply the truth. This is so until the end. At the end, when Stephen's development ceases, when he has very nearly acquired the shape that can't be changed, then he is troubling, and behind the device of the diary entries we may sense, a little, Joyce determined to withhold judgment.

It is a terrible, a shaking story. It brings Stephen where so many other potential Joyces have been brought, into a fixed role: into paralysis, or frustration, or a sorry, endlessly painful coming to terms. The most broken of the genre of beings to which Stephen belongs will be objects of pity and ridicule, like Bob Doran. The more fortunate will meditate on restful symbols, as Gabriel Conroy, cuckolded by a shade, turns toward the snow. All the potential selves we can admire stop short of what we are, and this is true however little we may be satisfied with what we are. Dubliner after Dubliner suffers panic, thinks to escape, and accepts paralysis. It is the premise of the most sensitive of them, such as Stephen Dedalus, that the indispensable thing is to escape. It was Joyce's fortune that having carried through Stephen's resolve and having escaped, he saw the exile he accepted as a means of being more thoroughly a Dubliner, a citizen of the city that cannot be escaped but need not be obliterated from the mind. He celebrated it all his life and projected the moods through which he had passed, and for which he retained an active sympathy, into fictional characters for each of whom the drab city by the Liffey, whatever else it is, is nothing at all to celebrate.

Notes

This essay is based on one I contributed to the *University of Windsor Review*, Spring, 1965.

1. James Joyce, *Ulysses* (New York: Random House, 1961), p. 36. Other Joyce editions cited in the text are: *Dubliners* (New York: Viking Press, 1967); *Finnegans*

Wake (New York: Viking Press, 1939); and *A Portrait of the Artist as a Young Man* (New York: Viking Press, 1964).

2. Published in *James Joyce: Two Decades of Criticism*, ed. Seon Givens (New York: Vanguard Press, 1948), pp. 132–74.

3. *Letters of James Joyce*, vol. 2, ed. Richard Ellmann (New York: Viking Press, 1966), p. 134.

4. Frank Budgen, *James Joyce and the Making of "Ulysses"* (New York: Harrison Smith and Robert Haas, 1934), p. 105.

The Elephant in the Belly:
Exegesis of *Finnegans Wake*   Clive Hart*

I shall lay my filing cards on the table from the outset: it seems to me that for many years the situation with respect to the explication of *FW* has been deteriorating, and that if current indications are to be believed the situation is likely to grow still worse before we see any improvement. The mass of inferior critical and exegetical material found its genesis in early and wildly speculative readings of the text which formed the basis of an in-bred school—if that is the right word—of Joycean studies, a school which has been established for so long that it hardly thinks of questioning its assumptions. But we must be careful in applying a corrective since this also is likely to have its dangers. I want, in this paper, to set out what seem to me to be the twin possibilities of extremism and to suggest a number of *points de repère* for future explication. I shall not attempt to develop a detailed theory of explication, but shall propose, instead, a limited number of simple working hypotheses and axioms.

FW has been a splendid encouragement to excess ever since the days of "Work in Progress." The colourful verbal revolutionaries of Jolas' transitional Paris have been succeeded by a less rebellious generation of critics and writers, but, although creative extremism has apparently had its day, critical standards still seem to undergo a strange shift of emphasis whenever people get a copy of *FW* into their hands. The book still represents to some readers—quite falsely, I believe—the high point of the die-hard literary movements of the early 30s, and there is still to be found a small band of critics who want to treat *FW* as they would the poems of Jolas and Hugo Ball, or the prose of Souppault and Eluard. Such criticism is so badly focused as to be negligible. Needing even less discussion are such matters as slovenly scholarship, inaccuracy of presentation, and garbling of facts. These things are to be met with in any

*This essay first appeared in *A Wake Newslitter*, No. 13 (May 1963) and reprinted with permission of the author.

branch of literary studies, and although they tend to be very frequent in published research on *FW*, and, perhaps because of the unfamiliar nature of the terrain and the difficulty of checking assertions, more dangerous in this field than in another, they are a general matter concerning all scholars and differ only in degree in this instance.

The really important issues are so simple that they often tend to be overlooked. They are all implied, in fact, in the intelligent layman's response to the explicator: "How do you know that these things really are in the text? Did Joyce intend them? If not, on what grounds do you justify them?" The layman is in strictly comparable difficulties with, say, *Hamlet*, but in the case of *FW* he seems to be much more at sea because he can rely on no easily discoverable system of values and commonly possessed standards from which to begin the exploration of textual possibilities more remote than those which appear on the surface. The fact that Joyce does indeed make use of such common critical and aesthetic property beneath the surface of the book is of little help to the layman, since these common possessions are buried under a mass of particulars so forbidding that only the initiate (in the present state of Joyce studies) can extract them. And so we turn in gyrogyrorondo.

For the average reader—and all too often for the average student as well—the common standards have been replaced by a set of publicly announced critical views on *FW* which have been taken for granted as the best basis on which to work. The highly flavoured dicta of the *Skeleton Key* have very often been accepted without question, while categorical statements about Joyce's methods of word-formation and word-association have been reiterated for years without their being subjected to scrutiny by application to selected passages of text. One suspects, indeed, that a great many people have written about *FW* without devoting to it even as much time as they would to *Ulysses*. Many a false trail has been started, many a chimera hunted through the dense pages as a result. The danger is not so much that incorrect readings will be offered (ultimately there is, I think, no such thing as an incorerct reading of *FW*), as that we shall lose our sense of proportion in assessing the relative importance of readings. I shall return to that point at the end of the paper.

The alternative danger—hitherto less familiar—lies in too great an insistence on the primacy of Joyce's initial and particular intentions, with the consequent undervaluing of, first, Joyce's general theory of *FW* and, second, the book's indications of its own "intentions" as distinct from those of its creator. While Joyce has clearly included words and word-parts with specific denotations, to ignore which would be to impoverish the sense of the text, there is nothing to suggest either that he wanted to hold the meaning of *FW* within these rigid limits, or that the book will appear less valuable if we allow our explications freer rein. Everyone is prepared, these days, to grant a certain measure of autonomy to poetry—*Dichtung*—and to allow sense and imagery to be to some extent self-controlling. The stumbling block with *FW* obtrudes because there we must take into account the further possibility that Joyce allows some autonomy to word-formation, morphology, and semantics. This is an entirely unfamiliar literary procedure which arouses a great deal of rather emotional opposition in some quarters. It is, apparently, well enough for the meanings of images to be undefined by an author, but it is not yet allowable for the denotations of individual words to be similarly indefinite. Now, at this stage I must stress that I am not on my way towards a justification of *FW* as cloud-material on to which we readers may project whatever sense seems best suited to our psyches. Far from it; I should like, indeed, to place the emphasis on the side of conservatism and reason, but I think it is as foolish to deny the validities of meanings which Joyce never consciously created as to deny them in the case of *Hamlet*—and few people, I suppose, will claim that *Hamlet* may be allowed to mean only what Shakespeare probably thought it meant. These considerations may seem elementary to the point of banality, but the extraordinarily lanate thinking of so much that has been said about *FW* in recent years makes some such approach advisable.

It is, of course, impossible to know exactly what Joyce consciously put into *FW*. Certain things can be discovered by recourse to the MSS, to the letters, and to other biographical sources, but we must be careful not to adopt too naïve an attitude to what the MSS tell us. Joyce seems to have been aware that his MSS would be read by future generations, so that they may not be the unswept literary workshop which they at first seem to resemble. It is, nevertheless, undeniable that their survival makes possible a fairly accurate tracing of the history and development of *one* aspect of the book: the constituent parts. One may wonder how legitimate it is to turn to the MSS for help; one may have one's doubts about the relevance of readings which only they can present; and Joyce's own attitude to their importance for the reader of *FW* seems to have been ambiguous, to say the least. But if we are enquiring about Joyce's conscious artistry they are of undoubted value. (On the whole they are most useful in the case of the chapters written earliest, since these tend to go through many draft stages—from a simple exposition in relatively plain English, to the complexities of the final text. As he got well into *FW*, Joyce started to write more spontaneously in his polyhedral style; many highly complicated sentences appear to have been written down in their final form without prior commitment to paper.)

An example of the pursuit of Joyce's intentions, and of the secondary help which the MSS afford by way of verification, was given us in the lists of Swahili words which Mr P. Wolff sent to *A Wake Newslitter*, and which were subsequently modified and corrected by Mr Jack Dalton.[1] Mr Wolff based his lists on his own knowledge of Swahili and on personal experience of Africa, while Mr Dalton relied on dictionaries, source-studies, and the text of *FW* itself. I am not now concerned with the matter of scholarly skill. Mr Dalton presented us with a model of accuracy and acumen in the pursuit of facts. What one may make of the facts themselves is of more importance. Mr Dalton has demonstrated that certain words may be seen functioning as Swahili in the completed text, while if verification should be needed, the MSS show to anyone with a suitably loaded microfilm-reader and half an hour to spare that a large number of Swahili words were added to the text of *FW* at the same time. People only casually versed in Joycean studies are often highly sceptical of the suggestion that such things as Swahili words *really* are in *FW*. One glance at the MSS will dispel any doubts that these words really are to be interpreted as Swahili—*at least in the initial stage of their addition to the text.* Whether they are to be so interpreted in the final version of the book is a more sophisticated question to which I shall return later.

By means which I shall not treat in detail here—such things as the recognition of quotations, misprints, special spellings, proper names—it is possible to retrieve at least the core of what Joyce *put into FW*. He himself helps the reader, as is now well known, by the introduction of clues to his sources and to his frames of reference. The danger—a very serious one, in my view—lies in thinking that if all these clues are discovered and followed up, the book will be elucidated. The relatively new tendency towards spareness and caution in interpretation and explication is very welcome; it will correct the extravagances of those who seem to keep their eyes on the ceiling rather than on the text; but it may lead in the end to a machine-like loss of sensitivity. Mr Wolff, for example, suggested that "rima" (200.33) and "tembo" (209.11) might mean "pit for catching large animals," and "elephant," respectively. In discussing these Mr Dalton says, first: "I'm afraid I'll have to draw the line on there being an 'elephant' in ALP's belly," and then hopes for a plethora of guffaws at the idea that Anna should be seen digging a Very Dip Pit for Heffalumps. These rejections show, I think, three things: first, rather too much insistence on a rational reading of the text; second, a certain lack of artistic sensibility; third, the unwarranted ignoring (in this instance, at any rate) of Joyce's use and abuse of the surrealist mode which was so popular during the heyday of the book's composition, and which he so richly parodies and cunningly pillages. I am not suggesting that the particular readings in question—elephants and pits—are necessarily of great aesthetic value, but I do suggest that they are by no means to be put aside merely on the grounds of their oddity, or because of their inconsistency with other levels of interpretation. We must not dismiss too lightly Joyce's delight in the chance meanings of words, the peculiar interaction often caused by their juxtaposition, and the power of verbal circumstance. That the accidents of language could stuff an elephant into Anna's world-bearing womb was the kind of thing that delighted Joyce—as his personal associates are unanimous in maintaining. Whether Joyce himself ever knew about the stuffing, in this particular instance, is quite beside the point. To dismiss such a reading as ridiculously incorrect is to ignore the better half of the book.

But let me move once more from the particular to the general. My principal objection to the logical and rational method of reading *FW* is that it may lead to the expulsion of poetry. I do not wish to equate poetry with disorder, but as soon as we start saying to ourselves that certain readings will not allow sentences to parse properly, we should ask whether we are not trying to turn *FW* into a prose palimpsest, each level of which can be stated in normal grammatical English. This is a grave literary sin. It seems evident that many readings of *FW* which are wholly acceptable will not "make sense" in any ordinary way. As I have already pointed out, it is certainly possible, by means of a reversal of Joyce's process of composition, rationally to extract and isolate the deposits of discrete pieces of denotation from which the book was originally compounded. I am not suggesting that this pursuit will lead to a denial of the interrelationships of constituent parts, nor that its exponents claim the whole to be no more than the sum of the parts. What I am suggesting, however, is that it constitutes a most restrictive form of fallacious intentionalism.

Now, I am well aware that the Intentional Fallacy can be, and too often has been, invoked to support over-personalized theories of the significance of works of art and, as I said, I do not hold that *FW* means just what each reader may want it to mean. But I do believe that Joyce's usual approach to his art supports the suggestion that he allowed his works at least some referential autonomy (which does not, of course, mean complete autonomy). I do not, therefore, wish to dismiss the importance of Joyce's intentions; in subsequent pages I shall frequently refer to them. Since, however, an anti-intentionalist reading of the text seems, paradoxically, to have Joyce's sanction—to have been, as it were, part of his intention—my occasional appeals to Joyce's practice and attitudes will be in support of both a closer examination of what he put into *FW* and a willingness on the part of the explicator to allow the relevance of readings beyond what Joyce consciously set out to achieve.

Although I agree that the first and most important thing to do in explicating *FW* is to deal with the material included by intention, it may not be so ridiculous as one at first imagines to allow the validity even of readings which Joyce never had *any possibility* of including. He seems to have wanted meanings to accrete in his text by hindsight as well as by means of his own constant redistortions of the vocabulary. Both referent and reference were for Joyce automonous and in a state of flux, their interrelationships constantly changing. This is a process which Joyce saw as continuous and endless. How else are we to interpret his delight in the Finns and the Russian Generals? Is not, by his own admission, the Finno-Russian conflict of the Second World War a minor theme in *FW*? Joyce wanted to be a prophet; the meaning of his book projects forwards as well as backwards, as the text repeatedly insists. This kind of thing can obviously and very easily be taken too far. But it may serve to emphasize that, in respect to details of the text, intent at the time of writing is not the only consideration.

The Dedalian withdrawal can also be exaggerated, of course. Joyce was by no means as detached as he often liked to pretend, and I believe the available biographical evidence shows him to have been much simpler, more committed, more bourgeois in his attitude to literature, than Mr Kenner, in particular, has depicted him. In the past we have read rather too much about manicuro-mania. And yet there always remains some truth in the image of the uninvolved Artist-God. I take a mid-position, then, and claim for *FW* no more than I claim for any poetry: that is to say, that it often means more than Joyce meant it to mean (just as it sometimes means less; that it is likely often to mean slightly different things to author and reader, and that this disparity is of no significance unless an artistically debilitating ambiguity results.

I should like now to set out in summary form my own present approach to this literary phenomenon. I think that Mr Atherton's view of *FW* as a cosmos governed by its own laws has been demonstrated beyond the need for further comment. It is from this position that I start. The concept of correctness must, I believe, give way entirely to pragmatism. A reading is to be accepted if it provides answers. But we must take care: by this method it is possible to prove literally anything. Take any passage at random and you can demonstrate that it is about, say, the twenty-four golden umbrellas of the King of Thailand. The method is, of course, applicable to any work of literature. Mr Dalton has suggested to me that the opening scene of *Hamlet* can be shown to be entirely concerned with sexual intercourse. The principle therefore seems to be a lunatic one, and yet I believe that in the case of *FW* it has a certain validity. Anything in *FW* is indeed about anything else—*but only in the last of an infinite regress of planes of meaning.* The all-important question, in my view, is how to get these planes of meaning into the right order, and into the right perspective. I have no doubt, myself, that all the planes are there.[2] But there is no point in assuming the book to be a meaningless jumble, which is the way it seems if we do not keep the frames of reference separated. To continue the analogy with the physical world: in the last plane everything is like everything else—a cricket cap is discovered to be identical with a cracked cup when the universe is an undifferentiated agglomeration of energy; in less remote planes various coherent configurations of world-material are stabilized and made apprehendable by the functioning of a variety of laws. In both the physical universe and *FW* chaos results if we do not distinguish between the laws of physics, say, and the laws of society, or between the world-views of scientist and mystic. I would ask the reader to remember the cricket cap and the cracked cup. That is genuine surrealism, producing a witty high-lighting of welded disparates. But it also leads towards a loss of identity. There is a point beyond which the flux ceases to be interesting.

There is a danger that the cultivation of one plane will lead to the exclusion of others of comparable importance. I think that some of the ambiguities and contradictions in Joyce's own statements about *FW* arise because he allows such a multiplicity of planes of meaning. Thus, he might tell one reader that a certain passage depends upon this or that particular piece of information, and tell another that specific allusions may be ignored. The letter to Frank Budgen about the Eastern and Western Churches is an example of the first,[3] while the famous statement to Professor Straumann exemplifies the second approach: "One should not pay any particular attention to the allusions to placenames, historical events, literary happenings and personalities, but let the linguistic phenomenon affect one as such."[4] There is a level, then, at which the Swahili words in ALP are probably not to be interpreted as Swahili at all—and I am not sure whether I think it more important to read them as Swahili or not. A lot of specific meanings emerge if we do so read them, but perhaps there is an even more valuable level at which the primary decorative nature of the Swahili references is overlaid by senses not dependent on this linguistic knowledge. I do not yet know where I stand on this issue—the factors involved are very complex—and I shall say only that I suspect, for example, that the English words "wend" and "wander" are *much* more important to an understanding of ALP than is our knowledge that "Wendawanda" (199.12) contains a Swahili word meaning virtually the same thing as the English word that follows it.[5] (I am not suggesting, of course, that "Wendawanda" means *only* "wend" and "wander," nor that Mr Dalton thinks it means only "a fingerthick." I am concerned here only with a priority for these two partial readings.) We must remember that, for all its pedantries, *FW* is a work of imaginative literature, and that imagination ought always to have the ascendancy over scholarship.

For whom, in any case, was Joyce writing *FW*? For a variety of audiences, no doubt, from the most erudite to the most naïve. Joyce's comments in his letters and in conversation make it quite clear that he had the common reader in mind as much as the literary sophisticate. He intended the book to contain something for everybody, hoped that readers from any part of the world would find rivers they could recognize, dialects with which they were familiar. He said that he was writing in a "Big Language." This is not to deny the value of the purely scholarly approach to *FW*, which can be made as relevant and as valuable as the scholarly approach to Shakespeare. But there seems every reason to approve of Mr Wolff's approach as well as of Mr Dalton's. Part of Joyce's aim, with his Big Language, was evidently to provide a level of significance to readers familiar with Swahili as living speech. To ignore the somewhat imprecise possibilities of meaning which thus arise, and to insist on "correctness" of interpretation as given by the source-dictionaries, is the more scholarly procedure, but it is also rather over-solemn. Without an appeal to the source-books, living experience will often lead the reader to interpretations at variance with Joyce's original specific intentions, as Mr Wolff's example shows. The consistency of the text is not alone sufficient to define the limits of those intentions. The text must first be used to lead to the sources (as it usually does, in the long run) and these in their turn examined to find the limits. This point seems to me to be of very great importance. Did Joyce expect his readers to root out the sources? In many cases, as recently published source-studies have shown, he does in fact encourage the scholar in these pursuits. But the scholar is only one among many classes of readers of *FW*. In so far as the Swahili in *FW* is there to be interpreted as Swahili, Joyce puts it into the book so that *those familiar with the language* will recognize it. The more his readers know, the more they will see (and also, as a corollary, the more doubtful readings they will reject). The limits of recognition are blurred, and I am not sure that Joyce would consider the originally intended meanings, or even the consistency of the text (as demonstrated by scholarly research) to be any more "correct" than the spontaneous and sometimes "inaccurate" readings of a Mr Wolff. The limits of scholarly and spontaneous recognition are not necessarily identical, and I see no reason to suppose that they should be. Consistency of the text is a comparatively new shibboleth which arose out of the rejection of intentionalism. It needs critical scrutiny, and may prove to be yet another Grand Fallacy.

The scholarly approach, which attempts to clarify and define with precision (and to which, I must add, I am myself ultimately committed) is a highly artificial way of reading *FW*. We are bringing literary experience to bear on it, rather than personal experience, and I have no doubt which of the two Joyce would prefer to see used. Of course, if we are to get beyond the limits of our personal experience, the richness of the text forces us into scholarship. But, having engaged in our literary researches, we must try to let our recondite bits of information develop in our imaginations into something more vital than facts if our reading of *FW* is to be of relevance to human beings. In case I may seem to imply the contrary, I shall add that I know that Mr Dalton recognizes this truth very well. Too many attempts to explicate *FW* fail, however, to progress beyond the facts.

Use of the imagination is in any case essential to an adequate perception of Joyce's planes of meaning. How far may we go in exercising it to discover new planes? I think that temperament probably determines the extent to which we spontaneously see relationships between words and images. To Mr Dalton's question: "does anyone honestly think ... that 'sufuria' or 'susurika' ... come close to 'susuria'?"[6] I answer, for myself, emphatically, "Yes, very close." As to his further question concerning "umvolosy" and "fuliza" I answer "No." Again, though "mbwa" is not, as Mr Dalton rightly says, "umbas," the latter word certainly suggests the former to me; and, furthermore, I am sure that it would do so to Joyce himself. (There are many examples in *FW* of suggestions much more remote than this—examples which can be demonstrated beyond any doubt, if need be, by recourse to the MSS.) Whether Joyce *intended* these suggestions is, of course, not in question at this point.

As I suggested above, I believe that Joyce's general attitudes to *FW* are more important than his particular notions about individual words, over which he does not exercise complete control. Ultimately, however, and perhaps more plainly than with any other work of literature, it is the direct relationship between the book and the reader which determines the value of an explication, the "truth" of a meaning. The truths enunciated by the scholars are no more, and no less, absolute than those enunciated, about the physical universe, by the scientists. My fears concerning the undesirable results which may possibly follow from too scholarly an approach to the text give way, however, to increasing dismay at the incoherencies of the opposite approach. I come down heavily on the side of the rationalists, at least for the time being, because I think that little progress of any value can be made in the more remote planes of significance until the nature of Joyce's central intentions is more fully documented. I shall conclude, then, with a few propositions about the reading of the book:

1: Every syllable is meaningful. *FW* contains no nonsense, and very little onomatopoeia, etc. Joyce deals principally in semantemes.
2: An explication is lacking unless it accounts for every syllable and justifies every letter.
3: Elements in an explication which are of widely disparate natures must—unless they can be seen to have hidden relationships—fit into a number of different but coherent planes of meaning.
4: If an element of explication does not fit into such a coherent plane it is probably irrelevant except on that last plane where meaning dissolves because everything corresponds to everything else.
5: The most important task of the explicator is to sort out the planes of meaning into an order of precedence.
6: *FW* is, throughout, a work of imagination and should not be read as a biographical or factual record of any sort, except in so far as James Joyce is a part of the world it describes.

Notes

1. *A Wake Newslitter*, no. 8, December 1962, pp. 2–4; no. 12, April 1963, pp. 6–12.

2. See such statements in *FW* as that at 109.27: "... capable of being stretched, filled out, if need or wish were. ..." And readers who doubt whether anything in *FW* can represent the author's own views might look at the letter to Frank Budgen dated 20 August 1939 (*Letters*, I, p. 406).

3. See F. Budgen, *James Joyce and the Making of* Ulysses. Bloomington, 1960, pp. 315–16.

4. H. Straumann, 'Last Meeting with Joyce', in *A James Joyce Yearbook*, ed. M. Jolas. Paris 1949, p. 114.

5. See, however, Mr Halper's excellent discussion of linguistic counterpoint, [*A Wake Digest*], pp. 54–55.

6. *A Wake Newslitter*, no. 12, April 1963, p. 10.

Book of Many Turns   Fritz Senn*

Joyce's works can be seen, with equal validity, either as one great whole or as a series of self-contained units. Seemingly contradictory statements can make good sense: Joyce kept reshaping the same material in more complex ways—he never repeated himself. The reiteration, even permutation, of some fundamentals is striking. We can trace the terminal actuality of *Finnegans Wake* from the germinal potentiality of *Dubliners*; but conversely we are also tempted to emphasize the unique whatness of every single work. Joyce kept repeating himself in metempsychotic succession—but if we highlight the individual incarnations, each of his major works is essentially and unpredictably different from its predecessors.

In coming to terms with Joyce's particular other world of words, we can choose between two different sets of terminology. Taking up Joyce's own, or Stephen Dedalus's, insistent metaphors, we can see literature as a process of conception and parturition. A quasi-biological vocabulary suggests itself which serves to describe an evolution of powerful, vital drives in a teeming world of luxuriant growth. In fact, such a monstrosity as the "Oxen of the Sun" chapter in *Ulysses* can be read as a hymn to fertility in its theme and by its very nature—a misbirth maybe, but the offshoot of some generative (perhaps too generative) force. If we were not trying to be so erudite about this chapter, we might be impressed by its sheer animal exuberance. It seems that all of Joyce's creations came into being through some analogous biological force and were subject to many changes during their prolonged periods of gestation. The works are not only separate, though related, but they all got out of hand in the workshop; they could not be contained within whatever original ground plan there was. They proliferated into something never imagined at the instant of conception.

Even the smallest elements in a literary universe, the letters of the

*This essay first appeared in the *James Joyce Quarterly*, 10 (Fall 1972) and is reprinted with permission of the *James Joyce Quarterly*.

alphabet, can be fertile. Long before Joyce thought of *Finnegans Wake*, he made one of the characters in his first short story reveal her ignorance with an illiterate "rheumatic wheels" (*Dubliners* 17). The life force, like everything else in the story, has gone wrong; it has been turned into decay. So, through a tiny change of two letters or one sound, an appropriate word "rheum" (suggeting a disease: natural development gone wrong) replaces another word.[1] In *Ulysses*, a typographical misbirth, which disfigures the funeral report in the newspaper, is called, with good reason, "a line of bitched type" (U 648), bitches being proverbially and indiscriminately fertile. The simple letter "l," whether superfluous as in "that other world" (*U* 77), or missing as in "L. Boom" (*U* 648), has a pullulating force and invites speculation.

But then it is exactly such exuberant, freakish offshoots as the "Oxen of the Sun" chapter that can be demonstrated to be the disciplined, programmed, calculated, systematic completion of an elaborate plan by a meticulous artificer—perhaps an obsessed one. Chaos resolves itself into the painstakingly structured order of layered symmetry, of catalogues and charts, schemas, correspondences, and parallels. The jungle is also a garden. Much of our labor actually consists of exposing the manifold coordinates in the system. To some of us the existence of such a system amounts to the major justification of a work of literature. To others, Joyce has become too exclusively a cerebral constructor and callous arranger.

In *A Portrait*, the two aspects are clearly interfused. We have now been trained to see its rigid structure as a verbal and symbolic system. But to early readers sheer disorder seemed to prevail. Richard Ellmann, drawing on internal as well as biographical evidence, uses biological terms to characterize the novel as embryonic (*JJ* 306–09).

I take my starting point from a different but related ambiguity. It is contained in the title of the novel, that oddly trailing, spiraling, threefold phrase: "A Portrait—of the Artist—as a Young Man." It looks like an attempt, pedantic and verbose, to fix the subject as accurately as possible. The incongruous effect is that the subject becomes all the more elusive. A less clumsily delimitative title might not have made us aware of the aim of portraiture to pinpoint quiddity in the way that those portraits adorning the walls of Clongowes Wood (*Portrait* 55) preserve something unchangeable for all eternity.

The title implies, however, that there is no portrait as such, that a choice must be made. Out of a wide variety, only *one* phrase or pose can be selected. So the implication is that there must be other poses or phases perhaps equally pertinent in the room of infinite possibilities. In the novel Joyce of course gives us a series of such poses and aspects, a chronological succession in which each phase extends and modifies the previous ones. Perhaps only in perpetual qualification can that quintessential quality be circumscribed which, in itself—as the title indicates—remains beyond our grasp. The specification "as a young man" is necessary to the nature of portraiture, but it also contradicts its concept.

In the title it is the unstressed but potent conjunctive particle "as" which seems to infuse the novel. This particle denotes, as the dictionary will tell us, something or someone "in the character, in the capacity" or "in the role" of something else. The *Portrait* is a sequence of such parts of character. Stephen, knowingly or unknowingly, assumes an amazing number of character roles as he grows up. Before he appears in the flesh, Stephen has already been transformed into a fairy tale character which is specifically glossed ("He was baby tuckoo" [*Portrait* 7]). He soon learns to play some parts, often protective ones, with varying degress of skill and success. Stephen learns to imitate and to pretend: on the second page he is already "feigning" to run. A number of roles are prescribed to him by the communities of family, school, church, and nation, and it takes some growing up to make him realize the reticular hazards involved. His reading provides a further set of models to be imitated. In the second chapter Stephen actually prepares for a stage performance in a school play, a take-off on one of his masters. He deliberately and, at times, histrionically rejects some roles, whereas he remains quite unaware of certain others. It is easier for us than it was for some earlier readers to recognize the stagey nature of some turning points in Stephen's career. Finally Stephen chooses to become an artist, that is, a creator of fictional roles. And in *Ulysses*, the same Stephen singles out, for a dazzling display of theorizing, the writer who probably created more roles than anyone else, Shakespeare (and Stephen is aware that Shakespeare also played real theatrical parts on the London stage). Stephen's artist is compared to "the God of the creation" (*Portrait* 215), and this God is immediately epiphanized in one particular pose—"paring his fingernails."

Somehow Stephen, who enumerates with such gusto the chosen roles of his father: ".... a tenor, an amateur actor, a shouting politician ... a taxgatherer, a bankrupt and at present a praiser of his own past" (*Portrait* 241), is a chip off the old block, with a self-written scenario that is just a bit more *recherché*. A predominant role is preordained in the family name, Dedalus, which was taken, along with the motto of the novel, from an ancient book of roles and transformation scenes entitled *Metamorphoses*.

All of this is carried over into *Ulysses* and magnified there. The conjunctive potential of that word "as" permeates all of *Ulysses*. But Joyce need no longer plant it into his title. The title *Ulysses* proclaims a role, one Leopold Bloom *as* Odysseus, or Odysseus *as* modern man. And once we catch on to this new game of aliases or analogies, there is no holding back. *Ulysses* is Joyce's *Metamorphoses*, a book of roles and guises, a game of identities, of transubstantiations. It is panto-mimic in the sense of imitating everything. Molly Bloom tells us that her husband is "always imitating everybody" (*U* 771). But even without Molly's corroboration it would be superfluous, after fifty years, to reiterate all the parts that all the characters play in the book.

It is sufficient, by way of recall, to mention the first appearance of a character in the novel. Joyce portrays a real Dubliner, Oliver St. John Gogarty, who was well known in Dublin and remains in Dublin memory just because he was able to carry off so many roles with impressive alacrity. In the book he immediately assumes one particular role, that of a priest, pretending to be a vicar of Christ and a follower of St. Peter. And one of Buck Mulligan's first mocking actions concerns the miraculous eucharistic metamorphosis of mundane into divine substance. He does it, profanely but tellingly, to the pretended acommpaniment of slow music, as an *artiste* in the music hall sense, a conjurer. And by means of electric current, as magic trickery, cunning deceit. His subject, however, *is* transformation, and he keeps transforming himself according to whim or opportunity. A true panto-mime, he becomes, in skillful mimetic turn, a priest, a military commander, patron of an artist, friendly adviser, medical rationalist, and so on. His repertoire transcends the boundaries of sex or humanity: he can imitate Mother Grogan or become a bird or an ascending Christ. His observer, Stephen, projects yet other roles onto him, while behind or beyond or above his handiwork an increasingly conspicuous author dangles another assortment of analogies. All of this takes place within some twenty pages comprising the first chapter.

It is no wonder that Gogarty, who could successfully bring off so many roles as doctor, athlete, poet, and later on as nationalistic senator, aviator, and carouser with the British nobility (quite apart from his histrionic talent *ad hoc*), resented the perpetuation of some post-adolescent roles in fictional permanence. Joyce had obviously and maliciously encroached upon his own chosen territory, and Gogarty was only paying back in kind when he revealed (to an audience of would-be Joyce idolators) the real, as he maintained, meaning of the term "artist" in Dublin parlance, reducing, in intention, Joyce's and Stephen's role to the limited one of a poseur.[2]

The simplest way of playing imitative roles is by repeating someone else's words: thus *Ulysses* opens with an explicit quotation. The first words spoken aloud, "*Introibo ad altare Dei*" (*U* 3), are not of that everyday common speech that Joyce could evoke so well; they are neither everyday English, nor even English, nor even speech. They are "intoned," in Latin, that dead tongue with which the Church until recently chose to transmit its messages. The stability of the ritual from which these words are taken contrasts of course with Mulligan's volatile flexibility and lack of principle. The words, in any case, are imitation, resounding for the millionth time, as prologue to the book whose characters play parts, whose actions often consist in acting, and many of whose words are quotation to an extent that the author never even attempted to single out individual quotes by customary typographical marks. A quotation also links the present occasion with a former one; it is a strandentwining chord back in time. So the first words uttered aloud in *Ulysses* take us even beyond the Roman Catholic Mass to the Hebrew Psalms of the Old Testament. They span several millennia.

One capsular reflection of the whole is this: that the novel, whose Latin title suggests a Greek hero based (as Joyce believed) on Semitic tales, begins like a play, with stage directions in the first paragraph and an opening speech by an Irish character whose language is English and who, with a flair for imitation, intones a sentence from the Latin Mass, which is in itself a translation of a Hebrew Psalm. The ethnological and literary multiplicity is already present, while on the surface of it we never for a moment leave a simple, realistic story.

Joyce, who reveals the identity of Buck Mulligan at the outset, keeps the question of who and what he really is suspended throughout. We first witness mimicry, mummery, and mockery; the first voice we hear is put on, and it continues to change. It would be hard to determine exactly where Buck Mulligan drops all of his guises and pretenses and speaks in his own voice, if ever he does. I think that for all his imitative zeal we can feel the man's character behind the sequence of adornments. But it is interesting to note how much at variance all our feelings are once we try to bring them into the open. And so, it is no wonder that critics disagree in their assessment of Buck Mulligan; this is in keeping with mercurial Malachi cheerfully contradicting himself while manipulating his various *personae*.

Hence *Ulysses* appears, from the start, as a reapplication of a principle evolved in *A Portrait*. The artist is re-portrayed as a slightly more disillusioned young man with some newly acquired roles. But the foreground is dominated by his mercurial counterpart, who condenses a whole portrait gallery of a vaudeville *artiste as* (to pick some more items from the script) a mocker, *as* St. Peter, *as* a sycophant, *as* Cranly, *as* a Homeric suitor, or, in the overall view, *as* a Shakespearean clown who sets the stage.

This stage will before long be occupied by Leopold Bloom, whose verbal and mimetic repertoire is much more limited. Mulligan's brilliance is set off against Bloom's lackluster commonness and common sense. Bloom's opening words could not possibly elicit the same sort of extended commentary that Mulligan's require. But with his trite "O, there you are" (*U*, 55), Bloom at least reaches his speechless partner, the cat, and attains whatever contact is called for. His concern for that partner is unfeigned. And the cat immediately responds with "Mkgnao," and two variations of the same theme: "Mrkgnao!" and "Mrkrgnao!"

The first book begins on top of a tower with imitative words and divine reverberations. The second book begins below ground in Bloom's kitchen, with simple words and onomatopoetic animal noises. It is intriguing to follow one reader, the Italian translator of *Ulysses*, who claims that the consonantic structure of the cat's "Mrkrgnao" utterance is a covert evocation of Mercury.[3] This would introduce either the Homeric messenger Hermes appropriate to the chapter, or else constitute an animal echo of Mulligan's mercurical role in the parallel chapter. As the novel moves on, Mulligan's brilliance can hardly be increased, while Bloom's earthy wit and less ostentatious resourcefulness have a way of growing on most readers.

But then of course Bloom is accorded a great deal of scope. Although he is remarkably awkward in acting out such roles as he might enjoy playing in real life, like Philip Beaufoy or Don Juan, he is unconsciously carrying a much greater load than all the other characters. Most roles (Mr. Bloom *as* Odysseus, Christ, Moses, Wandering Jew, etc.) have been well studied. I would like to single out a far less personal role. Within the totality of the novel, Bloom is also a part of speech. In purely grammatical terms, Bloom is also an all round man. His name is taken through all the cases of the singular: "Bloom. Of Bloom. To Bloom. Bloom" (*U* 453), and he seems to have become a grammatical case history. On occasion he resembles a noun with a relative pronoun in various inflections like "Bloowho" (*U* 258), "Bloowhoose" (*U* 259), "Bloohimwhom" (*U* 264), in passages that seem to bring out Bloom's relativity. An inflated version is "puffing Poldy, blowing Bloohoom" (*U* 434). At times perhaps Bloom appears more like a verb than a noun, the *verbum* of Latin grammar or else of the Gospel of St. John. In the course of the novel he seems conjugated in all tenses, past, present, and future; in the active and the passive voice; in all the possible moods—indicative, imperative, subjunctive, optative—not to forget participial forms like "blooming." He becomes a universal paradigm of the school book: if we can parse him, we can parse humanity. Beyond grammar, he is anagrammatically transformed into "Old Ollebo, M. P." (*U* 678). And "POLDY" is the basis for an acrostic (*U* 678).

Bloom's nominal existence is diverse too. He has been translated from Hungarian *Virag*, and he is translating himself into such fictitious roles as Henry Flower, to which Molly adds "Don Poldo de la Flora" (*U* 778), and the author such variants as "Professor Luitpold Blumenduft" (*U* 304) or "Senhor Enrique Flor" (*U* 327). Other transformations are geometrical, a concave distortion like "Booloohoom," or a convex "Jollypoldy the rixdix doldy" (*U* 434). Typography adds an insult, "L. Boom" (*U* 647), to the catalogue. Etymology extends the range further: Skeat's *Etymological Dictionary* relates "bloom" to "blood." Leopold Bloom does not read Skeat's by the hour, but he substitutes his own name for "Blood" in a throwaway (*U* 151), unaware of a momentary eucharistic function. No wonder there are Bloomites in the book, and that the hero is sartorially celebrated in "bloomers" and even citified into "Bloomusalem." Thus, on the merely nomenclatural level of this ominously cluttered novel, Bloom is awarded unprecedented scope as a paradigm.

We know that Joyce found in Homer's Odysseus the universal paradigm from myth that he needed. Hence, I would like to rephrase some of my remarks in the light of Homeric analogies. I have to admit first that I always thought these analogies meaningful, fruitful, and even helpful, even if some of our heavy-footed glosses may not be so. The Homeric ground plan provides another link with the past; it takes us back, as Joyce always tries to do, to first beginnings. Homer's epics are, for all practical purposes, the origins of Western literature. *Ulysses* comprises all literature from its Greek roots (as well as its Hebrew roots in the Old Testament) to its latest ramifications in Yeats and a just emerging Synge. In between, English literary history is amply documented, notably in "Scylla and Charybdis" and "Oxen of the Sun," and there are vestigial traits of Italian, French, and German literature throughout. Homer's highly finished art is a beginning for us, but it was in turn already the culmination of a long development now lost in obscurity. It is an end turned into a new beginning, which makes it all the more fitting for Joyce's purposes.

That the Homeric poems were not, originally, written down and read but passed on orally and recited with musical accompaniment moreover conveniently ties them to an oral tradition very much alive in Ireland. The art of storytelling was still practiced in Joyce's Dublin in those communities that had to be culturally self-sustaining.

Joyce preferred the *Odyssey* to the much more martial *Iliad*, not merely because of his pacifist inclinations nor because he needed more social relationships than a war report can provide, but also because the action of the *Iliad* is subsumed in its sequel. The *Odyssey* is wider in scope: temporal, topical, and simply human.

Even though the so-called Homeric parallels, the transposition of characters and situations, have definite purposes, it is sometimes useful not to insist on the strictly parallel nature of the correspondences: the pattern is often a crisscross one, and similarities often go by contrast. Perhaps the most pervasive Homeric features in *Ulysses* are not the one to one relationships that Stuart Gilbert began to chart for us, but principles or motive forces—such as the Protean force of transformation in the third chapter. Homer and Joyce both had the ability to condense certain overall principles into concise verbal form. Joyce was fond of condensing themes and techniques of his whole works into his opening words (as on the first page of *Ulysses*, which I have dwelt upon in the preceding pages). I believe that Joyce realized that the opening of the *Odyssey* is similarly fashioned, and that he was aware that Homer, much more pointedly and literally than Vergil, Milton, or Pope, put the subject of his poem right in front of us. The subject is Man. The *Odyssey* begins with that word—"*Andra*"—in the objective case, the central object, and Homer keeps it suspended over the first line. It is fortunate that Joyce, who knew little classical Greek (though a Zürich friend, Paul Ruggiero, taught him some modern Greek), recorded the first line of the *Odyssey* in the original, or very close to it. Ellmann implies that it was quoted from memory (*JJ* 585). It is misquoted, of course, and we can explain Joyce's faulty accents as the result of understandable ignorance or, maybe, as a shift in emphasis. At any rate, Joyce knew by heart, and was ready to scribble beside the only authentic portrait of Mr. Bloom we have, the well-known line:

Andra moi énnepe, Mōusa, polýtropon, hòs mála pollà[4]

It happens, fortuitously, that in Greek the accusative noun can be placed before us without a definite article and with its defining adjective being cleverly withheld for a few beats. Thus "Man" is placed before us in his most universalized form before the focus narrows to one particular individual. This obviously suits Joyce's purpose.

In the Homeric text the second noun is "Troy, the holy city" (*Odyssey* I, line 2). So even here Joyce's favorite coupling of the individual and the community of the city seems anticipated. But the word that is especially emphasized in Homer's first line and which is skillfully introduced after a weighty pause, is the epitheton that accompanies "man"—"*polytropos*." It has occupied commentators a good deal, and W. B. Stanford in his excellent study, *The Ulysses Theme*, devotes some pages to it.[5] Joyce could have found most of the glosses in reference books or in the standard Greek dictionaries that he was quite able to consult. Any Greek dictionary would have given him more or less the same information that Liddell and Scott provide: Literally, *polytropos* means "much turned," "of many turns." It is taken to mean that Odysseus is a man much traveled, "much wandering." But the meaning was soon extended to suggest characteristic resourcefulness—"a man capable of turning many ways," a versatile character. It acquired a pejorative use too: it came to mean "shifty" or "wily" (in this sense the adjective is applied to Hermes, i.e. Mercury). It can mean "fickle" or just "changeable," or become a vague term for "various" and "manifold."

I submit that all of these potential meanings of the one word[6] are, literally or figuratively, transferred into *Ulysses*. When Joyce described an early plan of his novel to Stanislaus in 1915, he referred to the central section as "Ulysses Wandlungen."[7] Since Stanislaus at the time was interned by Austrian authorities, the postcard had to be written in German. What Joyce probably wanted to say was "Wanderungen"—wanderings—but he was either confused by the intricacies of the German vocabulary (where the verb *wandeln* can mean both "to wander" and "to change") and hit on *Wandlungen* (which means "changes" but not "wanderings"), or he was trying to entertain his brother by a double entendre. The result, in any case, is that "Ulysses Wanderungen" happens to be an excellent summing up of the novel and also of the two main meanings of Homer's adjective, stressing the hero's travels as well as his versatility.

But to return to the Greek dictionary. Its philological lore seems to appear, in part verbatim, throughout the book. "Wily," for example, is an epithet reserved for the voluble sailor in "Eumaeus," whose pseudo-Odyssean role we have known all along ("such a wily old customer" [U 630]). He pretends to be much traveled, and he is in fact a resourceful inventor of tales. Another adjective, "shifty," is applied by Bloom to such "crawthumpers" as one of the Carey brothers who plotted murder and then turned on his accomplices (the negative side of Odyssean changeability): "there's something shiftylooking about them" (U 81). The other adjective of the dictionary, "fickle," occurs in "Nausikaa." The boy whom Gerty MacDowell admires in vain seems to her a "Lighthearted deceiver and fickle like all his sex" (U 362). Actually Homer's hero had appeared in just such unfavorable light to some of the early unsympathetic commentators.[8] Now I am not sure how far Gerty's boy friend qualifies for an Odyssean role of tertiary importance, but he is apparently capable of doing clever turns on his bicycle, and it is a nice touch that his name is Reggie *Wylie*. Since Joyce invites us to compare Odysseus with Leopold Bloom and since Gerty compares Bloom with Reggie Wylie, this may be a peripheral instance of Joyce's reserving some Odyssean versatility for minor characters as well.

Most editions of the *Odyssey* list, in their variant readings of *polytropos*, a different adjective "poly*krotos*." This is in fact usually the first textual note in the book. The meaning is generally given as "wily, sly, cunning" (which corresponds to "polytropos"), but originally it meant "ringing loud, resounding." Somehow this might contribute towards making L. Bloom a noise in the street. Stanford's interpretation of the adjective as "knocked about"[9] would also apply to Mr. Bloom. But even if this philological spectrum were outside of Joyce's ken, it is worth noting that Homer's first emphasized adjective was soon changed, distorted, or parodied—the earliest anticipation perhaps of Joyce's technique of meaningfully distorted readings.

The translation of the *Odyssey* by Butcher and Lang, which Frank Budgen assured me Joyce had used and for which Phillip Herring found notebook evidence, renders the first epithet as "the man, so ready at need." I cannot help being amused, perhaps coincidentally, by Bloom's being described as "a man and ready," and rising to make for the "yard," contemplating on his way Greek goddesses yielding to Greek youths (U 176–77). Immediately afterwards his elusiveness is commented upon. But this connection may merely be an instance of one reader's mind being polytropically affected.

Homer's Odysseus appealed to Joyce because of his universality and his encyclopaedic turns. In him the two opposites, the individual and the universe (poles that appear throughout in Joyce's works, from Stephen's geography book in *A Portrait* to Shem's riddle of the universe), are combined. I cannot help but think that Joyce was conscious of a translation of *polytropos* into Latin, which would yield *multi-versus*, the exact anthetical correspondence to *uni-versus*.

Naturally it does not matter too much whether some general principle in either the *Odyssey* or *Ulysses* finds one particular verbal incarnation. But Joyce had a way of expressing in representative detail what is also present in the organic whole. The preceding philological digressions are justified, perhaps, simply because Joyce was a philologist, in the etymological sense of being a lover of words and also in the sense of being a commentator of Homer. He attributed the art Philology to the chapter devoted to change and Odyssean flexibility.

Diverging from Homer, Joyce does not start with an invocation stating his theme, but he puts the principle into action by putting the most conspicuously *polytropos* man in the novel right in front of us, Buck Mulligan, whose shifting roles can now be reinterpreted as Odyssean. Buck Mulligan does not know how much he is in fact hellenizing Ireland (*U* 7). Fairly early he uses the Homeric type of adjective himself, both in the hackneyed original *"epi oinopa ponton"* and in parodistic variation "the scrotumtightening sea" (*U* 5). His early Greek samples, incidentally, refer to the eminently changeable elements of water ("ponton," "thalatta") or wine.

Mulligan is resourceful and skillful in dealing with any situation at hand. But he also incorporates these qualities of trickery and deceit that the detractors of Odysseus had pointed out in antiquity. Again there is the tenuous possibility that Joyce had heard of one such detractor who claimed that Homer's account was a tissue of lies. Stanford goes on to say that this critic, whose "oration is bland, persuasive and superbly argued," is hardly trying "to do more than dazzle and astonish his audience," his aim being "to gain admiration for skill in rhetorical technique."[10] There is something very Mulliganesque in all this, but what makes the connection particularly intriguing is that the name of the critic was—Dio *Chrysostomos*.

We are on safer ground by taking Bloom's word for it that Buck Mulligan is an untrustworthy but "versatile allround man, by no means confined to medicine only" (*U* 620). "Versatile" is, of course, the standard definition of *polytropos*; "allroundman" echoes Lenehan's grudging concession of Bloom as "a cultured allroundman" (U 235). It echoes, moreover, Joyce's conversation with Frank Budgen in Zürich about Odysseus as a complete all-round character.[11] Lenehan, as it happens, is a little Odysseus in his own small cadging way, wandering and wily and versatile (in "Two Gallants" he is described as a "leech" and is performing an Odyssey in a minor key). It is remarkable how frequently the Odyssean characters in *Ulysses* comment on each other, and often in Odyssean terms too: Lenehan comments on Bloom; Bloom on Buck Mulligan, Lenehan, Simon Dedalus, and on the Sailor; Simon Dedalus on Buck Mulligan ("a doubledyed ruffian," [*U* 88]); the Sailor on Simon Dedalus (his yarn presents Dedalus as polytropos, much traveled: "He toured the wide world" [*U* 624]); Buck Mulligan on Bloom, etc.

Our first glimpse of Buck Mulligan shows him literally and physically as a man of many turns. Within the first few pages he is choreographically living up to his polytropic nature: he faces about, bends toward Stephen, peers sideways, shows a shaven cheek over his right shoulder, hops down from his perch, mounts the parapet, and actually "turn[s] abruptly" (*U* 3–5).[12]

Polytropia in *Ulysses* then is not limited to any one feature, or level, or any one person—not even to persons. It is polytropically distributed and incarnated throughout. Animals too, like Stephen's protean dog on the beach or the dog following Bloom into the by-ways of "Circe," perform feats of amazing versatility. Even inanimate objects, such as Bloom's newspaper, his wandering soap, or Stephen's ashplant, are capable of transformation. One whole chapter hinges on the volatile mutability of all things, the "Circe" episode. It is made up of all the previous roles in the novel and a number of new ones, a gigantic transformation scene in pantomime, where old roles are continually permuted. Among its polymorphic turns are the deviate turns of the psyche, with such authorities as Krafft-Ebbing being responsible for parts of the script.

It is appropriate that Stephen comes to grief in this sequence, also because, for all the flexibility of his mind, he fails, or refuses, to be flexible enough to deal with a real situation and to evade a blunt danger. He is not trying to select a more opportune role, but rather continues a monologue that is unintelligible and must appear provoking to the soldiers, who of course are equally inflexible. The physical altercation in "Circe" is between characters who are rigid and might be called "monotropic." Stephen, in crucial moments, is scornful of such advice as Buck Mulligan has given him in the morning: "Humour her [his mother] till it's over" (*U* 8). Mulligan does a lot of opportunistic humoring, and Bloom is good-humoredly trying his best.

The culminations of "Circe" can be regarded as outgrowths of such mimetic features as are already present in the first chapter. "Circe" is made up almost entirely of Mulliganesque poses and projections. In the morning Buck Mulligan begins by quoting Latin from the Mass. Near midnight Stephen enters the scene by actually responding to Mulligan's opening words: "*ad deam qui laetificat juventutem meam*" (*U* 433). His version contains one small change (*deam* for *Deum*), but it is an entire perversion, a wholly new and utterly Circean turn. The first sounds heard in "Circe" are the call and answers of the whistles (U 429) which are an echo of the first page. The first words spoken aloud, "Wait, my love," are a variant of Mulligan's "Yes, my love" (U 429, 4). With his conjuring imitation of the transubstantiation, Mulligan has also prepared us for magic, the technique of the Circean transformations.

An interesting scene in the first chapter foreshadows many phenomena of "Circe." Mulligan, who has just challenged Stephen ("Why don't you play them as I do?") puts on some clothes with the remark that "we'll simply have to dress the character"—a dress rehearsal for the rapid costume changes in "Circe." Mulligan justifies the contradictions in his words and actions with a quotation from Whitman. In "Circe" all contradictions are staged. The paragraph in which Buck Mulligan is dressing (U 16–7) is, incidentally, the first in the book in which we cannot be certain which words are actually spoken by Mulligan and which are part of Stephen's thoughts. The distinction between speech and thought will make little sense in the hallucinations of "Circe." Thus we do not know whether "Mercurial Malachi" (U 17) is actually spoken by mercurial Mulligan or not, but Mercury, Hermes, the wily, roguish god, is also presiding over the "Circe" chapter just as he was instrumental in helping Odysseus.[13] Mercurial Malachi paves the way for the technique of "Circe."

In this view, then, an extravagant convolution like "Circe" is a polytropical reconjugation of familiar elements met before. Joyce manipulates his material in the most suitable manner. This technique—of adapting one's approach to the situation—is in itself an Odyssean one. Like Odysseus, Joyce chooses his speech, his role, and his narrative stance carefully and ruthlessly. Every style is a role adapted for some purpose. Part of our difficulty as readers is that we are too rigidly fixed to follow the abrupt turns, the changes of the stage, so that the verbal, situational, and narrative texture is too polytropic for our customary inertia.

Odysseus, as well as his presidential adviser, Athene, was not particularly scrupulous in the means he employed to attain a given end, and literal truth is not his overriding concern. Nor, in a way, is it Joyce's. He is not exclusively concerned with realistic verisimilitude and can depart from it entirely. The roles, the styles, the perspectives are chosen for optimal effect *ad hoc*.

Ulysses is Homerically polytropical. Voices change, characters are not fixed, language is versatile and polymorphous. The reader is puzzled by new turns. Where passages, or even chapters, are monotropic, their effect is parodistic, and they strike us by their inadequacy and incongruity; in their totality they add up to the most encyclopaedic mosaic in literature.

In the "Wandering Rocks" chapter the many turns are those of a labyrinth, solidified into the bricks and stones of the city. "Aeolus," the first of those extravagant chapters in *Ulysses* which draw attention to their form, is made up of all the traditional rhetorical figures. It is literally composed of many turns, of *tropes*—all the preformed roles available in human speech. Language is intrinsically metaphorical. Part of the dynamism of Joyce's prose arises from the contrast of figurative to literal meaning, or the ironic unfittingness of a metaphor or a cliché fixed in some no longer congruous roles. Language, the most polytropic invention of the human mind, fascinated Joyce. Skeat's *Etymological Dictionary*, a catalogue of the historical roles of words, makes us aware of morphological and semantic transformations. Joyce makes us aware, moreover, of the various roles that even the most ordinary and familiar words always play. Such a simple and seemingly unambiguous unit as "key," for example, is capable of amazing variety and change of identity. That it can refer to those domestic objects that Bloom and Stephen find themselves without, or to symbols of power (as with St. Peter), to musical notation in "Sirens," to a political institution (the House of Keys), to a name (Alexander Keyes), to connotations like a keyhole in "Circe," or else to a woman "properly keyed up," etc., is all very commonplace and generally unnoticed, but belongs to the polytropic potential that Joyce found in everyday language.

Fortunately for him, the English language is particularly flexible. Its powers of assimilation, its wide and varied vocabulary, but above all its lack of determining inflection, allow Joyce the scope he needed. In English the miraculous fact that "A belt was also to give a fellow a belt" (*Portrait* 9), which puzzles a young Stephen Dedalus, is easily possible—but perhaps only in English. Native English speakers may not realize, for example, what duplicity the simple title "The Dead" contains. A foreigner, especially if he wants to render it into his own language, may well wonder whether "Dead" is singular or plural. In the course of reading the story we could easily fluctuate in our view, at times taking the word in its more general sense until at one point it seems limited to Michael Furey before it is universalized again in the last paragraph. In other words, it seems to be a title that changes with our experience. Its flexibility is possible in English—in all other languages the meaning would probably remain fixed.

Bloom can beautifully make a trite phrase—"Another gone" (*U* 74)—do double duty, neatly referring, superficially, to Dignam's demise and internally to voyeuristic frustration. Once you try to do this in another language you will find that gender and inflection present some serious obstacles. Similarly, a "goal" scored in hockey cannot play the role of the great "goal" toward which all history moves (*U* 34) outside of the English language. English must be one of the most Odyssean languages; resourceful, pliant, homophonous, versatile, it allows Joyce to assume the voice appropriate for the occasion, multiple guises, mercurial transformations. Now the virtuoso performances of cunning and punning have appeared to some critics as questionable manipulations, forms of trickery. Interestingly enough, the two contradictory evaluations of Joyce's ways happen to reflect the two views held of the character of Odysseus—the superbly agile and ingenious hero, or else the artful, deceitful trickster. Not very surprisingly, the first one to take this negative view was the Homeric Cyclops, an early victim. It may be significant that his vision was troubled from the outset and worsened in the process. In his naiveté his one-track mind trusted words and names. For Polyphemus, at any rate, the pun on the name of Odysseus was a mean trick of some consequence, and it taught him the treacherous and potent nature of words. It taught him, one presumes, to trust no man and no man's words.

Language in the *Odyssey* and in *Ulysses* can be deceptive, elusive, often unreliable. "Sounds are impostures," says Stephen (U 622), and he says so in a chapter particularly suited to presenting the untrustworthy nature of all communication. The neatest instance is the funeral report in the newspaper. It contains untruths of two kinds. First the conventional hyperbolic formulæ that have little relation to a real emotional involvement which they pretend to express: *"The deceased gentleman was a most popular and genial personality in city life and his demise . . . came as a great shock to citizens of all classes by whom he is deeply regretted"* (U 647). This form of falsification is less conspicuous but more ubiquitous than such strident deviations from factual truth as the listing of mourners present like Stephen Dedalus, C. P. McCoy, L. Boom, and M'Intosh. The reader of the novel is contextually privileged; but readers of the *Evening Telegraph* would have been seriously misled. And the characters of *Ulysses* are being similarly taken in. Even the author himself at times assumes the pose of trusting speech and language naively, by pedantically transforming, in one case, a glib and bibulous and next to meaningless "God bless all here" into a prolonged scene depicting a ceremonial benediction (U 338-40), one example of the rigid belief in the literal meaning of powerful words. This happens in the "Cyclops" chapter, which shows the clash of the unifocality of view with the multivocality of language.

The reader, as against the more shortsighted of the characters involved, has enough information at hand to adjust his views. But even today it does take a reader with at least a minimum of Odyssean agility. After half a century of *Ulysses* we have learned to regard any information provided within the novel with skeptical, in fact Bloomian, reserve. On the other hand, we invest the words of the text with unusual trust. We know that "L. Boom" is, on the realistic surface of it, simply a piece of misinformation. But we tend to rely on the assumption that the distortion means something, and usually more than just one thing. A principle of obverse truth seems to pervade the novel: somehow, "Boom" is literally true and relevant; its incongruity serves intricate purposes.

And perhaps the Latin phrase from the Mass that is irreverently quoted at the beginning of "Telemachus" also indicates that the book is also perversely like the Mass. Not only because it deals with transubstantiations, significant changes, but also because in it, as in the liturgy, every detail—gesture, word, vestment, etc.—is meaningful, a product of a process of condensation and accretion, and generally overdetermined.

So language as a means of communication in *Ulysses* cannot be trusted and at the same time justifies unusual trust, within a hierarchy of potential contexts. An ignorant rendering of "metempsychosis" as "met him pike hoses" is plainly erroneous in one context, but it is appropriate, word for word, to the character who enunciates it and to some major themes of the novel. Bloom's innocent statement, "I was going to throw it away" (*U* 86) is met with distrust, and its unambiguous everyday meaning is disregarded. Bantam Lyons, a particularly biased person, considers it *purely* allusive and is even willing to back his trust in it as an allusion with hard cash. Reality then turns the initial error into unexpected truth, and the reader can rely on some further nonrealistic relevance. Sounds are tricky, but even their trickiness has a communicative value.

In the episode in which a false Odysseus tells obvious falsehoods, in which the novel's real Odysseus warns Stephen against trusting the novel's preparatory Odysseus, and in which Stephen declares sounds to be impostures, the language of even the tritest of clichés has an odd way of sidelighting some truths. I have had occasion to stress some similarities between Leopold Bloom and Buck Mulligan (they concerned me for the present purposes more than their patent dissimilarities). The two form an uneven pair each with Stephen in the respective chapters of Book I and Book III. Now, besides some parallels already mentioned and others easy to work out, I think a few different ones are potentially contained as homonymous asides in the first sentence of the "Eumaeus" chapter: "Preparatory to anything else Mr Bloom *brushed* off the greater bulk of the *shavings* and handed Stephen the hat and ashplant and *bucked* him up generally..." (*U* 612–13). I have italicized "brushed," "shaving," and "bucked" because to me they echo, unassumingly, a-semantically, and in-significantly, the first scene in which Buck wields his brush to shave himself. A few sentences later a connection is further made with Stephen's handkerchief "having done yeoman service in the shaving line." These frail links do not contribute much to the passage, but they do bring out, once more and in a different guise, the principle of the same elements being reshuffled within the novel, and here the elements are partly phonetic. The tiny point is that those signs singled out here are not *only* impostures. They contain a measure of oblique truth. (Incidentally, the vowel sounds of "shavings," "brushed," and "bucked" are the same as of "Stately, plump Buck.")

Or perhaps, to improve on my phrasing, these words and sounds are, literally and etymologically,[14] impostures, being imposed upon the text as an additional layer of gratuitous correspondence, ironic contrast, deviate reliability, or polytropical pertinence.

The novel's versatile and occasionally tricky resilience then can be accounted for as a quality that Homer ascribed to his hero. Joyce went on to write an even more *polytropos* novel with an entirely pantropical hero; also, among countless other things, an Irish Ulysses: "Hibernska Ulitzas" (*FW* 551.32). Because of its polytropic nature, *Ulysses* is capable of meeting us all on our own terms, or on any other terms we may think of. Strangely enough, we still tend to forget the lesson we might have learned and to fall back on monotropical statements of the form "*Ulysses* is basically this or that," and we can only do so by emphasizing one of the potentially multiple turns in our own Cyclopean fashion.

If there is any quintessential formula for *Ulysses*, I do not think it will be contained in a resounding, world-embracing YES, nor in an equally reductive nihilistic NO and rejection of our time, but in a modest, persistent, skeptical, Bloomian "Yes but."

Notes

1. Fritz Senn, " 'He Was Too Scrupulous Always': Joyce's 'The Sisters,' " *JJQ*, 2 (Winter 1965), 70–1.

2. "In Dublin an 'artist' is a merry droll, a player of hoaxes," Oliver St. John Gogarty, "They Think They Know Joyce," *Saturday Review of Literature*, 33 (Mar. 18, 1950), 70.

3. "Notice that the first time [the cat's meow] is spelled with Mk, the second time with Mrk, the third with Mrkr. . . . That's the Greek spelling of Mercury. The cat is Mercury." Sidney Alexander quoting Giulio de Angelis in "Bloomsday in Italy," *The Reporter*, 24 (Apr. 13, 1961), 42.

4. Joyce's version, as reproduced by Ellmann, *JJ* facing p. 433, is faulty and has here been substituted by the transcription of the standard Greek text.

5. *The Ulysses Theme: A Study in the Adaptability of a Traditional Hero* (1954: Ann Arbor: University of Michigan Press, 1968).

6. A selection of phrases with which translators of Homer tried to come to terms with *polytropos* is revealing: the hero fated to roam; who roamed the world over; who drew his changeful course through wanderings; that Great Traveller who wandered far and wide; an adventurous man who wandered far; of craft-renown that hero wandering; man of many changes; that sagacious man; resourceful; so wary and wise; various-minded; skilled in all ways of contending; steadfast, skilful and strong; for wisdom's various arts renown'd; who was never at a loss; ready at need; ingenious hero; the shifty; famous for cleverness of schemes he devised.

7. Reproduced in "Album Joyciano," p. 39 in Stelio Crise, *Epiphanies & Phadographs: Joyce & Trieste* (Milano: All' Insegna del Pesce D'Oro, 1967); it is also in the Frankfurt edition of Joyce: *Werke* 5, *Briefe I 1900–1916* (Frankfurt: Suhrkamp Verlag, 1969), p. 574. The postcard is dated June 16, 1915.

8. "The Grandson of Autolycus," in Stanford, pp. 8–25, et passim.

9. Ibid., pp. 260–61.

10. Ibid., p. 148.

11. Frank Budgen, *James Joyce and the Making of "Ulysses"* (1934; London: Oxford University Press, 1972), p. 15ff.

12. After this paper was read in Tulsa a member of the audience suggested that "plump," second word in the book, also somehow means "all-round."

13. "Moly is the gift of Hermes, god of public ways.... Hermes is the god of signposts: i.e. he is, specially for a traveller like Ulysses, the point at which roads parallel merge and roads contrary also. He is an accident of providence" (*Letters* I, 147–48).

14. Relying on etymological potential is a form of circuitous trust.

Miracle in Black Ink: A Glance at Joyce's Use of His Eucharistic Image   Robert Boyle, S.J.*

In his recent *Ulysses on the Liffey*, Richard Ellmann, through a consideration of Joyce's image of art as Eucharist, arrives at one of the most penetrating and powerful critical insights the last fifty years of *Ulysses* criticism have seen. This is his perception of Molly's (and the other Dublin women's) menstruation as intimately allied to the various consecrations throughout Dublin of Christ's blood and body. This paper aims at bolstering, specifying, and, hopefully, enlarging Ellmann's presentation.

Joyce's use of the eucharistic image can be readily traced from *Portrait* through *Finnegans Wake*, and the earlier and later uses help, it seems to me, to throw light on what Joyce does with the image in *Ulysses*. I will attempt to demonstrate, through the analysis of Joyce's own manipulation of a number of theological terms, how Joyce, bringing many centuries of Catholic tradition to bear on his vision of literary art, comes face to face with the ultimate mystery of human existence, and how he responds when that epiphanic *quidditas* demands expression. The terms are: transmutation, transubstantiation, consubstantiation, subsubstantiation, and transaccidentation.

I have written elsewhere of the theological oddity of "transmuting" in Stephen's careful statement in *Portrait* that "to him, a priest of eternal imagination, transmuting the daily bread of experience into the radiant body of everliving life" (*Portrait* 221). Stephen introduces a term from alchemical tradition into a context where the change from bread to Christ's everliving body would be most properly expressed, in Catholic terms, by "transubstantiating." That Stephen is aware of the distinction and implications involved becomes clearer as we trace the image

*This essay first appeared in the *James Joyce Quarterly*, 10 (Fall 1972) and is reprinted with permission of the *James Joyce Quarterly*.

through the transubstantiations of *Ulysses* into the transaccidentation of the "first till last alshemist" in *Finnegans Wake*.

In *Ulysses*, Joyce (or Stephen) with sophisticated skill shifts the terms, which operate in different ways when applied to different dogmas, from one theological context to another. The three principal mysteries involved, the Trinity, the Incarnation, and the Eucharist, are characteristically linked in this passage from the *Catholic Encyclopedia*'s article on "Eucharist" (the turn-of-the-century-theology of these volumes usually accords closely with the doctrines and theological speculations Joyce learned)—the movement is from the Trinity through the Incarnation to the Eucharist:

> According to a well-known principle of Christology, the same worship of latria (*cultus latriae*) as is due to the Triune God is due also to the Divine Word, the God-man Christ, and in fact, by reason of the hypostatic union, to the Humanity of Christ and its individual component parts, as, e.g. His Sacred Heart. Now, identically the same Lord Christ is truly present in the Eucharist as is present in heaven; consequently He is to be adored in the Blessed Sacrament, and just so long as He remains present under the appearances of bread and wine, namely, from the moment of Transubstantiation to the moment in which the species are decomposed (cf. Council of Trent, Sess. xiii, can. vi).

The term "consubstantial" changes its meaning in *Ulysses* according to the theological context. When it involves the Son's relation to the Father, the context is Trinitarian, and the term refers to the *one* divine substance shared by the two persons. When "consubstantial" shifts from a Trinitarian to a Eucharistic context, however, it then refers to *two* substances, the substance of Christ and the substance of the bread (or of the wine). When, in opposition to the Catholic view, both Christ and the bread are considered to be substantially present in the Eucharist, they are, in this view, "consubstantial." I take it that Stephen is using this notion in "Oxen of the Sun" (U 391) when he puts consubstantiality in relation to transubstantiality and subsubstantiality. "Transubstantiality" determines the Eucharistic context, since it has no meaning or use in other contexts. Then "consubstantiality" in its meaning of two contiguous substances could imply Mary's congress with a human male, and "subsubstantiality" a subhuman congress with a beast—panther perhaps, *sacré pigeon*, or, like Leda, a swan.

"Transubstantiation" is used theologically only for the Eucharist, where it refers to the mysterious (not available to observation, or to human reason unaided) replacement of the substance of the bread by the substance (and accidents) of Christ's body. Through the divine power, Christ, as it were, comes across ("trans") the void to replace the substance of the bread, though the accidents (or appearances) of bread remain, inhering in no substance at all, but somehow sustained in existence by divine power in some relation to Christ's body. Thus when I move the appearances of bread I really move Christ's sacramental body. Thus I can eat the living Christ as divine nourishment and a source of ever-living life for me. A new conscience—a *knowing-with* Christ, like what I take to be Stephen's basic meaning in forming a new conscience for his race, a *knowing-with* the artist—is thus nourished.

The term "transubstantial," then, involves divine action, direct intervention. On this base Joyce uses the term in contexts other than Eucharistic ones. He speaks (*U* 682) of Bloom as Virag's "transubstantial son," and of Stephen as Simon's "consubstantial son." This may imply that, since transubstantiation requires deliberate action of the priest and consubstantiation requires merely the acceptance of the natural situation, the doing of "the coupler's will" (*U* 38), Bloom's father wanted his son more intensely than Simon wanted his. But the theological auras of the words, I judge, suggest much more. In the first case, since the context involves Bloom's Jewishness as contrasted with Stephen's Christianity, the interest of the Jewish father in the divine activity in regard to his son seems to be involved: "and every male that's born they think it may be their Messiah" (*U* 338). In the second case, all Catholics accept the fact that Stephen and Simon share the same generic nature, and receive divine grace, if they do, not directly from God but from Christ operating through the sacraments, in the normal course of events. Stephen and Simon are therefore referred to here as consubstantial, because of their natural sharing of the human principle of operation. Also on page 38 the term is applied to them on the basis of their sharing of human nature, though in that instance their distressing duality as opposed persons is involved as well.

"Subsubstantiation" must be formed on analogy with "subhuman." Stephen uses it in his discussion of the "knowing" which resulted in Mary's pregnancy (a passage I discuss in "The Priesthoods of Stephen and Buck," in *Approaches to "Ulysses": Ten Essays*, ed. Staley and Benstock [Pittsburgh: University of Pittsburgh Press, 1970], pp. 47–52). Ellmann considers it as a discussion of the nature of Mary's own substance: "In other words, Mary was either of divine or of human substance, but in no case was she less than substance or had she less than sexual intercourse."[1] I read the pasage differently, since the context, as I now see it, does not deal with the question of the kind of substance Mary had. Her human substance is not here questioned, as it is not, as far as I know, anyplace in the book. Ellmann had earlier introduced the question of divine substance in regard to Mary: "Mariolatry and coyness resemble each other in that the one seeks to qualify the austere three-personed maleness of the Trinity by introducing a female presence into it..." (*UL* 128). That point may have some revelance elsewhere. Stephen speaks of "the madonna which the cunning Italian intellect flung to the mob of Europe," (*U* 207) as if this were a Vatican divine lure to enchant the world to weary ways. And maybe the idiocies of Mariolatry, which Stephen in *Portrait* amply illustrates, and the resentment of God as a stern Justius, a cosmic policeman, a Jesuit pandy-batter, might give some basis to Ellmann's introducing the possibility of any question of Mary's divinity—but not much, if indeed any. At any rate, in this passage (*U* 391), as I can now read it, the whole question is whether the human Mary has been impregnated by divine power, by human power, or, as Taxil's crude blasphemy, allied to Buck's, suggests, by subhuman power, *"le sacré pigeon."* As I see the matter now, then, it appears preferable to consider that "subsubstantial" refers here to "bestiality," and is allied to Buck's rationalistic attempt to reduce the death of Stephen's mother—and thus, by implication offensive to Stephen, Stephen himself—to a beastly event: *"O, it's only Dedalus whose mother is beastly dead"* (*U* 8). While Stephen is willing, in this discussion of Mary's conceiving the Word, to accept the notion of intercourse with God or with a human man, he pretends indignantly to reject the Leda-and-the-swan situation which Buck had vulgarized in his "Ballad of Joking Jesus."

Stephen orgulously goes on to mock, in terms more intellectual than Buck's, the problems Mariology had fussed over for centuries—e.g., "a body without blemish" thus would refer to the hymen of the inviolate Virgin, which many Mariologists asserted must have remained unbroken in the birth of Jesus, so that he passed through it as he passed through the locked door of the Upper Room some years later. Such matters, Stephen asserts, the faithful may assent to, echoing Mary's version of the Christian "Thy will be done," but the artist-priest and his ephemeral disciples will *with-stand*—perhaps in the old sense, stand *against* the dogma, and in the newer, stand *alongside* the artist-priest. He preaches, in any case, the human resolution of the situation: Mary had intercourse with Joseph (or perhaps with Panther). The lewd—that is the layfolk, *unlearned* in the Latin root of "lewd"; *vicious* in the Anglo-Saxon root mingled with the Latin—may accept anti-natural dogmatizing, but we artists, truly consubstantial with each other in this human Eucharist of alcohol, can withstand and, as speakers of the Word (Burke's it turns out), can with-say (*against* the Holy Spirit and speak *alongside* licensed spirits). Thus our will, not Nobodaddy's, will be done, and we show ourselves superior to the Blessed Virgin and her credulous admirers. This reading of the passage, while not totally satisfactory to me, nevertheless seems at the moment preferable to Ellmann's. But I certainly agree altogether with his main point, that "consubstantial" here refers to human substances as opposed to divine substance or to anything less than human substance (Ellmann seems to want to use "substance" as a synonym for human substance).

In his preparation for the statement of his great insight into Molly's role in the Eucharistic image, Ellmann states: "This synthesis was pre-pared for long before in the book; in the *Proteus* episode Stephen brooded on the oddity of God's transubstantiation into flesh occurring in so many communions in so many times and places . . ." (*UL* 170). That is not happily stated, since Ellmann introduces a confusion which I judge that the Catholic Stephen (and Joyce) would not allow in this context. In the Eucharist, God does not assume flesh (the term "transub-stantiation" does not at all fit into the context of the Word being made flesh); that is done in the Incarnation. In the Eucharist, Christ (not simply God, but God-made-man, anointed with chrism) assumes, as it were, without change of any kind in him, the accidents of bread and wine.

Stephen had considered this matter in "Proteus," when he thought of "the imp hypostasis" tickling Occam's brain (*U* 40). This considera-tion is most important in the eucharistic image Joyce develops, as Ell-mann perceives in linking these varied consecrations of the hosts to the menstruations throughout Dublin (and the whole human world, for that matter). I judge that Weldon Thornton is mistaken in stating, in his annotation on this passage that "Stephen's use of *hypostasis* here is mis-leading since hypostasis refers to the union of God and man in Christ, not to Christ's real presence in the Eucharist. . . ."[2] Stephen is consider-ing, as Occam did, that the hypostatic union effected in the Incarnation is the basis for the multilocation effected in the Eucharist. "Hypostasis" literally means exactly what "substance" means, and theologically it refers to the union of two natures, divine and human, in one divine person. Because that one person has both divine power and material extension, he can effect the transubstantiation of many diverse pieces of bread in different times and places and, without change in himself, become mysteriously present under their accidents (their extension, whiteness, and other sensible manifestations). It perhaps should be stressed that theologians do not operate on the basis of imagination, as artists do, so that Stephen's broodings on Occam's speculations might be quite novel to Occam. Stephen, like Joyce, is concerned merely to use the theological materials for his artistic and imaginative purpose. Here, his ultimate aim, as I conceive it, is to prepare for the image of the multilocation of the life-giving artist under the accidents of ink.

Now, if Stephen's thought is carefully considered, it will be seen *that* "transubstantiation" fits the bread very well, since the imagination tends to picture the substance of the bread (in the theological explana-tion Joyce most likely learned) passing, "transiting," into the potency of matter and disappearing altogether, while the accidents of the bread, those things which make it manifest to our senses, its extension, color, texture, etc., somehow mysteriously remain. How this can be merits some attention if we are to grasp the force of Joyce's later and most revealing Eucharistic coinage, "transaccidentation."

Human reason would surely judge, by available natural evidence, that where accidents appear there must be a substance in which they inhere. A baseless or rootless accident simply cannot be conceived or imagined, like a line with only one end. Or perhaps a faint analogy might be that engineless automobile which "Candid Camera" arranged to have apparently driven into a garage, to the stupified consternation of the observing mechanic. Yet some such situation does confront the Catholic theologian. The *Catholic Encyclopedia*, under "Eucharist," presents this solution: "If it be further asked, whether these appearances have any subject at all in which they inhere, we must answer with St. Thomas Aquinas (III, Q.lxxvii, a.1), that the idea is to be rejected as unbecoming, as though the Body of Christ, in addition to its own accidents, should also assume those of bread and wine. The most that may be said is, that from the Eucharistic Body proceeds a miraculous sustaining power, which supports the appearances bereft of their natural substances and preserves them from collapse." Now it is clear that the point of view of Christ and that of the bread, in this situation, will differ radically, as theologians have realized: "Accordingly, the continuance of the appearances without the substance of bread and wine as their connatural substratum is just the reverse of Transubstantiation" (*Catholic Encyclopedia*, "Eucharist"). I take it that this means that the losing of substance by the bread is the reverse of the gaining of a substance by the Eucharist. In any case, as I understand the play of Joyce's imagination with this notion, the situation of the bread which has lost its substance but, in some sense, gained Christ as a base is the reverse of Christ's situation, who has lost nothing but, in some perhaps applied sense, adopted the orphaned accidents of the bread. Thus Joyce the artist prepares to move, complete and living, under the accidents of his ink, more durable than flesh.

In the Eucharist, Christ has not changed at all, but the bread has changed more than the human mind, without faith, can grasp. Thus if we asked the bread, "What has happened to you," the bread (or the remaining accidents) deprived of its substance, could answer with fervor, "I have been transubstantiated." But if we ask Christ, who has not changed, not moved, and is yet really present, he can at most say, "I have been transaccidentated." He somehow supports accidents not proper to him, as if he had moved under them, and thus he becomes available to all throughout time and space.

This is Joyce's development of the Eucharistic image of the artist in *Finnegans Wake*, where Shem, having prepared a caustic ink out of his own body wastes, is described, after he has written human history on his own skin, as "transaccidentated through the slow fires of consciousness into a dividual chaos . . ." (*FW* 186). Thus the image which formally began in the smithy of Stephen's soul in *Portrait*, where he planned to forge with the fires of slow perseverance through millions of real experiences a conscience for his race, which could now *know-with* or *experience-with* him, comes to full flower in its reversed condition, where not the experience is changed but the experiencer. Now instead of the daily bread of experience becoming a record or reflection of the maker's own human experiences through transmutation as in alchemy, as we surely understood it in *Portrait*, it becomes the Artist himself, as the bread in the Eucharist becomes Christ. Thus, under the accidents of this human ink, composed of faeces and urine as the Eucharist is composed of bread and wine, the artist makes himself available to his race, to give them conscience—to make them share, as the *FW* passage makes clear, in all human history by plunging with the individual artist into the dividual human chaos, substantiated in the verbal chaosmos of *Finnegans Wake*. So Joyce as a human being, like Dublin as a city containing all cities, contains in himself all humanity, as the particular contains the universal.

One danger in stressing the ultimate implications of the Eucharist image, I might digress to observe, Ellmann has not, as it now seems to me, altogether avoided. About the Eucharist it is possible to say that the word "love" expresses best of all what it means and what it is. Ellmann says exactly that about *Ulysses*, too, so that, as with great insight he observes, all levels of the book "have their summit in love, of which the highest form is sexual love" (*UL* 175). My mind gives enthusiastic assent to Ellmann's stance, but on some subliminal level I feel a stubborn squirm of resistance. And I further feel that this doctrine of "Amor super omnia" is the source of Ellmann's finding in Joyce, writing the final stages of *Ulysses*, "a certain embarrassment and reticence. He speaks of love without naming it . . ." (*UL* 175). Indeed! Joyce's aim, I suspect, is different from Ellmann's, who seems to long for and find, so he thinks, though with infinitely greater depth and subtlety than Tindall, triumphant Beethovenian chords assenting to *Liebe über alles!*

I judge, with some reluctance, from what I can see and feel, that Joyce never totally abandoned the youthful cynicism evident in Number XXVII of *Chamber Music*:

> For elegant and antique praise,
>   Dearest, my lips wax all too wise;
> Nor have I known a love whose praise
>   Our piping poets solemnize,
> Neither a love where may not be
>   Ever so little falsity.

Ellmann, in his finding "a certain embarrassment and reticence" in this usually bold but now suddenly coy Irishman, seems to picture Joyce hanging back from the happy cosmic triumph, and suspects, as he goes on to say, that Joyce fears didacticism and is therefore embarrassed and reticent. I cannot at this moment see how Ellmann's attitude here totally avoids a tinge of Disney-like optimism. I myself suspect that Joyce did not name love as the word known to all men because he didn't see it or feel it that way. Love, in a human universe, does exclude a great deal—all negative, perhaps, but profoundly operative nevertheless. At Buck's Black Mass in "Circe," the server, Mr. Haines Love, hypostatically combines, like Butt and Taff in *Finnegans Wake*, the human moral opposites in one person. Joyce, as I see it now, is unwilling to exclude the opposite of love in his coal-hole vision, or to discount hell in his arrival at Paradise. He is not reticent. He is, rather, volubly cosmic—in the human cosmos. The word known to all men is in the cosmos ineffable, I suspect. It might come fairly close to being "Shantih," or perhaps even Justius's "Awmawm," but, as I can dimly see it now, it is not merely "love."

But to return to Joyce's image, the various Eucharists which touch the high points of its development deepen from the villanelle's "chalice flowing to the brim" through Buck's shaving mug, Bloom's tub, Molly's chamber-pot, until it reaches Shem's seemingly degraded yet amazingly elevated Grecian urn, in which he makes his eucharistic ink. The contrast of the two literary imagined chalices, Stephen's and Shem's, shows something of the increasing profundity of the image. Stephen's villanelle chalice, a fancy, somewhat romantically inflated vessel too eagerly fulfilling the requirements of the consecration of the Mass, recalls the "Araby" chalice borne so ineffectively through the Dublin streets. And the villanelle chalice, too, gathers about itself perverse, unhealthy vibrations, sounding with what I have elsewhere referred to as a Dracula tonality. The urn of Shem, once consecrated to sadness, more naturally receives the effusion from the bowels of his misery, and takes on its human ("consubstantial") rather than blood-brimming werewolf ("subsubstantial") tonalities especially in the context of Bloom's tub and Molly's pot.

Ellmann perceptively suggests that Buck, in his difficulty about "those white corpuscles" on the opening page of *Ulysses*, is looking down at the white beads of lather in his mug, beaded bubbles which could recall those presumably winking at the brim of the diseased beaker of the villanelle. Yet the tonality of Buck's relatively genial blasphemy is much healthier, by conventional norms at least, than Stephen's, if less profound. Buck the scientist is poking fun at dogma, but he is also out to dominate, to use, and perhaps to destroy the artist, as the prelatial patrons of the arts in the middle ages often did. His eucharist will be useful in cleansing and shaving, but will not be in any sense nourishing. Stephen's will have potentialities both for nourishing and, in its enchanting, baneful alchemical and diabolical aspects, poisoning ("and in the porches of their ears I pour" [*U* 196]).

Bloom's pleasant imagined tub, holding his body consecrated by nature to life ("the father of thousands"), offers the most humanly at-tractive eucharistic image that Joyce presents—pleasant to acquiescent Bloom as well as to the race which could, potentially, spring from his willing loins—willing, at least, in this eucharistic image. It is Bloom as priest, after all, who, having brooded over the Eucharist in the Mass he witnessed, says of himself in his imagined clean trough of water, "This is my body" (*U* 86). He can give, if not romantic ever-living life, real human life to others, which Stephen, priest of the eternal imagination, aiming to give a romantic reflection of the life his own twisted experience has revealed to him, cannot do, since, like another Prodigal, he squanders his substance among whores. Bloom's eucharist, less inflated than Stephen's, would indeed be human only and moral, but it would be complete. Stephen's literary sacrament of ever-living life, mixed with the seraphic and diabolic, surges either upward with Michael or downward with Lucifer in its Icarian effort to escape this mundane planet, this limited crystalline world. In its fear of and exclusion of earth and water, of death and urine, Stephen's frustrated soul wants both heaven and hell at once, and is satisfied with neither. If his eucharist could be mixed with Bloom's, the results might be good—or they might not.

Molly does a pretty good job of mixing the two. I cannot yet clearly see, as Tindall long has, that Stephen and Bloom become a satisfactory Bleephan in the eucharistic meal Bloom confects for Stephen. Maybe so, but far more satisfactory, as I can now perceive the matter, is the union that results from the chalice Molly confects of blood and urine. Here Ellmann's great insight into the mixing of the Dublin consecrations and the Dublin menstruations must be quoted: "But Joyce is establishing a secret parallel and opposition: the body of God and the body of woman share blood in common" (*UL* 171). And here too Molly brings in all that is good in the Eucharists of Stephen and of Bloom—the allure of woman and the potentiality for sharing life in the human body—and partially tends to correct what is bad—the destructive, cannibalistic voraciousness of female blood-sucking bat and sow and the fearful paralysis of the timid hedonist.

She alone of the eucharistic confectors has no idea at all, consciously at least, that she is involved in any sacrament, which may be one important reason why, as "only natural," she expresses most fully the "human only" experience of our race and, as the *clou* to immortality, best defies time. One surely must not leave out, in trying to perceive Joyce's whole vision, the complicating elements which make Molly share the diabolical (or quasi-diabolical) negative things in the previous Eucharists, but Ellmann's emphasis on love, if not carried too far, seems to me surely the right one. At least it operates in the book, and in me, as in Ellmann, with great force.

The fullest development of the eucharistic image, with all its possibilities and all of its positive and negative elements operative, can be found on pages 185–86 of *Finnegans Wake*. First the preparation of the materials, echoing faintly the instructions for the preparation of the host, emerges from the Latin passage on page 185, which may be translated thus:

> First of all, the artificer, the old father, without any shame and without permission, when he had donned a cope and undone the girdles, with rump as bare as on the day of birth, squatting on the viviparous and all-powerful earth, weeping and groaning the while, defecated into his hand; and secondly, having unburdened himself of black air, while he beat out the battle-signal, he placed his own faeces, which he entitled his "purge," in a once honorable vessel of sadness, and into the same, under the invocation of the twin brothers, Medardus and Godardus, he pissed happily and melodiously, continuously singing with a loud voice the psalm which begins, "My tongue is the reed of a scribe swiftly writing." Finally, from vile crap mixed with the pleasantness of the divine Orion, after the mixture had been cooked and exposed to the cold, he made for himself imperishable ink.[3]

This and the following paragraph describe the confection and effect of Shem's Eucharist. Analogous to Molly's chamber-pot, Shem's urn, now degraded (and, as it turns out, elevated) to receive the human waste which will, miraculously, provide "the radiant body of everliving life," brings in among other things cosmic Hellenic myths, astrological personages, canonized saints controlling the passing of waters, Old Testament prophets using their tongues as swiftly producing pens, Dublin editors rejecting Joyce's writing, epic and Miltonic and Uranian contexts, the wealth and power of the United States, the whole nineteenth-century literary effort to determine rather than to reflect reality as in Balzac and Wilde, the impact of Christianity, the domination of priest and king and their doom, and the squid's great miracle in black ink:

> Then, pious Eneas, conformant to the fulminant firman which enjoins on the tremylose terrian that, when the call comes, he shall produce nichthemerically from his unheavenly body a no uncertain quantity of obscene matter not protected by copriright in the United Stars of Ourania or bedeed and bedood and bedang and bedung to him, with this double dye, brought to blood heat, gallic acid on iron ore, through the bowels of his misery, flashly, faithly, nastily, appropriately, this Esuan Menschavik and the first till last alshemist wrote over every square inch of the only foolscap available, his own body, till by its corrosive sublimation one continuous present tense integument slowly unfolded all marryvoising moodmoulded cyclewheeling history (thereby, he said, reflecting from his own individual person life unlivable, transaccidentated through the slow fires of consciousness into a dividual chaos, perilous, potent, common to allflesh, human only, mortal) but with each word that would not pass away the squidself which he had squirtscreened from the crystalline world waned

chagreenold and doriangrayer in its dudhud. This exists that isits
after having been said we know. And dabal take dabnal! And the dal
dabal dab aldanabal! So perhaps, agglaggagglomeratively asaspenking,
after all the arklast fore arklyst on his last public misappearance, circling the square, for the deathfête of Saint Ignaceous Poisonivy, of the
Fickle Crowd (hopon the sexth day of Hogsober, killim our king,
layum low!) and brandishing his bellbearing stylo, the shining keyman
of the wilds of change, if what is sauce for the zassy is souse for the
zazimas, the blond cop who thought it was ink was out of his depth
but bright in the main. (*FW* 185–86)

The black ink of the frightened squid-artist squirted into this chaos,
available to the individual creator because he has penetrated through
the shell of self to the dividuality in which humanity shares, the *quidditas* common to allflesh, may, at least in its epiphanic defiance of Time,
be allied to Shakespeare's more conventional challenge in Sonnet 65:

> Oh, none, unless this miracle have might,
> That in black ink my love may still
> shine bright.

My friend Richard Kain, from his vast knowledge of Joycean materials,
referred me to the review of *Ulysses* from which Joyce draws his squid
image, N.P. Dawson's "The Cuttlefish School of Writers." The relevant
passage is: "For given a degree of talent, there is an increasing school
of writers who imitate the cuttlefish, and conceal their shortcomings by
'ejecting an inky fluid,' which is the definition the dictionary gives of a
cuttlefish. The Cuttlefish school would not be a bad name for these
writers who perhaps not being as great genuises as they would like to
be, eject their inky fluid, splash about and make a great fuss, so that
it is difficult to tell what it is all about, and it might as well be genius
as anything else."[4] The "crystalline world" of Joyce's passage might conceivably be influenced by Dawson's question, "Would we even find
'Ulysses' under glass in a museum?,"[5] though the major source, as I now
see the matter, is Milton's rational crystal universe hanging in chaos.

Thus Joyce's black ink like Shakespeare's will by a miracle have the
extraordinary power of bringing immortality (of a sort) to the artist's
love (perhaps both subjective and objective genitive). Shem's ink goes
through the shades of the Irish flag ("chagreenold [green and gold]
and doriangrayer ["or" and off-white]") to reach its black dudhud, im-
plying, I judge, that Shem's love, among others, is Ireland, even para-
lyzed, colorless, and dead. But mainly here, it seems to me, the Eucharistic image indicates two things: the concealment, sublimation perhaps,
of the creating artist in his art, and the quasi-sacramental victory over
time and space. The squid, in sending out into Miltonic chaos, among
the United Stars of Ourania, its protective ink, does screen itself effec-

tively from the crystalline world, but it also gives a message that it is there somewhere, a fact ("this exists") that we then know. As we know that God the Creator exists when we see his creation, though we cannot directly know what he is in himself, so we know that the artist-creator exists when we see his carefully formed ink. But we cannot—and the busy, busy Joycean psychoanalysts could well note this—with certitude tell what he is in himself.

More important, the image indicates that the artist is now transaccidentated under the accidents of ink, as Christ is under the accidents of bread. Now the Word that will not pass away (*U* 391; *FW* 186) can be carried to true believers, and through the mystery of himself we can share life more fully than Bloom can transmit it or Molly can assent to it. Stephen's image has reached a new cosmic depth, not divine but human only and mortal, but probably, the image implies, the best we are likely to find. Matthew Arnold might look up from his trimming of A. Lawn Tennyson in pleased delight, one guesses. And we can see now better Joyce's own attitude toward himself as the essential individual opening into that primitive dividual human chaos where the androgynous artist's creative efforts can bring forth his literary race to carry life, livable and unlivable, into the world.

Through his development of the Eucharist image, then, Joyce manages to reflect in Stephen the Romantic and Victorian fluctuations between the Shelleyan ineffectual angel and the Wildean, or perhaps better, Swinburnean perverse and rebellious devil, with their common abhorrence of ordinary humanity. In Buck he suggests along with some good qualities, an expedient common-law union of science and Catholicism, destructive not only of both of those but of humanity as well. In Bloom and Molly he does, through his uses of Catholic belief, far more than D. H. Lawrence could to justify sex's ways to man, and to set forth, without denying the human basis for hell, the tremylose terrian's drive toward some kind of heaven. In Shem he combines all that he has had before in his eucharistic image with a deeper imaginative apprehension of literature's cosmic worth to the human race. With this image Joyce reveals to us who choose to see that we are both gods and doggone clods, and then, faced with the ultimate question about the word known to all men, Joyce, without reticence or embarrassment, in his own prudent dudhud, imitates both Old Man River and Elijah's God: "Our Mr President, he twig the whole lot and he ain't saying nothing" (*U* 508).

APPENDIX

| Transubstantiation: | Stephen, who in *Portrait* prefers "transmutation"—aiming to make the divine (and diabolical) human. |

Subsubstantiation:	Buck as scientist-priest, Boylan as stud, Bella as enchantress—all aiming to make the human bestial.
Consubstantiation:	Bloom and Molly—aiming to make the human human, in flesh. Molly tends to bridge the human and at least some secular or humanistic "divine."
Transaccidentation:	Shem—making the human share the divine aspects of the Eucharist as well as the diabolical aspects of the Black Mass, in carrying the living human artist throughout human time and space, under the accidents of ink rather than those of bread.

Notes

1. *Ulysses on the Liffey* (New York: Oxford University Press, 1972), p. 139. Hereafter *UL*.

2. *Allusions in "Ulysses": An Annotated List* (Chapel Hill: University of North Carolina Press, 1968), p. 48.

3. For a detailed discussion of this translation, see my article "*Finnegans Wake*, Page 185: An Explication," *JJQ*, 4 (Fall 1966), 3–16.

4. "The Cuttlefish School of Writers," *Forum*, 69 (1923), 1182.

5. Ibid., p. 1184.

"The Dead": A Cold Coming   Bernard Benstock*

The motif of death is solidly established in the coda story of *Dubliners*, not only with Joyce's succinct title, but with the various rhetorical devices embedded in the terse opening sentence: "Lily, the caretaker's daughter, was literally run off her feet." Lily's tag-name, that of the funereal flower, serves as a symbol of death—as well as an ironic allusion to purity; the connotation of "caretaker" is mere innuendo, since we later realize that he is custodian of the estate, rather than of a cemetery, but by then the effect is unalterable, and the smell of the graveyard is in our nostrils; and the hyperbolic figure of speech ("run off her feet"), which although figurative, is offered to the reader to be accepted "liter-

*This essay first appeared in *James Joyce's Dubliners: Critical Essays* (London: Faber and Faber, 1965), and is reprinted with the permission of Faber and Faber.

ally." Yet this early impregnation of death symbolism is soon belied ostensibly by the pleasant Christmas setting, the musical entertainment, the sentimental speech, the "gourmeterring and gourmandising"—the *élan vital* of the story's surface. The hostesses bubble and flitter about; Freddy is hilariously drunk; Browne lecherously enthusiastic; and Gabriel Conroy himself seems the embodiment of contented self-importance. The dead appear far removed from the celebration of the Nativity.

The dead are very much in evidence, however, and death hovers over the feast at all times, emerging triumphant by the end. Three levels of these dead become apparent upon close examination: the deceased, the moribund, and the living-dead, the composition of the last group expanding with the progression of the story. Four of the "dear departed" remembered and acknowledged during the course of the evening's activities are: Gabriel's mother, whose "last long illness" he recalls in conjunction with her "sullen opposition to his marriage" to Gretta ("Some slighting phrases she had used still rankled in his memory; she had once spoken of Gretta as being country cute"); the two Patrick Morkans, "brother Pat" (Mary Jane's father, whose death terminated the residence of his sisters in Stoney Batter) and "the old gentleman" (whose horse Johnny had circled the equestrian statue of King Billy in mesmerized paralysis); and finally Michael Furey, whose spectre takes possession of the tale in a way comparable to Parnell's domination of "Ivy Day in the Committee Room." These in turn are represented by the array of opera singers conjured up during dinner (dating back to the Parkinson remembered only by the oldest participant) and even by the snow-covered statue of Daniel O'Connell.

Those obviously close to death are the three old women, Aunts Kate and Julia and Mrs Malins. Aunt Julia, whose "flaccid" face is grey with "darker shadows," has the "appearance of a woman who did not know where she was or where she was going." Aunt Kate, whose face is healthier, nonetheless has a face "like a shrivelled red apple," and is "too feeble to go about much." And Mrs Malins is "a stout feeble old woman with white hair." There is enough evidence, therefore, from Joyce's capsule descriptions of them, for the reader to realize, even before Gabriel's awareness late in "The Dead" of the imminence of Julia's death, that these old and sickly women are reminders of the final gasp of life. Their totems are the monks of Mount Melleray who sleep in their coffins "to remind them of their last end."

But old age is not the only requisite for inclusion among the moribund, as Gabriel also comes to realize, since time brings all men towards death: "One by one they were all becoming shades. Better pass boldly into that other world, in the full glory of some passion, than fade and wither dismally with age." Such passionate glory is denied to the living-dead, those who remain alive, but fail to live: the disillusioned, the self-destructive, the blighted and wasted lives. It is with these that "The

Dead" is most concerned. First there is the servant girl Lily, just out of school and already cynically world-weary, presumably because of a prematurely unpleasant experience with a man. The mature and proper Gabriel is actually shocked at her assertion that "The men that is now is only all palaver and what they can get out of you." And although we are informed that "she got on well with her three mistresses," a change is mirrored in Kate's recent disappointment: "I'm sure I don't know what has come over her lately. She's not the girl she was at all." (No longer a girl, Lily has been initiated into womanhood, and it is not difficult to speculate about what has come over her lately.) Less serious reminders are seen in Mary Jane, in her thirties and unmarried, who plays "Academy pieces" on the piano that no one listens to; Freddy Malins and Browne have their obvious vices; and Bartell D'Arcy, the much-praised tenor, is hoarse and consequently rather grouchy. Most important of course is the revelation that Gretta has been living a dead life in contrast to the remembered and cherished romance of her youth, a revelation that destroys the bubble of her husband's unreal existence, permanently deflating the self-assurance of his artificially bolstered world.

Even for those who are quick to perceive "the skull beneath the skin" of most of the characters in "The Dead," the Conroys at first seem to be a healthy contrast. Had there not been so much dynamic spontaneity associated with them, as they came in out of the snow much anticipated and warmly welcomed (Gabriel scrapes the snow from his shoes "vigorously"; his clothes emit "a cold fragrant air from out-of-doors," while Gretta goes upstairs with the aunts "laughing"), perhaps we might have been more suspicious of their poses. Surely the opening conversation contains enough indications that all is not sound as Gretta good-naturedly belittles her husband's prissy solicitousness: Gabriel is worried that his country wife will catch cold and has therefore engaged a hotel room in order to avoid the return home to Monkstown late at night. Gretta ridicules his insistence upon goloshes ("Guttapercha things," she calls them), and doubles her scorn by crediting his faith in them as both conformity and affectation: "Gabriel says everyone wears them on the continent." (Buck Mulligan sneers at Stephen: "O, damn you and your Paris fads.") Worse still, Gretta compounds his faults almost maliciously: "He's really an awful bother," she reports to his aunts in his presence, "what with green shades for Tom's eyes at night and making him do the dumb-bells, and forcing Eva to eat the stirabout." And finally she boasts of her successful rebellion against him, that on this particular evening she refused to wear her goloshes despite the snowfall. None of this, however, is as heavy as it might sound, extrapolated this way, but an important barometer of Gretta's effect on her husband's sensitivity can be seen from the changes in his attitudes as she babbles away: at first he answers his wife's glance with "admiring and happy eyes," and we learn that "Gabriel's solicitude was a standing joke" with the aunts, but the goloshes prove too sore a point ("Gabriel knitted his brows . . . as if he were slightly angered")—it takes Aunt Kate's tact to change the subject. Beneath Gretta's delightful banter, therefore, can be seen a slight but significant rift in the marital lute, and Mrs Conroy's objection to Gretta's country-cuteness might suggest a disparity in social levels, that her good looks have netted her the climb through marriage into the solid middle class.

Class distinctions are not irrelevant in "The Dead." Next to the son of a merchant-prince butcher in "After the Race," this last story gives the reader a glimpse into the best of the middle class in a volume whose range includes every aspect of the bourgeois spectrum. (There is almost a touch of Dickens when Gabriel thinks, "People, perhaps, were standing in the snow on the quay outside, gazing up at the lighted windows and listening to the waltz music.") But economic decline, an important factor in the depiction of the Dedalus family of A Portrait, is in evidence. The Morkans delight in living well, as attested by their annual fête and their general insistence upon the best in food ("diamond-bone sirloins, three-shilling tea and the best bottled stout"), but their rented floors in the "dark gaunt house" on Usher's Island represent a significant change from the house in Stoney Batter, and their zeal in preventing Mary Jane's pupils, who came from "the better-class families on the Kingstown and Dalkey line," from being discomfited by Freddy's drunkenness mirrors an attitude of social subservience. (Mary Jane personally serves as waitress for these pupils, offering them the best.) The three Graces have been reduced to selling their talents while nurturing their bourgeois assumptions that music is not a commodity like corn, the source of income for the Mr Fulham who owns their house and conducts his business on its ground floor. Ironically they also disclose their middle-class snobbery by insisting that the "old gentleman," their father, had owned a starch mill rather than a glue factory. ("Well, glue or starch," says Gabriel democratically, his intellectual snobbery sparing him the necessity of the snobbery of his class.) From affluent mill-owner to shabby-genteel music teachers indicates another Joycean irony. Yet the cause of the financial decline is somewhat unusual: it can be assumed that with the death of Brother Pat no male was left to run the business— the masculine line had run out, leaving only women. Pat's only child (at least from internal evidence) is also female, and only one of his sisters married, producing two sons, neither one of whom she groomed to soil his hands boiling starch (or glue). The priest and the teacher fulfil the family ideals of their class, rising above its mercantile level, but leaving the Morkans unable to reproduce themselves.

The musical Morkans by their very talent contain the seed of their own destruction. We have seen from "A Mother" the extent to which music is a dead end in Dublin; in a nation which considers vocal music its principal art form, a concert like the four-part series scheduled for the Antient Concert Rooms proves to be an acid test of the state of art in general in Ireland's capital city. Joyce has indicated that the trio of stories preceding "The Dead" ("Ivy Day," "A Mother," "Grace") concentrate on the public life of the city, isolating politics, art, and religion as areas of focus. The closing story summarizes this concentration as well as all themes inherent throughout *Dubliners.* Joe Hynes' sincere if ineptly expressed Parnellism is in healthy contrast to the betrayers in the Committee Room, but emerges as the narrow nationalism of Molly Ivors in "The Dead." The cash-register Catholicism of Father Purdon's sermon for businessmen is reduced to Gabriel's Christmas gratuity to Lily and Freddy Malins' Christmas-card shop, while the vestiges of Tom Kernan's Protestant objection to candles can be seen in Protestant Browne at the Morkans' party, in front of whom the Catholics fear that they are "giving scandal." In general, religion as a dead end is personified by the Mount Melleray monks in their coffins. And the failure of the concert series is prolonged in the reaction to Mary Jane's piano piece (which bores Gabriel and causes the four topers to slink away to the bar, returning only at the conclusion to offer the "most vigorous clapping"). D'Arcy's singing of "The Lass of Aughrim" receives a better response, although he himself proves irritable because of his hoarseness, but Gretta's reaction of intent rapture is due to personal nostalgia rather than critical appreciation. In contrast to these "failures," however, we seem to have the very substantial success of Aunt Julia's rendition of "Arrayed for the Bridal," where even the performer is moved by the applause which "sounded so genuine." Apparently a genuine response is a rarity (which in itself should make us suspicious), but Julia's triumph is tinged with irony. She is many years past her prime and in the process of being replaced by boy sopranos in the choir at Adam and Eve's Church. When Gabriel, who "applauded loudly with all the others" at the time, later realizes that he "caught that haggard look upon her face for a moment when she was singing," the full horror of the phenomenon should become apparent. "Arrayed for the Bridal," as incongruous a selection for the ageing spinster as "I Dreamt that I Dwelt" was for Maria in "Clay," is Julia's beautifully executed Swan Song.

Joyce's comment that he might have been "unnecessarily harsh" in his treatment of the moral state of affairs in Ireland (made after the first fourteen stories had gone to the publisher but before he wrote "The Dead"), may indicate that the added *novella* was in some way intended to offset the effect of the preceding epiphanies. Yet in dozens of small correspondences "The Dead" serves as a summation of the entire volume. The religion-art-politics of the immediate predecessors re-emerge here, while the breakdown of family relationships in those stories is paralleled as well: father-son in "Ivy Day" (not only the caretaker, Jack, and his profligate son, but the contrast established in Henchy between Joe Hynes and his father), mother-daughter in "A Mother" (although Mrs Kearney's domination of her husband is also important), and husband-wife in "Grace" (if Tom Kernan is a cross for his wife to bear, Martin Cunningham has one in his wife). The destruction of the superficial harmony of the married Conroys is well anticipated. And what are we to assume about the names Tom and Eva for the Conroy children? In "Counterparts" Farrington has a son named Tom whom he beats for letting the fire go out; by way of contrast, Gabriel, a very different sort of father, is concerned about his son's muscles and eyes. (Two adults are also named Thomas: Chandler and Kernan.) And is Eva to remind us of Eveline Hill? Her relationship with her father has certainly soured. With the reference to Kathleen Kearney in "The Dead" we find the first instance in which a previous *Dubliners* character is mentioned, the beginning of a process that Joyce went on to exploit faithfully, as both Kathleen and Gretta figure in Molly Bloom's thoughts.

The key words of the first paragraph of the first *Dubliners* tale (paralysis, simony, gnomon) are significant in varying degrees for every one of the fifteen stories, and reach their culmination in "The Dead." The whole process of the Morkans' soirée is a repeated one, so that even the reader (for whom this is a fresh experience) soon begins to feel an aura of *déjà vu* (Gretta caught cold after last year's party; Freddy can be expected to be drunk again). The participants themselves know the formula, as can be seen when Bartell D'Arcy, apparently a newcomer, at first refuses to allow his glass to be filled, until "one of his neighbours nudged him and whispered something at him"—the ceremonial toast is next on the programme. The "never-to-be-forgotten Johnny" is almost a parody of the theme of paralysis, and one might suspect that Daniel O'Connell, frozen in stone and covered with snow, is still another. The instances of simony are perhaps subtler, but the birth that took place in a manger among shepherds is being celebrated here in high style with the best of everything among the comfortable bourgeoisie, while irresponsible Freddy pays his debts after having cashed in on the Nativity by way of a Christmas-card shop. Even Gabriel is guilty of simony when, unnerved by his awkward conversation with Lily, he gives her a coin in order to cover his embarrassment, and when her attempt at refusal further discomfits him, he credits Christ as a precedent: "—Christmastime! Christmas-time! said Gabriel, almost trotting to the stairs and waving his hand to her in deprecation." The Euclidian gnomon, however, has drawn little notice from commentators on *Dubliners*, yet that "part of the parallelogram that remains after a similar parallelogram is taken away from one of its corners" (*O.E.D.*) offers us an insight into the author's technique in the book, where we come to understand the nature of the substance from its shadow. Father Flynn is that removed entity in "The Sisters," Mrs Hill in "Eveline," Mrs Sinico in "A Painful Case" (where the title itself is gnomonic), Parnell in "Ivy Day in the Committee Room," and of course Michael Furey in "The Dead."

Gabriel Conroy no more escapes the paralysis of Dublin than any of the other protagonists in the *Dubliners* stories, as he himself comes to realize during his epiphany. As a man of sensitivity and intelligence he becomes aware of the significance of the epiphany (like the boy in "Araby," James Duffy, and to a lesser extent Little Chandler). Material comfort, intellectual superiority, an important position, and distinction as a reviewer of books do not qualify him for exemption from the paralytic situation: he remains rooted in the centre of the paralysis. At best he is a part-time tourist, not an exile; a continental cyclist, not a "hawk-like man." He has reached the prime of life without realizing that he too shares the fate of the Freddy Malinses and Mr Brownes. Yet the surface evidence is at first deceptive (both to Gabriel and to the reader who takes him at face value): we can assume that his choice of a Browning quotation indicates a real degree of poetic appreciation (unlike Chandler's choice of Byron juvenilia), and that his book reviews reach an audience (unlike Duffy's sequestered translations and aphorisms). But the literary critic and the teacher of literature are poor substitutes for the creative artist, and vacationing on the continent is but temporary escape. Gabriel's self-deception is as serious as Chandler's or Duffy's and has been far more successful until the night of the Morkan party. We never learn whether Gabriel's epiphany redeems him, but we can assume that he is redeemable: he is a younger man than James Duffy and has not cut off all avenues of contact with the outside world; unlike the adolescent in "Araby" he is mature enough to cope with "anguish and anger"; and he is spared the intellectual pretention of Chandler, while country-cute Gretta will obviously prove less of a burden than the pretty-faced Annie.

The road leading to the destruction of Gabriel Conroy's inflated ego is lined with a succession of women. It is highly ironic that his lack of sophistication in handling women should prove to be so instrumental, but the entire evening is progressively ruined for him by this shortcoming. Perception in dealing with the masculine world is apparent in Gabriel: he is elected to apprehend Freddy upon his arrival and gauge the severity of his drunkenness; he can determine from the "indelicate clacking of the men's heels and the shuffling of their soles" that he "would only make himself ridiculous by quoting poetry to them which they could not understand"—and he makes his adjustment accordingly.

With men his defences are air-tight, but with women he is virtually defenceless. He starts out on the wrong foot with Lily and never recovers his equilibrium, yet the barely literate girl should hardly be a match for the articulate and worldly Gabriel. Only a year or so out of school, she is hardened into a cynicism which shreds the mature man's naiveté with a single ungrammatical sentence. He has no sooner recovered from this encounter than his own wife has her chance at him (goloshes, dumb-bells, eye shades, stirabout), the worshipful aunts, whose "favourite nephew" he is, joining in ("Gabriel's solicitude was a standing joke with them"). Then Molly Ivors all but demolishes him. Her intentions seem to be honourable: "I have a crow to pluck with you," she says, and we can conclude that she proposes a friendly discussion over a difference of attitude; there is also her invitation that he join her and her faction on their Irish vacation. Her tone is one of flirtatious teasing and it is again a commentary on Gabriel's lack of *savoir faire* that his hackles rise (Richard Rowan certainly handled Beatrice Justice with far greater dexterity). She is coy, she is cute, she squeezes his hand, whispers in his ear, smiles at him and gazes into his eyes, but Gabriel is made nervous, he blushes, he tries to "cover his agitation" and finally concludes that she "had tried to make him ridiculous before people, heckling him and staring at him with her rabbit's eyes." Even when he has recovered, the best he can do is gallantly offer to see her home when she attempts to leave. There is no doubt that Gabriel is ripe for Gretta's final twist of the knife. His self-delusion of strength is merely a matter of his never really having been challenged before.

Gabriel yearns for escape. He may appear to be at home in the warm surroundings of the social event, in his "well-filled shirt-front," but he dreams of being outside, detached from it all. (Mr Duffy "lived at a little distance from his body," but Gabriel lives too close to his.) Waves of anxiety mix with moments of self-confidence, as each discomfort is compensated for by a minor triumph. Lily's disdain for his paternalism at first causes him to doubt the success of his speech ("He would fail with them just as he had failed with the girl in the pantry. He had taken up a wrong tone. His whole speech was a mistake from first to last, an utter failure"). But the gush of affection from his aunts dispels his pessimism, and he responds to Gretta's opening volley of teasing with "happy eyes." When Gretta goes too far, he again sinks into a sombre mood, "as if he were slightly angered," until his successful shepherding of the tipsy Freddy restores him. So the pattern develops: he finds Mary Jane's piano piece too academic but lacks the courage to be as impolite as the four young men in the doorway and walk out on it; instead he remains, although his eyes are "irritated by the floor, which glittered with beeswax," and only a picture of his mother soothes him (until he remembers her contempt for Gretta). It is Miss Ivors' turn then to chip away at his ego, and his contemplation of revenge, public insult incorporated into his after-dinner talk, assuages him, so that he can afford to be magnanimous in offering to escort the "retreating" Molly. But before his plan has taken form in his mind, Gabriel leans against the window and realizes: "How cool it must be outside! How pleasant it would be to walk out alone, first along by the river and then through the park! The snow would be lying on the branches of the trees and forming a bright cap on the top of the Wellington Monument. How much more pleasant it would be there than at the supper-table!" Thoughts of the masculine symbol, erect in the park, revive him, but his dreams are in vain of course; he is committed to the supper-table and the party for the entire evening. It is Molly Ivors who escapes, whose "retreat" further accentuates her victory over paralysed Gabriel. Yet he misinterprets the significance of her departure, and gains ebullient self-assurance: "Here I am, Aunt Kate! cried Gabriel, with sudden animation, ready to carve a flock of geese, if necessary."

With malicious Molly gone, the hero begins to achieve a series of victories to offset her effects. Carving the goose is the first: "He felt quite at ease now for he was an expert carver and liked nothing better than to find himself at the head of a well-laden table." He misses the irony that he who had yearned for the cold outdoors should content himself with his indoor employment, "for he had found the carving hot work." When he is about to begin his speech, he again thinks of the outdoors ("The air was pure there")—his fingers are "trembling" and he smiles "nervously." But the speech is a grand success, minus the bothersome quotation from Browning, for which he has substituted the dig at Miss Ivors. (That she has escaped his barb does not seem to faze Gabriel, who seems quite satisfied with his hollow victory.) This second irony is followed by still a third: in the hallway before departure, Gabriel scores his finest social coup of the evening in recalling the anecdote of his grandfather and the never-to-be-forgotten Johnny, apparently for the edification of Mr Browne of all people. The worm has turned: it is Gabriel's turn to tease and taunt now, as he tells his version of the story about the "old gentleman," against the gentle protests of Aunt Kate. "A very pompous old gentleman," Gabriel labels him, unaware of his own pomposity, his "well-filled shirt-front." In fine humour he finally emerges into the cold night air, achieving his escape at last, and contemplating enjoyment of the spoils of victory.

The contrast between cold and warmth hints at a symbolic understructure in "The Dead" that is far more complex than in any of the previous stories. Critics have suggested that the fire in "Ivy Day," for example, indicates a scene in Hell (giving neither warmth nor light), when in actuality Joyce employs fire often in *Dubliners* with just this sort of emphasis: as fire in "Counterparts," "Clay," and "Ivy Day in the Committee Room"; as artificial lights and candles in "The Sisters," "Araby," "The Boarding House," "Two Gallants," and "Grace"; sunsets and sunrises in "Eveline," "After the Race," "A Little Cloud," and "A Painful Case." In summation "The Dead" contains all of these. The artificial lighting in the Gresham Hotel is out ("The porter pointed to the tap of the electric-light and began a muttered apology"), but Gabriel rejects the candle ("I bar the candles!" Tom Kernan had declaimed in symbolic rejection of the entire *Lux upon Lux—Lux in Tenebris—Lux in Tenebrae* confusion). Gabriel prefers the gas lamp glow from the street:

"—We don't want any light. We have light enough from the street. And I say, he added, pointing to the candle, you might remove that handsome article, like a good man." But the preferred light proves to be "ghostly," and Gabriel soon learns about Michael Furey ("He was in the gasworks," Gretta informs him), a handsome article that had been removed but is now present nonetheless. This gas motif has been prepared in three earlier instances: Gabriel notices that Lily is made to look paler by the "gas in the pantry"; Aunt Kate comments on Browne: "He has been laid on here like the gas ... all during the Christmas"; and Gretta listening to D'Arcy's song is described as: "standing right under the dusty fanlight and the flame of the gas lit up the rich bronze of her hair which he had seen her drying at the fire a few days before." If we tend to conclude that Gabriel's self-betrayal is mechanically mirrored in his acceptance of warmth and gaslight in lieu of the cold outdoors, we overlook the significance of the most persuasive symbol in the story, the snow (which has evoked the most confusing range of interpretation from critics). Joyce employs the snow for double service in "The Dead": what begins as representative of Life and of Gabriel's view of himself as standing apart from others modulates into a symbol of Death and of Gabriel included among the living dead ("Yes, the newspapers were right: snow was general all over Ireland").

The seed of self-destruction is as inherent in Gabriel himself as the suggestions of death are throughout the weave of the story: Gretta "takes three mortal hours to dress herself"; upon her entrance the aunts "said she must be perished alive"; resentment towards his mother's insult of Gretta "died down" in Gabriel's heart; Molly Ivors nods her head "gravely"—as does Mrs Malins; when Gabriel begins to eat he asks the company to "kindly forget [his] existence"; his speech invokes the memory "of those dead and gone great ones whose fame the world will not willingly let die"; Aunt Kate worries that "Mrs Malins will get her death of cold"; and upon entering the hotel Gabriel "felt that they had escaped from their lives and duties." Yet it is difficult to see much fault in Gabriel Conroy: what sin has he committed that he should be punished by a lifelong awareness of a rival he can never conquer or even combat? He is a far cry from the bullying Farrington, nor is he the pleasure-seeking hedonist like Jimmy Doyle. He has committed no indiscretion comparable to Bob Doran's nor turned his back on his fellow creatures as James Duffy had, and he is in every way superior to the envy-riddled Little Chandler. His bit of pomposity is venial enough, and his feelings of superiority seem legitimate. Nonetheless he suffers a fall as serious as Duffy's or Doran's.

It has been suggested by John V. Kelleher[1] that Gabriel has sinned against the past: that in making the "old gentleman" the butt of his triumphant jest Gabriel has broken faith with his heritage. Yet is it not his subservience to tradition, to the past, to dead conventions that Gabriel himself blames when he undergoes his epiphanic experience in the hotel room? "A shameful consciousness of his own person assailed him. He saw himself as a ludicrous figure, acting as a pennyboy for his aunts. . . ." Actually, it is to the future that Gabriel has been disloyal: although he considers himself an advocate of liberal and advanced ideas, he allows his wounded ego to cause him to betray the future and sell out to a dying past. If he had gone ahead and quoted Browning over the heads of his audience, he would at least have been faithful to his own values. But injured pride sidetracks him into attempting to retaliate against Molly Ivors (who does keep faith with at least *her* idea of the future). They have clashed over Irish nationalism and the language question, areas in which Gabriel assumes that Molly is reactionary, attempting to revive a dead past, and he is progressive in looking forward to an international and cosmopolitan future. Despite the nature of his approach to these questions, he master-plans a speech to demolish Miss Ivors, a speech of sentimental clichés of reverence to the past. He denounces the "new generation" and opts for the qualities of "an older day." He himself reveals the danger of his approach ("were we to brood upon them always we could not find the heart to go on bravely with our work among the living"), and claims to avoid that danger ("Therefore, I will not linger on the past"); but linger on the past he does, until that past in the figure of Michael Furey rises up to destroy him. Until this evening Gabriel has had no idea how limited his ability to embrace life has been; he actually saw himself as a passionate man, and maintained a faith with what he saw and believed. When he betrays that faith, he is vulnerable to the blinding revelation. The Christ of the future, of renewal and resurrection, is repeatedly betrayed during this Irish Christmas celebration.

There has been some speculation about the Christmas setting for "The Dead," but little of it has been germane to this central idea of betrayal and self-awareness. There is no mistaking the yule season in the story, and a precise placement of the significance of this setting is vital to an understanding of it. We know that it is "Christmas-time! Christmas-time!" from Gabriel's gratuity to Lily; Freddy Malins has sold Christmas cards and Mr Browne has been "laid on here like the gas . . . all during the Christmas." Yet it is neither Christmas Eve nor Christmas night, nor is it Boxing Day nor New Year's Eve nor New Year's Day. Florence Walzl[2] is quite correct in announcing that the Morkan party is taking place on January 6, the Day of the Epiphany, but she has neglected the one piece of evidence that makes that choice of date almost conclusive: Freddy Malins is drunk despite the fact that "his poor mother made him take the pledge on New Year's Eve." This could hardly refer to *last* New Year's Eve—no one would be shocked that he violated a pledge taken a year ago. A mere six days have elapsed since New Year's Eve and it is still Christmas-time. The Day of the Epiphany is a perfect Joycean choice for the final story of a volume in which climactic situations give way instead to a technique Joyce labelled "epiphanies."

What should disturb us about "The Dead" is the total absence of Christianity from the Christmas festivities. Only money earned and offered are reminders of Christmas, unless monks sleeping in their coffins will satisfy a demand for Christian seriousness during the occasion. No grace is said before dining; the dinner oration conjures up pagan Graces instead, but no mention of Christ. No single clergyman is among the guests, and surely Dublin is not short of priests to participate in a Christmas-time party. One such priest comes easily to mind, Father Constantine Conroy, Gabriel's brother and as much a nephew of the old aunts as Gabriel. We learn that Gabriel was "their favourite nephew," but surely his brother should have been invited too. Gabriel came into town from Monkstown, and is staying the night in Dublin to avoid the trip back; Constantine is at this time "senior curate in Balbriggan," a mere twenty-two miles away, and could have made the journey almost as easily to the Morkans' fest. Joyce tells us just enough about Father Conroy for us to be aware of his existence and conscious of his conspicuous absence. Not only are priests absent, but Father Healey of Adam and Eve's Church is disparaged by Aunt Kate: "if I were in Julia's place I'd tell that Father Healey straight up to his face. . . ." When discouraged from maligning the Pope in the presence of a Protestant, she directs her attack against the priest instead.

The irreverence of Joyce's depiction of Epiphany Day nineteen centuries later is the crucial element of "The Dead," a reminder that throughout the work of James Joyce it is spiritual death that is at the core of the paralytic condition, the hemiplegia of the will, the death of the heart. And it is the Church in Joyce's Ireland that is primarily responsible for this spiritual annihilation. The conflict of Gabriel and Michael, archangels who were never intended to be antagonists but in harmony with each other, again indicates that there is a serious disjunction, and Gabriel Conroy is no more able than Hamlet to "set it right"—much less so. But he has it in his power to understand the situation, one which he has conveniently ignored until this epiphanic evening. If we allow the suggestion that there is a reduplication of the original Epiphany here, we become aware of an incomplete but interesting pattern. It is true that during the course of the story three arrivals take place at the Morkan House, Gabriel, Gretta and Freddy Malins—all the other guests are already there before the story begins, or at least we never learn of any new arrival other than these three. But they do not come at the same time, and they certainly do not have equal value as individuals—they are hardly kings or magicians. If Joyce is obliquely paralleling the journey of the

Magi to the crèche of the Christ child, he has probably meant that Gabriel Conroy should represent all three kings—his name Conroy has already attracted attention as containing *roi*, the French for king.

That Gabriel, a single magus, should be pressed into service to represent all three Magi seems as commonplace as St. Patrick's shamrock, but Joyce probably had a more esoteric source for his whimsical condensation. Joyce was probably well aware that the tradition of a trio of Magi comes from an Irish source. Ludwig Bieler, in *Ireland, Harbinger of the Middle Ages*, notes that "Irish Biblical expositors are responsible for the fact that the unnamed and unnumbered magi from the East who came to adore the newly born Christ became, in western legend, the three holy kings, Caspar, Melchior, and Balthasar. Among the several 'trilingual' sets of names of the magi in the Irish commentaries on St. Matthew we find Melchio, Aspar, Patisara."[3] These stem from the reverence for the three "sacred" languages, Hebrew, Greek, and Latin. Joyce's magus has only two names, Gabriel Conroy, which metrically scan like Melchior and Caspar, but Lily's low Dublin accent gives him a third: "Gabriel smiled at the three syllables she had given his surname"—so that Con–o–roy parallels Balthasar.

Gabriel arrives on this cold night, having travelled a long distance (so far, in fact, that he does not intend making the journey home that night). He comes from the east, or at least from the south-east (it would have been impossible to make a long journey from due east, and the Conroys could not be expected to live in Dublin Bay or in either the Poolbeg or North Bull lighthouses), and his town has a fine ecclesiastical name, Monkstown, a second reference to monks in "The Dead"—that important reminder that the elaborately spread board is in sharp contrast with vows of poverty, with Christian austerity, with the economic conditions of the original manger scene. (Note that Gretta left her "grandmother's house in Nuns' Island" to go to the convent, and now lives in Monkstown.) Does he bring gifts? The offer of gold is mirrored in the coin he gives to Lily (although it probably was not gold), but nowhere do we find myrrh or frankincense, or any fragrance or incense, unless the following is intended to be relevant: As Gabriel is taking off his coat, "the buttons of his overcoat slipped with a squeaking noise through the snow-stiffened frieze, a cold fragrant air from out-of-doors escaped from crevices and folds."

Such parallels, if actually intended at all, are certainly sardonic and tangential, although the Joycean method allows for this sort of speculation, particularly at this point in his development, when the approach was becoming highly refined and was still quite unselfconscious. But are we then to conclude that the Christ child that the magus beholds is the roast goose? that Gabriel, a tame goose at best, aware of the tradition of the Wild Geese who had fled Ireland, sees himself as a cooked goose? More germane and far more serious is the revelation of Michael Furey that is brought to Gabriel during the later part of the evening, a Christ figure who sacrifices himself for his ideal. It would certainly be concomitant with Joyce's oft-quoted criticism of Christ as having shirked the major burden of life by not living with a woman, so that manly Gabriel, who has accepted that burden but is embarrassingly naïve in his contact with women, is again a parodic figure. The important point of such an investigation of "The Dead" is that Joyce is holding up Irish religious practices and theory for scrutiny, that he chooses to pit his latter-day archangels Gabriel and Michael against each other, revealing Michael as the traditional victor—though belated and retroactive—and Gabriel much deflated. Even the structure of the story is suspect from this point of approach. We have been informed that Joyce intended that "Grace," the penultimate story and originally the last one in *Dubliners*, parallel the three sections of Dante's *Commedia*. The horizontal structure of "Grace" conforms to that of a triptych, with the central segment of *Purgatorio* as the major section. This three-part structure is also available in "Clay," with the *Dublin by Lamplight* laundry as the *Inferno*, the Dublin streets as *Purgatorio*, and the Donnellys' home as an ironic *Paradiso*—as ironic as the Gardiner Street Jesuit Church of "Grace." If "The Dead" follows this pattern—and there are definite space breaks indicated in the text—the Morkan household at Christmas-time is Hell indeed for Gabriel, while the carriage trip to the Gresham serves as a period of purgations, and the hotel scene of revelation is a third ironic paradise. The three portions in this case diminish in size as the story progresses.

In viewing "The Dead" as a tale of the Epiphany, we see Joyce at an interestingly close juncture with Yeats's attitude in "The Second Coming." Christianity as a dynamic force has dwindled to a mockery of itself: self-contradictory, as Gabriel belatedly and effetely opposes Michael, and self-betrayed, as simoniac symptoms of the commercialization of Christmas become apparent. Its priests die of paralytic strokes, demented and disillusioned; they leave behind them rusty bicycle-pumps and suspect books with yellowed pages, or have gone off to Melbourne or are responsible for evicting spinster sopranos from their choirs in favour of boys. Gabriel as king considers himself above the common paralytic situation, and as magician he has his magical books and his quotations from Browning to keep him uninvolved. But on the Night of the Epiphany Gabriel Conroy follows his star to the Morkans' house on Usher's Island—not a new star, but the same one that has brought him there so often—expecting in his reconquest of Gretta to renew himself and sharpen the distinction and privilege which keep him safe from the doomed, the unbaptized, the unanointed. But on this night he comes face to face with his predecessor and with his own self, with the past that has claimed all the others and the future that he has betrayed in order to maintain his comfortable position on the outside. The enigmatic sentence that has bothered so many readers of "The Dead" ("The time had come for him to set out on his journey westward") indicates his awareness of his new responsibility: Gabriel must begin the quest of self-discovery to arrive at the real epiphany, to follow his star. After many false starts of self-deception, the "rough beast, its hour come round at last, slouches toward Bethlehem to be born."

Notes

1. John V. Kelleher, "Irish History and Mythology in James Joyce's 'The Dead,' " *The Review of Politics*, XXVII, July 1965, pp. 425–7.

2. Florence L. Walzl, "The Liturgy of the Epiphany Season and the Epiphanies of Joyce," *PMLA*, LXXX, Sept. 1965, p. 449.

3. Ludwig Bieler, *Ireland, Harbinger of the Middle Ages*, London, 1963, p. 14.

NOUVELLES CRITIQUES

Nodality and the Infra-Structure of
Finnegans Wake
David Hayman*

Joyce's last book is most remarkably a play of structures, a game the reader exerts himself to play and which in turn vigorously plays the reader. Whereas most texts incorporate the figure Genette has called the *narrataire* (or "ideal reader"), implicitly, *Finnegans Wake* manipulates and teases in the reader's name and virtually in his person. But, for this to be so, for the experience of reading to be one of making, the *Wake* must give the appearance of randomness when in fact it is organized down to its least unit. In demonstrating such order we can, of course, point to various macro-structures, beginning with the Viconian $3+1$ of the sections, noting, for example, that part of Book One divides neatly into four male chapters and four female which can be doubled over to make an equivalence:

$$\frac{1\text{-}2\text{-}3\text{-}4}{8\text{-}7\text{-}6\text{-}5\text{-}} \qquad \text{or} \qquad \begin{array}{cc} & 45 \\ 3 & 6 \\ 2 & 7 \\ 1 & 8 \end{array}$$

Clive Hart's *Structure and Motif* shows how we can impose yet other schemes (circles, crosses, counterpoint, etc.) upon the larger matrix of the *Wake* without distortion.[1] Such schematization, perceived generally by hindsight, is what stands in for broad narrative development in the *Wake*, making its huge bulk more manageable. It certainly helped Joyce erect his wall of words.

If the macro-structure is the most accessible of the *Wake*'s devices, its infra-structure tends to be even more pervasive, more immediately

*This essay was first published in French in *Poétique* 26 (Spring 1976) as "Réseaux infra-structurels." It has since appeared in Spanish as "La infraestructura nodal de *Finnegans Wake*) in *La Casa de la Ficcion, Espiral*, revista 3 (1977). Reprinted from the *James Joyce Quarterly*, 16 (Fall 1977 / Winter 1978) with permission of the editor.

relevant to the dynamic of reading, better integrated into the texture of the *Wake*. Hart's account of the "motif" demonstrates one aspect of Joyce's method (an aspect of what might be called the *Wake*'s micro-structure). But Joyce's practice suggests another approach which, rather than the individual motif, would focus the coherent clusterings of motif-like materials and might be called "nodalization." The key element here is the "prime node" or apex of the "nodal system," a passage where some act, activity, personal trait, allusion, theme, etc. surfaces for its clearest statement in the text, is made manifest, so to speak, and in the process brings together and crystallizes an otherwise scattered body of related material. This prime node is the generative center for lesser and gener-ally less transparent passages devoted to its elaboration or expansion and strategically located in the text. The latter are reinforced by more numerous but briefer allusions to one or more of its attributes. As the units diminish in size, their distribution becomes increasingly, though never truly, random. Taken together, all of these components constitute a single nodal system though on occasion one prime node may generate more than one system and though such systems always tend to be inter-related. As in more conventional narratives some nodal systems are thematic, constituting centers of signification, but the category and its attendant principles are structurally more important than the term theme or even the term motif would suggest, since they constitute a major source of interest and coherence and take precedence over any vestiges of or allusions to narrative and plot.[2]

Joyce's manuscripts and letters provide us with clues to the history and function of what I am calling his nodal systems. They indicate that early in 1923 he composed from his own notes a group of non-narrative or minimally narrative episodes, evoking carefully culled shards and husks of a dormant culture. When he had sent drafts of these sketches to his benefactress Harriet Weaver, he wrote her: "...these are not fragments but active elements and when they are more and a little older they will begin to fuse themselves" (*Letters I* 205). The impor-tance of Joyce's remarks should not be underestimated. The main struts of the *Wake* are indeed those early passages, the *Wake*'s focal nodes, which portray in a variety of burlesque conventions crucial instants in the male cycle, suggesting stages in the history of Ireland, of mankind, and of the individual. Dating from the first six to eight months of 1923, they constitute along with the ALP Letter the only existing structural paradigm of the *Wake*—Joyce's approximation of an outline, written be-fore the advent of the puns or the Vico structure at a time when the book was to portray simply (!) the "nightmare of history" from which mankind, like Stephen Dedalus, is striving to awake.

In terms of mode, the early sketches recall the pastiches-parodies of "Cyclops," the chapter of *Ulysses* most transparently concerned with history. The difference here, an important one, is that Joyce does not

propose these sketches as adjuncts to narrative and to meaning, as sur-
real or mock-commentary on a seemingly coherent text. Rather these
snapshots function as texts or pretexts to which the rest of the *Wake*
will be added as commentary, or shadow text. Instead of telling tales,
establishing perspectives, eliciting suspense, these narrative fragments
become contexts, centers of significance. It would appear, therefore,
that their function and nature were fixed virtually from the start, that
is, even before the final structure of the book had been established. But
this is a matter which can be left to conjecture. More important is their
ultimate placement and function.

Originally, there were five sketches, in order of composition: "Roderick O'Conor" (*FW* 380–82), "Tristan and Isolde" (*FW* 383–99, but
interlaced with a slightly later "Mamalujo"), "St Patrick and the Druid"
(*FW* 611–12), "St Kevin's Orisons" (*FW* 604–06), and the "Here Comes
Everybody" passage which was originally to have opened the book
(*FW* 30–34). To these we should add the earliest version of the ALP
Letter, which was probably written in December 1923 before Joyce began to compose Iv. It is now located near the end of Book IV where
it serves to introduce the concluding monologue (*FW* 615–19).

Significantly, these passages mark the beginning, middle, and end
in good mock-Aristotelian fashion. But even more importantly, with the
exception of the "HCE" which was published as part of chapter Iii in
1927, none of them saw print before 1939 and none of them grew much
either in length or complexity. Perhaps, like the title, about which Joyce
made such a fuss, these pieces were felt to be keys to the book and
hence aspects of overall suspense structure. Even when inverting the
norms of fictional discourse Joyce was conscious of himself as belonging
to a timeless tradition of tale-telling and mystification.[3]

These are not true tales, unless we think of the "shaggy dog tale"
as a conventional narrative, a tale which is all tail, one completely lacking in point and punch line. In another sense, like *Ulysses*, *Dubliners*,
and the epiphanies, these vignettes, in terms of their narrative content,
convey pauses in the action, stills, anticlimaxes which bring into focus
the moment as a transparency through which significance may shine.
They characterize Joyce's view of history as not so much a continuous
sequence of significant action / reaction as an impasto of activities breed-
ing and feeding upon one another, producing nothing but more of the
same in a slightly different order: "Yet is no body present here which
was not there before. Only is order othered. Nought is nulled" (*FW*
613.13–14).

In the infra-structure, which is the *Wake* experienced most directly
by the reader, the sketches help compose and flavor with specificity the
life cycle of mankind. They constitute primal moments, strategically
placed reference points for those who feel themselves "lost in the bush"
(*FW* 112.03). Thus, they bridge the gap between the macro- and infra-

structures and contribute to readability. Further, for all their remarkable range of parodic styles and materials, they established early on the dominant pantomime-farce mode of the text, being its broadest statement in the sense that the clowning and gesticulation is most readily available on first reading. Together, they compose what might be called a primary structure to which everything else is at least secondary in terms of accessibility and / or strategic placement.

Since the book is circular and subject to multiple readings (none of which is truly the first, though each may have the impact of a first reading thanks to the density and variety in the text), it makes no difference, theoretically, where the sketch or prime node falls. The fact that a node has been stated early alters only slightly the suspense or interest generated by the nodal system since the fleshing out of a system is itself a source of interest. Once nodality, the existence of a focused nodal system, has been discovered, it inevitably contributes to the structure of interest. If the prime node falls in Book IV as do the St. Kevin, the St. Patrick, and the ALP Letter, it both illuminates earlier passages and provides light for later readings.

The nodal systems guarantee the constant presence of varieties of narrative experience if not a developing thread of narrative discourse. References to the Letter of ALP or to the romance of Tristan and Isolde or to the fall of the great man are filled with predictive mystery, subject to fulfillment which will satisfy our craving to know, much as would the evolving action of a romance, a melodrama, or a tragedy. The dawn implications of St. Kevin (whose construction of a nine-circled island-womb is a birth metaphor) or St. Patrick's bringing light to the gentiles by plucking a green trinity from the ground, evoke and condense and focus elements of utopic and pastoral narrative, to say nothing of hagiography. Thus the tradition of narrative-dramatic genres is at once conserved as an aura in suggestive contexts and destroyed by a text which refuses sequential presentation.

This is perhaps best understood in relation to two major nodal systems, both based in the early passages: the Tristan and Isolde tale, and the Letter of ALP. The former is crystallized in IIiv during the voyeuristic narrative of the four old men, the gospellers, the chroniclers. The Letter is not fully aired until Book IV where we finally read what ALP said in defense of HCE to Shem and what was contained in the letter delivered to HCE by Shaun.

The Tristan and Isolde system is patterned rather strictly after Bédier's reconstruction which Joyce suggested Miss Weaver might read for background. Both the approach he took and the material he used were already available in notes dating from 1922–23 (under the *Exiles*).[4] Even the uninitiated reader may, once he has been alerted by the text, pick up and retain certain familiar details from a well-known narrative.

But if the recognition of such details arouses interest, their random and achronological distribution obviates conditional suspense.

By contrast, the tale of the writing and delivery, and the account of the contents of the Letter will be new to him, requiring a good deal of piecing together and ultimately yielding the illusion of narrative progression. As we might suspect, Joyce plays coyly with this suspense element throughout. In Chapter Iv, where the theme is first developed, we have the questions what, how, and who applied to the Letter's genesis through scholarly detective work. A second treatment occurs during the children's lessons in IIii when Issy writes a practice letter, reproducing the tired format but revealing nothing (*FW* 279–80). In IIiii, HCE returns from the outhouse having perused and used a "sacred" text (*FW* 356–57): "I have just (let us suppraise) been reading in a (suppressed) book—it is notwithstempting by meassures long and limited—the latterpress is eminently legible and the paper, so he eagerly seized upon, has scarsely been buttered in works of previous publicity wholebeit in keener notcase would I turf aside for pastureuration. Packen paper paineth whomto is sacred scriptured sign." (*FW* 356.19–25). In IIIi Shaun is questioned concerning the Letter's content (*FW* 412–14, 419–24). Finally, the mystery is solved, in a text which is both exceptionally brief (a bit over four pages in the published version) and remarkably clear. What has been a major narrative development and what is certainly a major nodal system have come simultaneously to their climax. Here, for the first time, the voice of ALP is heard clearly and without interference, a voice which holds itself up to ridicule as does that of Winifred Jenkins in *Humphry Clinker*, one of Joyce's principal models. But then the letter is not ALP's true medium as we see when the "Soft Morning" monologue wipes the slate clean, giving us a persona as vigorous, articulate, and delightful as Molly Bloom herself (though not as bawdy) and illustrating a principle of balance in the *Wake*, where compassion vies with ridicule and frequently wins.

Ultimately, the narrative development climaxed by the presentation of the Letter is of less moment than the Letter as a prime node in a nodal system; for the suspense generated by this motif is not dissipated by the revelations in Book IV. Neither is suspense at any point crucial to the reader, who hardly needs to solve the mystery of the pre-text when the text itself remains a source of endless surprises and everchanging vistas. Rather, the Letter tends to coalesce with other motifs, themes and narrative elements to fascinate by the proliferation of its implications. The Professor's question "who in hallhagal wrote the durn thing anyhow" (*FW* 107.36) is importantly beside the point, being precisely the question one does not ask of the *Wake*.

As suggested above, the Letter read to us (by us) in Book IV has as its secondary nodes four longish and elaborate passages: 1) the description of the manuscript, its discovery and its presumed origins; 2) a treatment of Issy as the young ALP practicing writing the Letter; 3) HCE telling the pub(lic) his reactions to the document he has wiped himself with; 4) Shaun telling a Shemish questioner about the Letter and his obligation to deliver it. These secondary nodes are not chronologically ordered in the text, a fact which reinforces the essentially anti-diegetic nature of the nodal systems. Further, though in both Chapter Iv and Chapter IIii we find what Clive Hart calls "major statements" of the Letter motif (see *FW* 111, 113, 116 and 279F1, 280),[5] these "statements" do not constitute the substance of any of the secondary nodes.

Each of these secondary nodes is itself the source of at least one further nodal system. For example, the professorial account given in Iv, points up among other things the sacred book analogy, turning the text dug up from a dung heap by a neighborhood hen and rescued by a schoolboy into a fragment of the lost past, a mysterious scripture. It also illuminates a stage in the development of religions, the moment when scholarship brings rumor and superstition into rational focus and begins the process of evolving a code of belief and practice. Further, using a male voice to describe *the* female event, it introduces the sub-dominant nocturnal force, which hides its subjective energy behind a mask of scientific (male) objectivity. Or, again, we have the metaphor both for the creation of this book and for aesthetic creation in general, a mystery which haunted Joyce from the very start of his career. Thus a subordinate node is itself the base for further systems subject in their turn to elaboration. Such systems are also secondary in respect to the overall structuration of the *Wake*, though the reader need not perceive this organization. They are all, however, clearly generated by the primary node established in the early days of the *Wake*'s history, and they must be seen as modifying and elaborating upon it.

The interrelatedness of these secondary nodes is supported by manuscript evidence, as is the primacy of the nodal system. To the completed first draft of the Letter Joyce added: "Alone one cannot [know who did][6] it for the hand was fair. We can suppose it that of Shemus the penman, a village soak, who when snugly liquored lived, so."[7] Unclear and unpolished though it may be, this passage must be seen as the source of Chapter Iv. It also generated Ivii, the Shaunish description of and condemnation of Shem in his role as counterfeiter / writer. The second bit of evidence is a longish passage written after the drafting of Iv. In it we find a description of Shaun delivering the Letter in his "emptybottlegreen jerkin," a discussion of his "qualifications for that particular post," a paragraph on ALP's reasons for writing her "petition," and one on HCE's reactions.[8] Here, though the sequence is not quite chronological, we are somewhat closer to a conventional narrative development in the manner of a chronicle or at least of a reportage. What interests us is the fact that in these short passages Joyce outlined the secondary level of the nodal system, that both were generated by the previously written Letter, and that they formed a pendant to the Letter from the very start.

With this in mind we can point to the components of the tertiary level of the Letter system, passages, which, while significant and relevant, are somewhat more oblique in their rendering of the nodal subject, and function mainly as brief asides. Usually, they garble the message, presenting it in a more sublimated form; yet, as Hart's listings indicate, they are recognizable by virtue of the number of key allusions worked into their texture and by their dominant subject matter.

For example, on pages 11 and 12 in Chapter One, we find a description of the "gnarleybird" scavenging on the field of battle, an avatar of the hen Biddy Doran who scavenged the Letter from the dung heap. It is normal that scraps of Letter find their way into such a passage, but an extended treatment would be out of place. Thus the catalogue of detritus ends as do certain versions of the Letter "With Kiss. Kiss Criss. Cross Criss. Kiss Cross." This is followed by a macabre salutation (a play on the name Anna Livia Plurabelle) and signature: "Undo lives 'end. Slain." Since this passage treats the salvaging of the lost, hence the mending of reputations, we need not be surprised to find the next paragraph ending with a reference to the enigmatic tea stain ("the tay is wet") with which the Letter examined by the Professor in Chapter Iv is signed.

The treatment on pages 301–02 of Shaun's reaction to Shem's account of the truth about his mother is a stronger example of the tertiary node. Indulging in a bout of self-pity Shaun contemplates among other things, writing a letter to his lady: "Dear and he went on to scripple gentlemine born, milady bread, he would pen for her, he would pine for her . . . And how are you, waggy?" (*FW* 301).[9] Allusions to the Letter occupy only a fraction of the published passage, but in the first draft where the subject was more clearly enunciated, we find mixed in with the aftermath of the Geometry Lesson an account of Shem's letter-writing lesson leading directly to an attack on him by his desperately confused brother. The present version, though over three pages long, submerges the letter motif and introduces references to a number of other nodes including the Tristan and Isolde. On the other hand, it joins the Letter to the secondary system Letter / literature which relates directly to HCE's account of his reading in the outhouse (see the secondary node in IIiii, 363–66).

Three other tertiary nodes can be listed briefly: the "Nightletter" which concludes IIii (*FW* 308), a ghoulish juvenile spoof; the account of ALP as secretary bird / scavenger which briefly interrupts the pub-jury's deliberations to summarize schematically the Letter's history and mark the decline of the hero (*FW* 369–70), and a few lines from Issy's response to a departing Jaun in IIIii during which her gift handker-

chief (a reference to Veronica's cloth) is identified as a letter and
signed with "X.X.X.X." (*FW* 457–58). It should be clear from this partial listing that while none of these passages adds significantly to our
sense of the nodal subject, each of them furthers the system by connect-
ing the Letter to other facets of the night world increasing its physical
presence and range. Further, the location is in each case fitting, pointing up some aspect of the nodal subject which has been developed elsewhere.

The three strata of the system outlined above suggest at least two
further levels which will broaden the base of the pyramid. Thus on the
fourth level we find a strongly marked allusion to the Letter hidden
in an account of the growth of the alphabet (*FW* 18.30). Somewhat less
accessible, at the base of the structure, is an isolated allusion to the
catch phrase "it begins to appear" somewhat randomly pasted onto a
passing allusion to *Ulysses*'s critical and publication history: "it agins
to pear like it" (*FW* 292.08). Such flitting references are probably the
most numerous, but they are also the hardest to locate and chart. They
will be found in appropriate places but more widely scattered and quite
unaccented. We may think of them as constituting a large if tenuous
fifth nodal level, one which may slip beyond the range of Hart's motifs,
blending into the allusive subsoil of the text.

The Tristan and Isolde nodal system is of a different order and mag-
nitude, though it too is based in a rather conservative principle of plot.
The primary node of this system falls near the middle of the book in
IIiv where the seduction of Isolde (or by Isolde) is witnessed by the
senile four. The immediate source of Joyce's account is the first act of
Wagner's opera, but the treatment owes much to Jules Laforgue among
whose mock-*Moralités* we find revisions of *Hamlet*, *Herodias*, and *Lohen-
grin*. Like the other primal nodes, the account of the seduction is remarkable for the clarity of its presentation and, despite the intrusive
comments of the "four," for its logical development. Joyce has managed
to meld two distinct sequences while retaining the rhythms of both and
without significantly altering the texture of the early Tristan skit to
which he added many of his early *Scribbledehobble* notes:

> It brought the dear prehistoric scenes all back again . . . and after that
> now there he was, that mouth of mandibles, vowed to pure beauty, and
> his Arrah-na-poghue, when she murmurously, after she let a cough, gave
> her firm order, if he wouldn't please mind, for a sings to one hope
> a dozen of the best favourite lyrical national blooms in Luvillicit,
> though not too much, reflecting on the situation, drinking in draughts
> of purest air serene and revelling in the great outdoors, before the four
> of them, in the fair fine night, whilst the stars shine bright, by she
> light of he moon, we longed to be spoon, before her honeyoldloom, the
> plaint effect being in point of fact there being in the whole, a seatui-

tion so shocking and scandalous and now, thank God, there were no more of them . . . listening, to Rolando's deepen darblun Ossian roll, (Lady, it was just too gorgeous, that expense of a lovely tint, embellished by the charms of art and very well conducted and nicely mannered and all the horrid rudy noises locked up in nasty cubbyhole!). (*FW* 385–86)

The seduction is a high point in the book's development, a seemingly satisfactory and delightfully explicit mating sequence. But it also mediates between the much more obliquely rendered mating of earth and water (mountain and stream, HCE and ALP) in Iviii, and the grotesque and explicit intercourse of Mr. and Mrs. Porter in IIIiv, a passage which comically turns the aging couple into a landscape of love, a map of the Phoenix Park, and hence a symptom of renewal out of bitter ashes. Thus the central love sequence contributes to a second nodal system, one that is tributary to the elaborately developed Tristan and Isolde.

The primary system resonates throughout the book developing allusions to chapters and incidents in Bédier's version of Tristan and Isolde. If the most explicit sequence is the Wagnerian kiss-philtre episode in IIiv, secondary sequences recount more or less clearly other adventures. A passage in Chapter Iiv (*FW* 94–96) deals with king Mark of Cornwall (an avatar of HCE). The irreverent narrative voice lets the senile four ("fourbottle men, the analists"—*FW* 95.27) extend their vicarious or voyeuristic experience without once mentioning Tristan and Isolde by name (except in terms of "dear Sir Armoury, queer Sir Rumoury" and "trickle trickle trickle triss"). The role of Mark ("old markiss their besterfar" and "marcus") is only one of several roles played here by HCE, the deceived father / husband. He is also Sinbad ("Singabob, the bedfather") and Pantaloon, the Commedia dell'Arte father figure ("Dirty Daddy Pantaloons") and identified as "that old gasometer with his hooping coppin and his dyinboosycough," with a "big brewer's belch." The intratextual reference to Mark and the events of chapter IIiv are unmistakable, but the ship has been replaced by a field and forest, Issy has become identified with a flirtatious Molly Bloom, and the seducting hero coalesces with the pub-crawling dun of "Cyclops," and even with Lenehan, the aging parasite: "O breezes! I sniffed that lad long before anyone. It was when I was in my farfather out at the west and she and myself, the redheaded girl,[10] firstnighting down Sycomore Lane. Fine feelplay we had of it mid the kissabetts frisking in the kool kirkle dusk of the lushiness. My perfume of the pampas, says she (meaning me) putting out her netherlights, and I'd sooner one precious sip at your pure mountain dew than enrich my acquaintance with that big brewer's belch" (*FW* 95.18–26). This passage continues with a reference to the babes in the woods and the sly adultery aspects of the Tristan myth (see their exile in the wood of Morois) as the four discuss "her whose-before and his whereafters and how she was lost away away in the fern and how he was founded deap on deep in anear,[11] and the rustlings and the twitterings and the raspings and the snappings and the sighings and the paintings and the ukukuings and the (hist!) the springapartings and the (hast!) the bybyscuttlings and all the scandalmunkers and the pure craigs that used to be . . . (FW 95.28–35). As so often happens with well-developed secondary nodes, the passage has taken on its own vitality, and fallen by associative linkage within a number of other nodal systems. But if we sort out those elements which refer us to the Tristan myth, we find them to be preponderant. Hence the passage belongs to a system generated by a sequence the reader will not encounter for 300 pages.

We may speak of IIIiv as belonging to the same family as other chapters (Iiv, Iviii, IIiv) telling of the fatal love encounter. Though the central event (after the parents have been awakened by a crying Shem) is the unsuccessful lovemaking of the aging couple, a bosky love encounter between Tristan and Isolde by the pine in the garden constitutes an interlace secondary action and a prelude to the parents' act. The sequence of allusions follows this pattern: p. 556, Issy-Isolde and the forest theme; p. 561, Issy-Isolde and the philtre; p. 562, Shaun as Tristan the opportunist; p. 563, Shem as sad romantic lover of Isolde; p. 564, Shem as Tristan by the pine and carving messages in wood chips; pp. 570–72, a map of love recording the erotic zones of the parents conceals, among other things, the trysting lovers.[12]

> This place of endearment! How it is clear! And how they cast their spells upon, the fronds that thereup float, the bookstaff branchings! The druggeted stems, the leaves incut on trees! Do you can their tantrist spellings? I can lese, skillmistress aiding. Elm, bay, this way, cull dare, take a message, tawny runes ilex sallow, meet me at the pine. Yes, they shall have brought us to the water trysting, by hedjes of maiden ferm, then here in another place is their chapelofeases, sold for song, of which you have thought my praise too much my price. O ma ma! Yes, sad one of Ziod? Sell me, my soul dear! Ah, my sorrowful, his cloister dreeping of his monkshood, how it is triste to death, all his dark ivytod! Where cold in dearth. Yet see, my blanching kissabelle, in the under close she is allso gay, her kirtles green, her curtsies white, her peony pears, her nistlingsloes! I, pipette, I must also quickingly to tryst myself softly in this littleeasechapel. (FW 5713–18)

The passage from Bédier farcically distorted here is the assignation made by Tristan who sets cleverly carved chips afloat in the stream that passes through the royal palace, asking Isolde to meet him by the pine. The names of the lovers are cunningly disguised and distributed throughout the passage: "tanttrist . . . trysting . . . sold . . . sad one of Ziod . . . my sorrowful . . . triste . . . blanching kissabelle . . . tryst. . . ." It is precisely this sort of distribution of variously broad and subtle

hints and particularly the allusions to proper names which marks the
secondary nodes to which we have been alluding.

We may begin to see how Joyce completed or gave an aura of integrity to the secondary level of the Tristan and Isolde system. If IIiv
has a couple orientation, focusing more or less equally on Tristan *and*
Isolde, and Iiv focuses mainly on king Mark, IIIiv emphasizes the Isolde
role. Joyce seems to have worked out the permutations of focus which
are completed by an extended parenthetical reference to "Dolph, dean
of idlers," in IIii, an avatar of Shem, in which Tristan's voyages to Ireland are discussed along with those of St. Patrick. That passage interrupts the boys' Geometry Lesson, so the emphasis on the young male is
as appropriate as the Isolde orientation is in IIIiv, where a description of
the female genitalia follows an extended description of HCE / Porter's
Wellington Monument. Like all the other secondary nodes, it is recounted from the perspective of the "four." By including it in a central
chapter, Joyce has achieved a semblance of formal balance on the secondary level while preparing for the fuller treatment in IIiv.

The Tristan and Isolde system proliferates throughout the text, taking on different colorations in different contexts, frequently blending
with other systems but achieving exceptional coherence and consistency.
We can point to six fairly distinct levels: 1) the central statement of
the myth in IIiv; 2) tributary statements where the theme is elaborated
(Iiv, IIii, IIIiv); 3) extended passages where, despite allusions to the
personae and aspects of the myth, the myth itself is subdominant; 4)
passages of a line or two which coherently evoke "Tristan and Isolde"
but in an alien context; 5) passages containing allusions to correlative
myths like the Dermot and Grania tale or the various Arthurian legends;
6) brief and generally unsupported references to the chief personae or
to some central attribute. By far the largest category is number six in
which we find items like "Chapelldiseut" (*FW* 236.20), whose spelling
emphasizes both the French origins of this village name and the character of our heroine, but whose context while suggestive of young maiden-
hood or girlhood is one of several versions of the famous Edgar Quinet
passage. If we look carefully in the vicinity of this allusion and of others
in this category, we frequently find passages which belong to categories
4 or 5. On page 238 in a context that bristles with allusions to Oscar
Wilde's career and which foreshadows Jaun's sermon in IIii, there are
three clear references to Isolde of Brittany and fidelity: "isaspell . . . ishi-
billey," "for sold long syne"; and one veiled reference to Tristan who
died at Penmark. To this same category (4) belong relatively coherent
allusions like this one to the bath given Tristan by Isolde: "An they bare
falls witless against thee how slight becomes a hidden wound? Sold-
woter he wash him all time bigfeller bruisy place blong him" (*FW*
247.20–23). On the very next page we find an item from category 3,
an allusion both to the kiss and to the adventure in the forest which

includes references to Isolde and Mark but which also alludes to St. Kevin and to Arthur Rimbaud in his role as *le voyant* (*FW* 248.23–249.04).

Not all Joyce's early sketches generated systems as full and elaborate as those relating to the Letter and the Tristan and Isolde. But statements of HCE's vulnerable eminence, his mature vigor, and his mysterious crime all devolve from and refer back to the "Here Comes Everybody" sketch. The fall from eminence along with aging and impotence are most clearly stated in the "Roderick O'Conor." From the "St Kevin" we may trace not only references to the Kevin myth but also Shaun's (false and sentimental) piety, his youthful innocence, and his identity as a solar being. Similarly, there is the large and virtually unexplored system of allusions to St. Patrick, to the confrontation of brothers, to victories won by sleight of hand. As indicated earlier, these systems frequently overlap and interlace to complicate the texture of the book. Inevitably, like everything else in the *Wake*, they contribute to a single overriding system of allusions to the fate of post-fall man as subject to the daily, seasonal, life cycles and to the vicissitudes of history and human relations.

The interlocking systems, so sketchily outlined here, are only gradually unveiled by the process of the text; they are probably never fully perceived by any reader. Further, these primal nodal systems seen in context constitute only the first of at least eight categories which I shall list in something like their order of importance but not attempt to discuss here:

1. The early sketches plus the Letter.
2. Passages devoted to character exposition: the profiles and monologues.
3. Symmetrical passages like the three brother-confrontations and the fables.
4. Expositions of major themes: the fall, the flood, the crime, historical decay, sexual deviation, writing, etc.
5. Developments of aspects of the landscape: river, mountain, ocean, tree, stone, city, park, etc.
6. Allusive parallels drawn from history, religion, and literature: Oscar Wilde, Shakespeare, Ezra Pound, Humphry Clinker, Christ, Buddha, etc.
7. Key rhythms of rhythmic clusters: the tonality of the river, the legalistic "tion" passages of the twelve patrons / judges, the Quinet passage, HCE's stutter, the thunder words, song tags, etc.
8. Foreign language word clusters.

Clearly, we may add to this list and elaborate on the categories. Further, just as the two systems analyzed above deviate from each other, we may expect to find considerable variation among systems on all levels. Readers may differ over the precedence and content of certain categories, but the fact remains that a complex or hierarchy of nodal systems governs our (subliminal) perception of the *Wake*. It makes little difference whether or not the systems focused by the early sketches are *perceived as* more important than those in categories 2, 3, and 4. The principle established by Joyce's decision to build around them has controlled the organization of the rest of the book.

In composing *Finnegans Wake* over a period of eighteen years Joyce was not simply filling in the blanks of a structural plan or indulging in free association. The process was more like running after one's own language, adding allusions or picking them up in an effort to gain and regain mastery over a text which aimed for at least a semblance of comprehensiveness, an all-bookness similar to the one posited by Stéphane Mallarmé. His effort was partly to make language obey *his* rules rather than its own, partly to exploit the givens of language. It is the result of this process which the reader reacts to and experiences in his mirror struggle to master the "proteiform graph" that has immeshed him. Like the writer's, his is an effort to assert a self (by imposing a pattern or a flux of patterns) or rather to win a self back from the language over which he repeatedly gains and as often loses mastery. To this process the "proteiform" network of nodal systems contributes importantly through its imposition, on the very texture of the text it now permeates, of rhythmic orders with recognizable if unfixed dimensions.

In pointing to such an infra-structure we are approaching the essence of the *Wake*'s contribution to subsequent forms, one which may even surpass the contribution of its language to the liberation of the word.

Notes

1. *Structure and Motif in Finnegans Wake*, (Evanston: Northwestern University Press; London: Faber and Faber, 1962).

2. Clive Hart's "Leitmotif" overlaps with and foreshadows our concept of nodalization, but it functions in very different ways. Though he deals with several longer "complexes," Hart focuses mainly on brief allusions which would be placed low on any nodal scale. His practice of building up from the minimal evocative marker or motif to the larger cluster leads him to posit the "motif agglomeration" of which there are two sorts, the first a simple grouping of disparate motifs, the second and more important the "true interacting *leitmotiv*-complex, of which the Letter is the most outstanding example" (*Ibid.*, p. 180). I would suggest that this sort of "complex" is more handily viewed as a primal node, that it is used in *Finnegans Wake* far less "sparingly" and with more system than Hart claims, and that it should be seen as generating as well as bringing together motifs. Hart also makes use of the term node. But for him "nodal point" occurs when in his catalogues Joyce halts the "narrative for a moment . . . filling the pause with . . . concentrations of motifs" so that the "reader can contemplate the primary materials at his leisure" (*Idem*). For our purposes nodes are effectively primary materials and the prime nodes halt, not the narrative (which they may in fact constitute in its purest form), but the flow of the rhetoric before they once again break down into their component

parts. I believe that this distinction is crucial if we are to understand how the nodes help structure the book.

3. Significantly, one of the more coherent series of early notes in the *Scribbledehobble* notebook for *Finnegans Wake* concerns the oral tale and its conventions: the notes under "The Sisters," first of the *Dubliners* tales. *Scribbledehobble*, ed. Thomas E. Connolly (Evanston: Northwestern University Press, 1961), pp. 25–27.

4. *Ibid.*

5. *Scribbledehobble*, p. 232.

6. We can only approximate these words.

7. *A First-Draft Version of Finnegans Wake*, ed. David Hayman (Austin: University of Texas Press, 1963), p. 81. For a fuller account of the process by which not only book III but also Iv and Ivii were generated see my introduction and consult the text of the *James Joyce Archive* volume containing facsimiles of chapters Iiv–v (New York: Garland Press, 1978).

8. *Ibid.*, pp. 90–91.

9. This sentence is annotated with a letter to "Erosmas" from "Grunny Grant" but all of the footnotes are in the hand of Issy.

10. Isolde in IIiv has "nothing under her hat but red hair and solid ivory"(*FW* 396.09–10).

11. This is a clear enough reference to ALP's origins as a brook in the hills of county Wicklow (see Iviii) and to HCE as the Norwegian Captain, an avatar of the sea (see IIiii).

12. In this latter passage we find as a secondary subject a reference to Oscar Wilde and sodomy. The emphasis is reversed on page 588, where a passage devoted to Wilde's crimes, trials, and incarcerations includes references to "Issy's busy down the dell" and to a variety of trees.

A Beginning: Signification, Story, and Discourse in Joyce's "The Sisters"[1]   Thomas F. Staley*

I

Just as beginnings in fiction delimit possibilities, they simultaneously awaken expectations; in beginnings the signifying structures of art and life are surely similar. A number of narrative beginnings have become signatures in our memories of the literary landscape: "Mother died today" or "Happy families are all alike" or "riverrun, past Eve and Adam's." How beginnings become beginnings is an equally compelling question for life as well as art. It is perhaps arbitrary to call "The Sisters" a beginning and confine one's discussion only to the beginning of the story at that, for its composition in its various stages was not Joyce's initial creative activity. Yet "The Sisters" is surely a beginning in Joyce's life-

*This essay first appeared in *Genre*, 12 (Winter 1979), and is reprinted with permission of the editor.

work: in this story in its final version Joyce's major importance as a writer is initially revealed. Its exploration of the resources of language and its method of construction and intention also reveal, if only in embryonic form, the direction not only of Joyce's art but one of the formative stages in the unfolding of modern literature. "The Sisters" is important as the beginning of an entire trajectory of literary accomplishment in prose from *Dubliners, A Portrait, Ulysses,* and finally to *Finnegans Wake*; therefore, it is worthwhile to explore more precisely a few aspects of this beginning.

There are only subtle indications to the contrary that during the planning and in the first published version of "The Sisters" Joyce was not predominately concerned with his subject matter, both personal and historical—Dublin, Dubliners, and his own personal attitude toward the city and its subjects.[2] His letters reveal that wounds done to him both real and imagined were very much on his mind. It is only in the later stages of the genesis of the stories that we get a strong sense that Joyce shared the modernist aspiration of Flaubert that subject and author be refined out of existence. *Dubliners* was not to be a work of "almost no subject," "dependent," as Flaubert said, "on nothing external, which would be held together by the strength of its style." Joyce indicated that these stories of Dublin life would be told with "scrupulous meanness," and written in "tiny little sentences," phrases which addressed economy of language more than tone, but the subject was of foremost importance. His concern at this stage was primarily with "moral history," the world of Dublin and its people—Dublin because it "seemed to be the centre of paralysis." The title of the stories is itself a "synecdoche," as David Lodge has pointed out, in "that the book describes a representative cross-section or sample of the life of the Irish Capital."[3] There is, in short, little to indicate from Joyce's letters and the first appearance of "The Sisters" that the work would not fall primarily within the traditions of late nineteenth-century realism.[4] *Dubliners* in its final form, however, while retaining many of the conventions of this tradition, is a work of a different literary order. Like a new species in its evolution, it retains several of the more visible and commonplace characteristics but is essentially different. The various versions of "The Sisters," and especially the opening paragraph, reflect in their evolution not only the expanding dimensions Joyce gradually conceived for *Dubliners*, but the increasingly mature vision of his art.

Lodge sees *Dubliners* as a transitional work, lying between the metonymic and metaphoric poles of Roman Jakobson's scheme: "the stories do not quite satisfy the criteria of intelligibility and coherence normally demanded of the classic readerly text."[5] Lodge's language seems itself schematized, but he is working within an important and cogently rendered argument. He carefully supports and expands his point by citing Barthes' definition from S / Z where Barthes contends that in the readerly text, the dominant nineteenth-century model governed by metonymy, "everything holds together." As Barthes goes on to explain, "the readerly is controlled by the principle of non-contradiction, but by multiplying solidarities, by stressing at every opportunity the *compatible* nature of circumstances, by attaching narrated events together with a kind of logical 'paste,' the discourse carries this principle to the point of obsession."[6] Barthes' own text turns from here to an almost strident argument against the readerly text. Later, this essay will look at several other features of Barthes' arguments, but there is another aspect of this transition to mention and that is the literary-historical context of Joyce's generative process. Herbert Schneidau has made observations similar to Lodge's concerning *Dubliners* as a transitional work within this context of the general development of modernist writing.

> As we all know in Joyce's later writings Dublin, including the associated themes of betrayal and paralysis, remained the "subject" while the aims of the portrayal were universalized in almost unprecedented ways. Consequently the notion of "subject" mutates almost beyond recognition; no one had ever used a city in such ways before. In the *Dubliners* stories Joyce had been willing to risk severe attenuation of apprehensible plot, story, action. Obviously he anticipated with some relish complaints that these stories were not "about" anything. He knew what they were about. But even Joyce's friends were nervous. Ezra Pound felt himself obliged to come to the defense of "Araby" as "better" than a story: "it is a vivid waiting." In *A Portrait* and *Ulysses*, subjects are specifically much more in evidence, but Joyce is so evasive about climaxes, "big" scenes, and other standard developments as to make convention-minded readers very uneasy. The hesitant and patronizing reader's report on *A Portrait* by Edward Garnett is probably typical.
>
> Joyce is supposed to have said, in later years, that he wrote about Dublin because "if I can get to the heart of Dublin I can get to the heart of all the cities of the world. In the particular is contained the universal." This is a highly ingenious statement of a rationale that carries the Western theory of representation as far as it will go, but in some ways it is misleading and fails to reach into the heart of the Modernist strategy of particularization. For one thing, Joyce was not portraying some essence of *civitas* in his work, though that aspect enters into his ironies. And even though Pound chimed in with a quotation from an unnamed Belgian who said that *A Portrait* was "as true of my country as of Ireland," Joyce cannot be said to have chosen as subject peculiar parochialisms of modern culture. The reverence of Modernism for precise renderings of particulars demands still further rationalization.[7]

Somewhere between the original conception of the *Dubliners* stories and their completion, Joyce moved along a path similar to the one that was to transform the manuscript *Stephen Hero*, a prose work in the tradition of late nineteenth-century realism and naturalism, into *A Portrait*, a novel that retains many conventions of the realistic text, such as the Christmas dinner scene, but is dominantly a modernist text. *Dubliners* is itself a beginning, and the opening paragraph of the final version of "The Sisters" makes clear that for Joyce, although preserving the facade of this tradition, the stronger impulse was to take seriously the overture of John's Gospel, "In the beginning was the word." (This "beginning" itself echoes the opening line of Genesis that reveals how God brought an orderly universe out of primordial chaos.) Among other things, the beginning of "The Sisters," while not rashly innovative, places radical emphasis on language and in turn on the text as text. In *Dubliners* Joyce begins to give priority to the word over the world.

II

> There was no hope for him this time: it was the third stroke. Night after night I had passed the house (it was vacation time) and studied the lighted square of window: and night after night I had found it lighted in the same way, faintly and evenly. If he was dead, I thought, I would see the reflection of candles on the darkened blind for I knew that two candles must be set at the head of a corpse. He had often said to me: *I am not long for this world*, and I had thought his words idle. Now I knew they were true. Every night as I gazed up at the window I said softly to myself the word *paralysis*. It had always sounded strangely in my ears, like the word *gnomon* in the Euclid and the word *simony* in the Catechism. But now it sounded to me like the name of some maleficent and sinful being. It filled me with fear, and yet I longed to be nearer to it and to look upon its deadly work.
>
> "The Sisters"
(Beginning paragraph, the final version.)

Upon reflection, while attending a Greek Mass in Trieste, the first reader of "The Sisters" thought its early version "remarkable."[8] Once it was finally written, Joyce almost left it at that, content to smile cunningly and pare his fingernails, but not so subsequent readers; by and large those who have written about it affirm the work's imaginative inconsistencies, curious ambiguities, gaps in the discourse, and the general uncertainty it casts on every level from beginning to end. And if the beginning of a text is, as Edward Said has so eloquently told us, "the entrance to what it offers and the first step in the intentional production of meaning,"[9] readers need to explore sufficiently these initial codes, the ensemble of rhetorical markers (the code of connotations), the stylistic codes, the conventional structures—in other words, the full range of the linguistic activity of the text.

The most apparent conclusion, among many, that can be drawn from a study of the evolution of "The Sisters" in its progressive versions is its movement away from the "readerly" text. In reworking "The Sisters" Joyce became increasingly aware of the potential of language itself. This awareness was to change the course of his writing, and, although this point is obvious when we read *Ulysses* and *Finnegans Wake*, his larger assumptions concerning language are clearly visible in *A Portrait*. As Richard Poirier has observed, "the cultural implications of Stephen's language are from first to last what concerned Joyce."[10] From Stephen's early preoccupation with words, to his later posturings in the style of Pater, the reader is drawn constantly to a wide range of implications of the language of the text as it calls attention to itself.

Much has been made of the opening paragraph of "The Sisters" because there is so much to engage and perplex, so much more suggested by the language than the events and circumstances of the text seem to reveal. The first paragraph of "The Sisters" is more than the narrative event which opens the story; it draws the initial line of a larger narrative enclosure, and is every bit as much the beginning of the first movement in the orchestration of *Dubliners* itself. It has already been noted that the various versions of "The Sisters" evolved with Joyce's expanding aims, but some were more immediate, such as his desire to integrate the stories thematically as well as chronologically. Following the collective title of the stories is the slightly foregrounded title of the first, "The Sisters," which he retained throughout all the versions because of its special importance. Initially the title seems ironic in its reference to the vestal virgins Eliza and Nannie, but in the final version it becomes more prominently the first instance of the verbal playfulness of the text in its Elizabeth-Ann, Beth-Annie, Bethany, Lazarus, death associations.[11] There is a persistent self-consciousness in the language of the entire text. The language, too, shadows and alludes to biblical and liturgical references which generate further signification and meaning in the narrative, and these will be discussed later.

Without carrying this first association too far, we can at least see that the title itself offers the first indication of the self-conscious nature of the text. Perhaps it is more obviously so in another way—negatively, for the title is curiously inappropriate for a story that ostensibly narrates the mysterious relationship and the effects of old Father Flynn's death on the young boy narrator. The title signals us away from the traditional slice-of-life, naturalistic sketch that one could expect from the realistic collective title of the stories. Critics who have read "The Sisters" as a realistic text have had enormous difficulty accounting for the title. Even those who declare it as a signaled break from the realistic mode and a gesture of the story's symbolic portent, find the title awkward and even unsatisfactory. The enigmatic title of the first story conflicts with the precise naturalistic title of the collection. From the start "The Sisters" begins to reveal meaning in ways that go beyond the consistencies of a readerly text. Further, it is Joyce's intention to combat the assumptions of such a text. He would write in a mode that would reflect the realities of a new century and create what we have come to call the modernist text which depended upon a new set of cultural assumptions and has been open to charges of obscurity. With "The Sisters" Joyce has just begun a deconstructive process, and the title is the first announcement of a new awareness of the potentiality of language.

To acknowledge the opening paragraph as an overture for the themes, conflicts, and tensions that were to be evoked and stated again and again, not only in the story itself, but throughout all of *Dubliners*, has been critical commonplace.[12] That this final version of the beginning is more than an introduction or overture to the story and the collection has come more slowly to assert itself on the critical consciousness. The virtual nature of the work pointed to so consciously by the text only slowly reduced the certainty and compulsion of critics to assign meanings and thus ultimately abridge the range of possibilities.[13] In these early readings with their rigid and frequently fanciful assignment of symbolic meanings, the potential of the language field itself was abridged, and the fuller range of the text's amplitude was ignored.[14] The asymetrical activities of the text were excluded, too, in the interest of finding exact correspondences. Much of the criticism of "The Sisters" in its desire to account for an exact relationship between symbolic and realistic elements fails to construct a grid which allows for the interplay of the various levels of the text, both horizontal and vertical.[15]

Several recent critics of *Dubliners* stories, such as Robert Scholes in his essay on "Eveline," have attempted to account for the wider potential of the texts by their use of different theoretical models. Scholes's essay, for example, is as much a small-model demonstration of the critical resources in the theories and methods of Todorov, Genette, and Barthes as it is a reading of the story. His application of Barthes' codes is an attempt to demonstrate the deeper and more various levels of the text and their associations both within and outside the text, especially as they relate to language, mode, genre and culture relationships, and assumptions of the author.[16] The present essay avoids Barthes' terminology and does not attempt to apply his codes rigidly to the beginning of "The Sisters," nor does the writer ascribe to their frequently arbitrary application in S / Z. Nevertheless, the reader of Barthes will recognize in this essay an agnostic's imperfect debt along with the measure of doubt: Barthes' work does provide important avenues of adventure in his engagement with a text. And it is Barthes who also cautions us to refrain from structuring a text in large masses and not to delegate a text to a final ensemble, to an ultimate structure.

Given the special importance Joyce assigned to beginnings, the heightened role of the beginning as part of the fundamental boundary and frame in a verbal artistic text, and the beginning as a defining and modeling function, it is worthwhile to confirm this theoretical significance.

Jurij Lotman, for example, has assigned crucial importance to the coding function of the beginning of the narrative text: "When a reader starts reading a book or a spectator watches the beginning of a film or play, he may not know for sure, or may not know at all, into what system the proffered text has been encoded. He is naturally interested in getting a total picture of the text's genre and style and those typical artistic codes which he should activate in his consciousness in order to comprehend the text. On the whole, he derives such information from the beginning."[17]

The beginning paragraph of "The Sisters" not only propels the reader into the various levels of the text and the special network of codes it generates, but it functions as a model for the entire story; the paradoxical realism, the hint of an extravagant presence of the artifice, the allusive tracery of the architectonics which calls attention to the text as text—all of this as though reality itself were dependent upon artful consciousness—a mode that forecasts an entire avenue of discourse as well as story. The responses to this kind of text have, of course, been varied, but it has been generally agreed that from this beginning the work hovers between the two fundamental modes of writing, the metaphoric and metonymic.[18] To see the balance Joyce achieves between these two modes has been the principle aim of the best criticism of this work. Rather than reconcile these two metaphysical orders, it is a more open and far richer experience to ponder their interplay in Joyce's text. Our response comes through engagement not conclusiveness—suspension, rather than closure; suggestion rather than assertion. It comes from situating itself at a beginning of the crossroads of the two fundamental modes of writing. As Colin MacCabe has pointed out, from the earliest stages of his career, Joyce gave special attention to the correspondence between word and world, and the many languages or discourses of the text. MacCabe cites the early paper, "Drama and Life," where Joyce draws such distinctions:

> Joyce sets himself against a drama which comes complete with its own interpretation and caught within the stereotype of its age, a drama which Joyce describes as purveyor supplying plutocrat with a "parody of life which the latter digests medicinally in a darkened theater." For Joyce, real drama is to be found in works, like those of Ibsen, which give us the pleasure "not of hearing it read out to us but of reading it for ourselves, piecing the various parts and going closer to see wherever the writing on the parchment is fainter or less legible." The contrast between a text which determines its own reading and a text which demands an *activity* of reading was central to Joyce from an early age.[19]

The first sentence of "The Sisters" turns us to the thought of death: "There was no hope for him this time: it was the third stroke." With its tone of finality and certainty, this opening begins the circle of death for

Dubliners, a circle clear enough from the last lines of the final story, "The Dead," and clearer still from the pulpit rhetoric of the priest that closes "Grace,"which at one stage in Joyce's plan was to be the final story, when he advises his audience to set right their accounts with God. Besides the emphasis on the word "time" in the first half of this sentence, the rhetorical arrangement and the colon give added emphasis to the temporal where death and dying are in the order of things, and from the beginning of the story priesthood and death are aligned in some seemingly immutable way.

In the second sentence the boy narrator states that "night after night" he had passed the stricken priest's house (we, of course, do not yet know that the victim and object of his compulsive concentration is a priest; this information is inferred later in the paragraph). The intensity of his gaze narrows his focus to the "lighted square of window." The house with its lighted window begins to fill his imagination and memory. As Bachelard tells us, "in the most interminable of dialectics, the sheltered being gives perceptible limits to his shelter. He experiences the house in its reality and in its virtuality, by means of thought and dreams."[20] Because of the priest's illness, the narrator is excluded from the house, a house now protected and presided over by the two sisters, where the priest lies dying. A perspective both imaginary and actual begins to take place and will be sustained throughout the text; the levels of discourse are expanded. The antithesis of outside and inside is thus initiated, and it governs certain other textual arrangements and strategies which will be developed. From the outside, the narrator keeps his own vigil and studies the faint and even light from the window to look for a sign, "the reflection of candles on a darkened blind." Although we have had the religious foregrounding in the title, the candles and their part in the ritual of death offer the first overt suggestion of a religious element on any level.

Appropriately the religious significance is tied in with death from the first—here the candles would act for the boy, at least, as sentinels for the priest's death—and all forms of religious connotation, object, sacrament, and symbol are clustered and bonded. But equally important is the context of this overt religious association: the narrator says, "I knew that two candles must be set at the head of a corpse." The word "must" alerts us from the first to a world where religious form will be mandatory and religious forms control behavior. This fact has already penetrated the boy's consciousness—a religion that places form over substance is to become a central theme of the story. Religious practices will be associated with malevolent paralysis, which with its symptom of perversity is an apt metaphor for a religion whose sacraments rather than outward signs of grace seem to have become not only arid rituals, but signs and gestures of a neurotic abandoned people. In rich detail the text plays almost systematically on the perversion of the Church's sacraments and rituals as a symptom of neurosis and haunting fear, but the very decadence of these church rituals and mysteries have drawn the boy compulsively to the priest. And this mysterious conversion of an almost metaphysical order is what attracts the power of the text's language, the force of its signs and meaning. The language associated with the boy and his descriptions of the priest, with its richness of connotation and possibility, stands in bold contrast to the pedestrian dialogue of the other characters.

The narrator also gives special emphasis to the frequency of the boy's visits to the lighted window—visits which seem to take on their own repeated ritual: "Every night as I gazed up at the window I said softly to myself the word *paralysis*." Each time he gazes upon this scene his memory and imagination go to the fears and secrets that the priest had evoked and passed on to him. The word "paralysis" is the first of a cluster of signifiers which begins within the hermeneutic code, whose meanings are not fully clarified either individually or collectively by the text. This signification, however, extends to other levels of the text. Colin MacCabe has observed that "the reader is introduced to a set of signifiers for which there is no interpretation except strangeness and an undefined evil."[21] The relationships of the words, "paralysis," "simony," and "gnomon," however, seem to foreground each other, by their arrangements as well as meaning, so that beyond the strangeness and undefined evil, there is also a bonding of religious practice with maleficience and perversion. This triad of words produces in the boy the emotions of fear and longing, and, if as MacCabe contends, the words are part of an opening which displays a "certain excess of the power of signification,"[22] they also support the inexplicable power over the narrator who is unable to assimilate in his consciousness their meaning or full evocation, only their deadly charm and attraction for him. It is the confluence of meaning, only dimly understood by the boy and the reader, of these three words as much as their individual signification that generates their mystery, a mystery that sets up the mood and tone of the dream sequence which takes the boy "into some pleasant and vicious region." Words themselves not only have seductive power over him, but they signal the boy's separation from all of the other characters in the story and his alignment with the priest.

No matter how divergent their conclusions, those who have written about "The Sisters," and *Dubliners* generally, have sought to codify the various ways in which this first paragraph of the story generates meaning in its introduction of the various codes for the entire story and the collection itself. Primarily the discussions have centered on these three crucial words of the paragraph, "paralysis," "simony," and "gnomon." Because the words emerge from the boy's consciousness, many of the interpretations have centered their discussion exclusively on the significance of the words for the boy, hence confining their reading to only one level of the text's meaning. But the boy is only the figural medium of the fictional world. Seen only on the one level the words remain incomplete and illusive and in their shadowy significance for the boy they become so for the discourse as well. But beginning from different assumptions there are other possibilities for the reader to explore. It is, of course, in the boy's consciousness that the vague and mysterious connection between "paralysis," "simony," and "gnomon" begins, but their connotations as well as their clustering bring additional semantic elements to the text, thus extending their significations.

The boy murmurs "paralysis" to himself each night as he gazes up at the window until it becomes almost a part of his nightly ritual, which gives the first clue that the sounds of words are as important to the boy as their semantic connotations and referential meanings. The two latter words are also triggered in his consciousness, initially at least, as much by their sounds as by their strange meaning for him. The word "gnomon," for example, seems to confirm the eminence of sound, and sound as meaning, for the word has only remote lexigraphical signification for the boy. But because of its remoteness it calls attention to the power of the word as word, and its geometrical meaning establishes another tracery throughout the text, but one independent of the boy's consciousness.

The emphasis on all three as words is enforced syntactically in that each is preceded by the same word, "word." But their signification extends to cultural and connotative codes as well as the hermeneutic. We draw them into a relationship by virtue of their syntactical locations as well as through the common strangeness they have for the boy, but more than this we are able from them to begin to "thematize" the text. Already alerted to the potential playfulness, extended ironies, and the latent verbal resources of this text, we are able to recognize as many critics have, that "simony" and "paralysis" when run together, as they are nearly so in the boy's mind, suggest the word "syphilis" and broaden the associative power of the vague air of corruption that undergirds the entire story and becomes thematic throughout *Dubliners*. Richard Ellmann first offered the hint of this disease, known as it was at the turn of the century as the general paralysis of the insane, and Burton A. Waisbren and Florence L. Walzl have concluded that Joyce deliberately implied that Father Flynn had central nervous system syphilis,[23] which is now described medically as "paresis." Their extreme interpretation takes suggestiveness to finality, but their analysis reveals the persistent strength of the associative possibilities and latent significations that the text renders. Mystery and suspicion are a part of the language itself as well as the narrative it unfolds. Further, and equally important, is the way in which these three words initiate and establish, as the narrative eventually makes clear, a bond between the priest and the boy—a bond of fear and longing —but nevertheless a union is initiated. This union lies submerged as well in the narrative and establishes something far more suggestive than the boy's own confused and vague association with the priest.

It can be mentioned at this point that the entire language of the opening paragraph also has a seminal foregrounding function which we realize retrospectively. The passage is immediately followed by the most trivial dialogue between Old Cotter and the boy's uncle as they reveal their vapid imaginations and verbal incapacities in contrast to the careful verbal ordering of the first paragraph, which, among so many other things, displays the boy's rich if puzzled fluency. The richness of language is not displayed again until the boy is alone in his room lying in bed between sleep and dream imagining the priest confessing to him. Richard Poirer, in contrasting the modernism of Frost to Eliot's and Joyce's, makes a broad and an important point about the form of a modernist text and cites this contrast in the language of "The Sisters" as an example:

> In saying that Joyce and Eliot were compelled by historical conditions while Frost, for the most part, was not, I do not mean that the form of their writings was predetermined by historical circumstances except as they and their readers came to *imagine* that this was the case. Temperamental or psychological alienation played a crucial part, so did a disenchantment with inherited literary forms, but both feelings preceded those broader encounters with historical plights which in the later works seem to be the source and justification for these feelings. "Modernist" skepticism about "any small man-made figure of order and concentration" is apparent in the earliest, least historically rooted and least allusive writings of Joyce and Eliot. Joyce's "The Sisters," in the contrast it establishes between the poetic elegance and balance of the young boy's language when he is alone in his bedroom as against the fracturing banalities of all other conversation in the story, could be a case in point.[24]

The long scene that concludes the story, dominated by the attenuated dialogue between the boy's aunt and Eliza, with the latter's account of her brother's strange fate, reflects the same incapacity for language as the earlier dialogue. These sharp linguistic contrasts point not only to the text's emphasis on the language field, but contribute to the meaning of the larger cultural and thematic structure of the story.

The multiple dimensions of this beginning paragraph and the course that it set for the entire verbal structure of the story derive in part from Joyce's obsessive autobiographical notions regarding the relationship of priesthood and artist, a relationship of central significance in *A Portrait*. Throughout his discussions in *Portrait*, Stephen constantly refers to the artist and his creation in religious and liturgical language and imagery. In a sense art was the performance of the artist of a sacred rite similar to the priest's at Mass. It is more than merely an analogy, it was partially an aesthetic source for what Joyce would come to define as the priesthood of art. The deeply religious and specifically Roman Catholic saturation of Joyce's texts have particular functions on various levels. All of his texts, in a way, are rooted in the assumption that art replaces religion in a fundamental way—not that art dissolves religious constructs, but that it uses them by reconstructing them. Joyce did not want to remove God from the cosmic structure, but he wanted for the artist God's power of creation.

In the same letter to Stanislaus in which he begins by telling his brother about attending the Greek Mass and recalling "The Sisters," Joyce is referring to the version of the story with the following beginning:

> Three nights in succession I had found myself in Great Britain Street at that hour, as if by providence. Three nights I had raised my eyes to that lighted square of window and speculated. I seemed to understand that it would occur at night. But in spite of the providence which had led my feet and in spite of the reverent curiosity of my eyes I had discovered nothing. Each night the square was lighted in the same way, faintly and evenly. It was not the light of candles so far as I could see. Therefore it had not yet occurred yet.
>
> On the fourth night at that hour I was in another part of the city. It may have been the same providence that led me there—a whimsical kind of providence—to take me at a disadvantage. As I went home I wondered was that square of window lighted as before or did it reveal the ceremonious candles in the light of which the Christian must take his last sleep. I was not surprised, then, when at supper I found myself a prophet.[25]

In this version the beginning of both story and discourse is much closer to the conventional mode of the realistic text, but the nexus between the boy and the priest is not nearly so clearly drawn. The boy is led to the priest's house by "providence," but the mystery and attraction that suffuses the language of the final version of the beginning is notably far less intense. A phrase of special interest in this earlier version is "I found myself a prophet." It is given an added measure of significance by a revealing passage in this same letter to Stanislaus when Joyce details the actions of the priest at the Greek Mass he was observing that brought his story to mind:

> The altar is not visible but at times the priest opens the gates and shows himself. He opens and shuts them about six times. For the Gospel he comes out of a side gate and comes down into the Chapel and reads out of a book. For the elevation he does the same. At the end when he has blessed the people he shuts the gates: a boy comes running down the side of the chapel with a large tray full of little lumps of bread. The priest comes after him and distributes the lumps to scrambling believers. Damn droll! The Greek priest has been taking a great eyeful out of me: two haruspices.[26]

Whether or not he recalled this experience in the later rewriting of "The Sisters" we do not know. But the union Joyce draws between himself and the priest in his letter becomes far more pronounced and important in the final version of the text, especially the beginning. It is in the priest's performance of the ritual Greek Mass, a ritual Joyce found exotic and even flambouyant, that Joyce identifies himself with the priest with the word "haruspices." The roles of artist and priest are joined in the word which means one who foretells events through observations of natural phenomena, a prophet. As the simple bread through the priest's power becomes the body of Christ and retains the appearance of bread as he offers it to the people, so, too, does the artist transform life to art through language. The priest gives significance to the most mundane, so, too, for Joyce does the artist. Language has the same resources and power of the sacraments such as the Eucharist. Herbert Schneidau has commented that: "The characteristic Joycean strategy, embodying the sacramentalist ideal, is expansion: a bare nugget or kernel is transformed, by a kind of explosion of the stylistic potentialities latent within it, into a many membered, multilayered construction. Far from collapsing levels of significance, Joyce seeks constantly to add to them."[27] This strategy of development in Joyce's texts is apparent in the beginning of "The Sisters," especially in the final version where we begin to see this attempt to create a text of multilayered construction through the emphasis on the resources of language itself. The style of the entire story, for example, not only reinforces the themes, it also discovers and manifests them.

As Hugh Kenner has told us, Joyce's earlier fiction is filled with discarded portraits of himself, portraits he might have been or had the potential to become. The first of these is the boy narrator who is simultaneously enchanted and repelled by the priest and his office, an office in which the priest is a failure, for the priest is the leader of ritual and a community's ritual functions to support and draw it together. For the priest the burden, however, is too heavy; the sacrament becomes a perverse sign of his enfeeblement, his incapacity to perform the rites and rituals of his office. Joyce the artist, the creator of form through the medium of language, views the boy through a retrospective prism which generates not only a figural medium, but an authenticity of focus from which to view the fictional world. Such a perspective, once realized, forged a new beginning for his art and what was to become a dominant art of the century.

The changes that took place in Joyce's progressive versions of "The Sisters" represent an initial and tentative movement—and it is no more than that when considered in light of *Ulysses* and *Finnegans Wake*—from the metonymic to the metaphoric, from the "readerly" to the "writerly," from the realistic / naturalistic to the modernist text, but we are able to see from this development a growing and abiding concern on the part of the author for the nature and potentiality of language itself.

Joyce saw language not only as a vehicle but as the informing structure for art in all of its communicative capacities. In "The Sisters" he was writing language over a dead ritual, a dead communion of people, but, at the same time, he was using the motive power of the sacrament as sign analogously to the power of the word as sign in art. However much the boy in this story is a victim, he has escaped the fate of the adult world and the priest, because he is attuned to the potential and transforming power of the word itself, and this story can be read at one level as the fulfillment of Joyce's own conversion. The beginning of "The Sisters" is, then, as we noted earlier, an embryonic stage, or maybe only an imperfect impulse, in Joyce's mature development, but, it, nevertheless, signals the direction his art would take in its own radical restatement of the nature of art and language. If the reader of *Ulysses* must differentiate constantly between the linguistic possibilities of style and the possible nature of the world, the reader of *Finnegans Wake* is aware from the beginning, wherever the beginning is, that the world has become the word, hence with *Finnegans Wake* the beginning is only in the word.

Notes

1. From Tzvetan Todorov and the Russian Formalists, I draw partially my distinctions: *story* comprises a logic of actions and a syntax of characters, and *discourse* comprises the tenses, and aspects and modes of the narrative. These are discussed in much more detail in Todorov's *The Poetics of Prose* (Ithaca, New York, 1977).

2. The most comprehensive discussion of the various versions of "The Sisters" is in Florence L. Walzl's essay, "Joyce's 'The Sisters': A Development," *JJQ*, 10 (1973), 375–421; see especially page 376. *The James Joyce Archive*, Garland Press, contains reproductions of the Cornell and Yale manuscripts, as well as a photographic reproduction of the story as it appeared in *The Irish Homestead*. Throughout I will cite from The Viking Critical Library edition of *Dubliners*, ed. Robert Scholes and A. Walton Litz (New York, 1969), when referring to the final version as it appears in *Dubliners*.

3. David Lodge, *The Modes of Modern Writing* (London, 1977), p. 125. I am generally indebted to Lodge's study, and I feel his work is an important bridge between recent European and Anglo-American criticism.

4. The Viking Critical Library Edition conveniently reproduces the first complete manuscript version of "The Sisters" which is a similar version to the one published in *The Irish Homestead* (Yale ms.).

5. Lodge, p. 125.

6. Roland Barthes, *S / Z*, trans. Richard Miller (New York, 1974), p. 156.

7. Herbert N. Schneidau, "Style and Sacrament in Modernist Writing," *The Georgia Review*, 31 (1977), 433–34.

8. Letter to Stanislaus Joyce, 4 April 1905 in *Letters of James Joyce*, Vol. II, ed. Richard Ellmann (New York, 1966), 86.

9. Edward Said's brilliant work, *Beginnings* (New York, 1975), has brought the whole idea of literary beginnings to mind with such force and possibility that I have yet to assimilate the work's impact on my thinking, but it is considerable.

10. Richard Poirier, *Robert Frost* (New York, 1977), p. 33.

11. The biblical possibilities of this association were first pointed out by Peter Spielberg in his brief article, " 'The Sisters': No Christ at Bethany," *JJQ*, 3 (1966), 192–95.

12. The most suggestive article on the language of "The Sisters" and still one of the most provocative generally, is Fritz Senn's " 'He was too Scrupulous Always,' Joyce's 'The Sisters,' " *JJQ*, 2 (1965), 66–71. His article is based on the conviction "that even in his earliest published prose Joyce wrote in a most complex, heavily allusive style, different from its later convoluted intricacies in *Ulysses* and *Finnegans Wake* in degree only" (p. 66). For articles which discuss the previous criticism see especially: Donald T. Torchiana, "The Opening of *Dubliners*: A Reconsideration," *Irish University Review*, I (1971), 149–60; Bernard Benstock, " 'The Sisters' and the Critics," *JJQ* 4 (1966), 32–35.

13. Although I am not in full agreement with Wolfgang Iser's views, his discussion of the virtual nature of the literary text I find illuminating; see *The Art of Reading* (Baltimore, 1978).

14. It is pointless here to list those critics to whom I am referring. Rather, the following discussions of "The Sisters" I find most illuminating and interesting and not necessarily so because I am in accord with their views: Lodge and Senn have been previously cited; Charles Peake, *James Joyce: The Citizen and the Artist* (London, 1977); Therese Fischer, "From Reliable to Unreliable Narrator: Rhetorical Changes in Joyce's 'The Sisters,' " *JJQ*, 9 (1971), 85–92. Arnold Goldman's discussion of the story in his *The Joyce Paradox* (Evanston, 1966) is especially revealing in its argument that the boy is not permanently ensnared by the paralysis that pervades the adult world.

15. This point obviously needs further development because of the assumptions it makes regarding the nature of the text and the relationship of the reader to the text, but to do so here would require extended discussion. An extreme position on the nature of this relationship can be found in Maria Corti, *An Introduction to Literary Semiotics* (Bloomington and London, 1978).

16. Robert Scholes, "Semiotic Approaches to a Fictional Text: Joyce's 'Eveline,' " *JJQ*, 16 (Fall 78 / Winter 79), 65–80. Briefly, Barthes' codes are proairetic, the code of actions; hermeneutic, code of enigmas; cultural, the text's references to things already known; connotative, the location of themes; and symbolic fields.

17. Jurij Lotman, *The Structure of the Artistic Text* (Ann Arbor, 1977), p. 216.

18. For an extended discussion of these two poles of writing, see David Lodge's work, cited earlier.

19. Colin MacCabe, *James Joyce and the Revolution of the Word* (London, 1975), p. 28.

20. Gaston Bachelard, *The Poetics of Space* (Boston, 1969), p. 5.

21. MacCabe, p. 34.

22. MacCabe, p. 34.

23. Burton A. Waisbren and Florence L. Walzl, "Paresis and the Priest, James Joyce's Symbolic Use of Syphilis in 'The Sisters,' " *Annals of Internal Medicine*, 80 (1974), 758–62.

24. Poirier, pp. 40–41

25. The Viking Critical Edition, pp. 243–44.

26. *Letters*, II, 86–87.

27. Schneidau, p. 441.

Doing Things In Style: An Interpretation of "The Oxen of the Sun" in James Joyce's *Ulysses*

Wolfgang Iser*

I

Shortly after Joyce's *Ulysses* was published in 1922, T. S. Eliot saw in the multifarious allusions to the literature of the past the fabric indispensable to the literature of the future. "In using the myth, in manipulating a continuous parallel between contemporaneity and antiquity, Mr. Joyce is pursuing a method which others must pursue after him. They will not be imitators, any more than the scientist who uses the discoveries of an Einstein in pursuing his own, independent, further investigations. It is simply a way of controlling, of ordering, of giving a shape and a significance to the immense panorama of futility and anarchy which is contemporary history."[1] If the Homeric myth in *Ulysses* is to be regarded as a means of giving shape to a world of futility and anarchy, then clearly a link must be established between past and present that will enable the myth to exercise its "ordering" function. The nature of this link is something that has caused many a headache to Joyce critics down through the years. Is the Homeric epic to be viewed as an "objective correlative"[2]—as defined by Eliot in his "Hamlet" essay—that enables us to grasp the modern situation in the first place? Or does the literary parallel reveal a structural principle that moulds the modern world just as it did the ancient? These two lines of thought represent the two basic approaches to the function of the Homeric parallel. According to both, the apparent chaos of the "Welt-Alltag"[3] (World Weekday) of June 16, 1904, is related to the sequence of adventures in the *Odyssey*, and through this connection is to bring to life in the reader's mind the outlines of an order which is to be read into the events of that day. This view has gained currency through the fact that in the modern world we are denied direct insight into the meaning of events, so that the Homeric parallel appears to offer a way of projecting a hidden meaning onto the chaos of everyday life. But herein lies the inherent weakness of this approach, for it says nothing about the way in which myth and the present day can be brought together.[4]

If Homer's epic contains the meaning, and Joyce's novel contains only a confusing plethora of appearances interspersed with allusions to Homer, such a view must lead ultimately to a Platonizing interpretation of the modern novel. The *Odyssey* will then act as the ideal, while Bloom's wanderings are nothing but the copy of a homecoming which

*This essay first appeared in *The Implied Reader* (Baltimore: Johns Hopkins University Press, 1976) and is reprinted with permission of The Johns Hopkins University Press.

for *Ulysses* means completion, but for Bloom entails just one more grind in the ceaseless monotony of everyday life.[5] Whenever interpretation is dominated by the idea of an analogy, one is bound to be dogged by the consequences inherent in the old conception of the *analogia entis*.[6]

There is, however, another possible interpretation of the Homeric parallel to *Ulysses*, and Joyce himself offered certain indications of this. He called the *Odyssey* "the most beautiful, all-embracing theme" in all world literature.[7] Going into details, he suggests that Ulysses embodies the most vivid conglomeration of all human activities, so that for him the Homeric hero becomes an archetype for humanity. Some Joyce scholars have tried to couple this statement with the idea that the modern novel is an attempt to renew Homeric archetypes.[8] And so the concept of literary permanence comes to the fore whenever the critic concerned makes a fetish of the "unbroken tradition" of Western literature. But such a naive view of permanence demands a blind eye for all the differences between Joyce's novel and Homer's epic. Even though the permanence interpretation of *Ulysses* does not insist that Bloom is nothing but a return to Ulysses, it does insist that he *is* a Ulysses in modern dress.[9] Such a metaphor, however, obscures rather than illuminates the intention of Joyce's novel. Indeed both "schools of thought"— that of analogy and that of permanence—even though they are backed up by some of Joyce's own statements, by existing parallels, and by the actual grouping of the episodes in the novel, shed light only on starting-points and not on intentions.

A hint as to the intention might be found in the oft quoted conclusion of Joyce's *A Portrait of the Artist as a Young Man:* "Welcome, O life! I go to encounter for the millionth time the reality of experience and to forge in the smithy of my soul the uncreated conscience of my race."[10] This corresponds to what we have come to expect in modern times of our novel-writers. Ernst Kreuder, in his treatise on the *Unanswerable*, has described it as follows: "We expect the novelist, by virtue of his imagination, his inventive energy, his story-telling art, and his creative vision, to take us out of an exhaustively explained world of facts and into the inexplicable. . . . The aim of the epic poet can be called a paradoxical one: the completion of the unbounded. The leading of the reader up to the indecipherableness of an existence that flows without end."[11] In the light of such an expectation, the Homeric parallel takes on a very precise function. If the novel is to uncover a new dimension of human existence, this can only present itself to the conscious mind of the reader against a background made recognizable by allusions and references which will thus provide a sufficient amount of familiarity. But the "uncreated conscience," which the novel is to formulate, cannot be the return of something already known—in other words, it must not coincide purely and simply with the Homeric parallel. Harry Levin has rightly pointed out that the links between Joyce and Homer are paral-

lels "that never meet."[12] While the Homeric allusions incorporate into
the text a familiar literary repertoire, the parallels alluded to seem rather
to diverge than to converge. Here we have the conditions for a rich interplay that goes far beyond the lines of interpretation laid down by the
analogy or permanence theories. Indeed there arises a certain tension
out of the very fact that there is no clearly formulated connection between the archaic past and the everyday present, so that the reader himself is left to motivate the parallelism indicated as it were by filling in
the gaps between the lines.

This process only comes to the fore if one in fact abandons the idea
of the parallels and instead takes the modern world and the Homeric
world as figure and ground—the background acting as a sort of fixed
vantage point from which one can discern the chaotic movements of
the present. By means of the allusions, Bloom's and Stephen's experiences are constantly set off against this background, which brings home
to the reader the great gulf between Joyce's characters and those of
Homer. If Bloom is, so to speak, viewed through Ulysses, and Stephen
through Telemachus,[13] the reader who knows his Homer will realize
what is missing in these two modern men. Thus greater emphasis is
thrown on those features which do not coincide with Homer, and in this
way the individuality is given its visible outline. Individuality is therefore constituted as the reverse side of what is suggested by the Homeric
allusions; being conditioned by the very nonfulfillment of the expectations arising from these allusions. Joyce's characters begin to take on a
life of their own the moment we, the readers, begin to react to them, and
our reactions consist of an attempt to grasp and hold fast to their individuality—a process that would be quite unnecessary if they were immediately recognizable types representing an immediately recognizable
frame of reference. Here the reader is compelled to try and find the
frame of reference for himself, and the more intensively he searches, the
more inescapably he becomes entangled in the modern situation, which
is not explained for him but is offered to him as a personal experience.

The Homeric repertoire is not, however, only a background enab-
ling us to grasp the theme of modern everyday life. The interaction can
also be two-way, with Ulysses occasionally being viewed through the
perspective of Bloom. This is significant in the light of the fact that for
Joyce, Homer's hero epitomized humanity.[14] How, then, could he lack
something which Bloom has simply by not being identical with Ulysses?
Obviously because humanity never coincides completely with any of its
historical manifestations—it is a potential which is realized differently
at different times. Even if Ulysses is an ideal manifestation, this only
becomes apparent through the Bloom perspective, which mirrors not just
the ideality of Ulysses but also—and much more significantly—the fact
that humanity, whatever its outward circumstances, can only be apprehended as individual manifestations arising out of reactions to historical

situations. And so the Homeric myth itself takes on another dimension against the foreground-turned-background of the "Welt-Alltag"—a dimension aptly described by S. L. Goldberg as follows: "Once divorced from their origin in implicit, pious belief—and that is the only condition under which we now know the myths of Greece and, for most of us, the myths of Christianity as well—their meanings are perpetually created in our experience, are the colouring they take on from the material into which we project them. The myth is like a potentiality of meaning awaiting actualization in the world we recognize as real, in a specific 'now and here'."[15]

II

The actualization of this potential is not left to the discretion of the individual reader. On the contrary, the manner in which he perceives and conceives events will be guided by the stylistic technique with which they are represented. In *Ulysses* the function of style is so important that a whole chapter is devoted to it. For Joyce, style as the technique of communication was of prime significance. When Stanislaus wanted to discuss fascism with his brother, Joyce remarked laconically: "Don't talk to me about politics. I'm only interested in style."[16] The chapter entitled "The Oxen of the Sun" sheds a good deal of light on this obsession, although Joyce critics generally have tended to look on it with a certain amount of embarrassment,[17] regarding the linguistic experiments as an obvious digression from the novel's apparent subject matter—everyday life in Dublin. The most acceptable explanation for this widespread unease is given by Goldberg, though he too has certain qualms about this chapter:

> The "symbolic" scheme so violently obtruded into these chapters from "Wandering Rocks" to "Oxen of the Sun" attempts much the same effect as the Homeric parallel, but without its foundation and enactment in the characters' own lives and in the reader's belief in the abiding poetic truth of the original myth. The trouble with these chapters in short is that their order is not "aesthetic" enough. Perhaps this is the necessary price for the attempt Joyce makes to shift our attention from the represented reality to the shaping activity of the artist. Given the strategic need to bring himself, as artist, into the action of his book, Joyce could hardly use the old tactic of direct authorial commentary. That would draw attention to him, but not as a dramatis persona and certainly not as an unmoved mover suggested within yet beyond the action. What he did, however, is in its way very like intruded authorial comment.[18]

If Joyce's "failure" lies in the fact that here he discloses his technique instead of continuing the dramatization of individual attitudes, by unraveling this technique we should be able to gain a good deal of insight into its function within the novel's overall framework of presentation. Here we might bear in mind Ezra Pound's pronouncement: "I believe in technique as the test of a man's sincerity."[19]

The subject of this chapter is Bloom's visit to a maternity hospital. There he and his friends wait for Mrs. Purefoy's confinement. The conversation is mainly about love, procreation, and birth.[20] The linguistic presentation of these themes takes place on different, contrasting levels of style. The chapter begins with an enigmatic invocation, and this is followed by an equally cryptic succession of long and tortuous sentences, which seem to lose their meaning as they progress. Immediately after these comes the sequence of historical styles that takes up the whole of the chapter. The subjects of love, procreation, and birth are dealt with in all the characteristic styles of English literature, from alliterative prose right through to pidgin English. "The Oxen of the Sun" starts with three sentences, each of which is repeated three times. An impression of some sort of magic arises out of these triads. The sentences are: "DESHIL HOLLES EAMUS. Send us, bright one, light one, Horhorn, quickening and wombfruit." And finally the Dada sounding "Hoopsa, boyaboy, hoopsa."[21] These three sentences, deciphered, convey the following: Bloom feels an urge to go to Holles Street, where Dr. Horne's maternity hospital is situated. There is an invocation to the art of Dr. Horne to help the fruit of the womb to come into the world. And finally we have the threefold delight of the midwife as she holds the newborn babe in her hands.[22] These banal contents leap to life through the use of Latin words, Latin-sounding turns of phrase, a rhythmic beat, and an incantatory evocativeness. But they also take on a peculiar sort of tension, for the simplicity of the content and the complexity of the presentation seem out of all proportion. Are linguistic montages and magic incantations necessary to make us aware of ordinary, everyday events? This question, right at the beginning of the chapter, is symptomatic of the whole, and indeed here we have a technique which Joyce uses frequently in *Ulysses*: individual chapters begin with a sort of codified theme which is then orchestrated by the narrative process.[23] The invocation then gives way to a completely different style. With long-drawn-out, mainly unpunctuated sentences, an attempt is made to describe the nature and significance of a maternity hospital. But it is only after very careful study that the reader begins to discern this intention. The lack of punctuation excludes any logical linguistic pattern, and behind this there obviously lies the fear of making any concrete statement about the object to be described. Joyce himself gives voice to this fear: "For who is there who anything of some significance has apprehended but is conscious that that exterior splendour may be the surface of a downwardtending lutulent reality."[24] His awareness of the danger that he will capture only the surface view of things makes him approach the object as it were from all linguistic sides, in order to avoid a perspective foreshortening of it. And so the long appositions are not set out as such, and dependent clauses are left unmarked, for divisions of this kind would involve premature definition of the object concerned. At the same time, however, the language makes wide use of specialized vocabulary and precise nuances of meaning, and this gives rise to the impression that the institution is to be described with the utmost exactitude, although in fact it tends to become more and more blurred. Through this effort to depict the object from as many sides as possible, the maternity hospital seems almost to become something living and moving. And this is a stylistic feature typical not only of the chapter in question, but also of important sections of the whole novel: language is used not to fix an object, but to summon it to the imagination. The multiplication of perspectives will blur the outline, but through it the object will begin to grow, and this growth would be stunted if one were to try and define, since definition involves restriction to a chosen viewpoint which, in turn, involves a stylization of the reality perceived. It is therefore scarcely surprising that practically every chapter of *Ulysses* is written in a different style,[25] in order—as Broch puts it—to transfer "the object from one stylistic illumination to another," for only in this way is "the highest degree of reality"[26] to be achieved. The constant change of perspective modifies the definition inherent in each stylistic variant, and so reveals the object as something continually expanding. In this way, even the most commonplace things seem potentially illimitable.

From the invocation that opens this chapter, we may conclude that only a cryptic form of language can succeed in making statements about even the simplest of things. The relation between language and object becomes a mystery, and the tension arising from this is extended by the next stylistic form which, as it were, sets the object in motion through its changing nuances of observation. Thus the basis is laid for the subsequent array of styles emanating from the history of English literature. If one bears in mind the fact that the two different levels of style at the start of the chapter seek only to set us on the road to the maternity hospital and to evoke the nature of such institutions, whereas now we are to be confronted with the great themes of love, procreation, and birth, one might expect the gap between language and object to reach unbridgeable proportions. If the simple themes at the beginning were difficult to deal with linguistically, surely these much broader subjects will totally exceed the capacity of language. And yet, surprisingly, this is not so. Although he may be confused at first, the reader actually needs only a basic knowledge of English literature in order to understand completely all that is going on. Without doubt, Stuart Gilbert's commentary offers some very useful guidelines on this,[27] but critics have never really accepted the parallelism he suggests between the sequence of period styles and the development of the embryo, or the many other references and cross-symbols he worked out as a ground plan for *Ulysses*. Goldberg ends his critique of Gilbert's book with the question: "But if Mr. Gilbert's way of interpreting it [i.e., *Ulysses*] is generally felt to be wrong, what is the right way, and why?"[28] As far as "The Oxen of the Sun" is concerned, a provisional answer must be: because Gilbert's equation of the individual styles with embryonic development is too rigid—not unlike the analogy theory that always seeks to establish precise equivalents in *Ulysses* and the *Odyssey*. Gilbert overlooks the latent comedy that runs through the imitations and shows up the degree of deformation brought about by each individual style.

We can gain a closer insight into the nature of the historical sequence of styles by having a look at a few examples: first, in imitation of old English poetry, we are given an alliterative prose impression of Dr. Horne's maternity hospital. A mainly substantival style captures the outside of things and sets them side by side *en bloc* and unconnected. It seems as if the articles of equipment described are simply there for their own sake, although the alliteration does hint at certain unformulated connections.[29] The function of the individual items remains hidden from perception, so that they take on an element of incomprehensibility which transforms their practical value into some secret sort of reference. The style itself brings about an effect of contrast, insofar as this austere, alliterative prose follows on directly from the attempt, through extreme nuances of language, to describe the nature and importance of a maternity hospital. The consequences of the next style are quite different: events in the maternity hospital are recounted in the form of a late medieval travel book. Everything seems somehow to be tinged with excitement. The surface description of things is conditioned by the need to understand the new in terms of the familiar. However, this technique gets into severe difficulties when the traveler is confronted by a tin of sardines in olive oil. The resultant comedy derives from the incongruity between a style rigidly seeking to define the object in its own gallant terms, and the mundane object itself. The determinant pressure exerted by this style is so great that the advertising agent Leopold Bloom suddenly becomes the medieval "traveller Leopold."[30] Then the language changes again: the characters waiting in the hall of the maternity hospital converse in the style of Sir Thomas Malory.[31] Once again the unifying tendency of the style affects the very identity of the characters. The medieval traveler Leopold of a moment ago now becomes "Sir Leopold." The highly stylized discussion concerns traditional moral problems connected with birth (e.g., whether a wife should be allowed to die for her baby), and then suddenly Stephen raises the subject of contraception. Now neologisms creep into the conversation[32] as signs of human independence, defining man's interference with the God-given order of things. Here it becomes evident that the style shaped by the ideal of Christian knighthood is no longer capable of coping with the multifarious problems under discussion—namely, of love and procreation. Nevertheless, the attempt is made to use the system of references inherent in the ideal of the Christian knight in order to work out an idea of love that cannot be fitted into this system. This incongruity between style and object is apparent all through the series of imitations from one century to another. After a love passage in the language of the Arcadian shepherds, there arises an inner indignation against the trend of the conversation, and this is expressed in the form of a Bunyan allegory.[33] The spiritual conflict transforms the maternity hospital and its trappings into "the land of Phenomenon,"[34] with an unreal outer world giving way to the reality of the inner. The hidden thoughts and feelings of the people concerned are externalized as allegorical characters that enact the ensuing conflict. But here, too, the relation between object and style becomes absurdly unbalanced, as the lusts of the characters are suddenly allegorized, bringing about an extraordinary sort of psychomachia. In medieval literature, allegory personified the Christian moral code. The personification of sexual urges, carried to extremes by Joyce, destroys the whole principle of the form as it had been used up to and including Bunyan.

As a sort of relief from all this personified "inwardness," there now follows a minute description of the external events of the evening, in the diction of Samuel Pepys.[35] The most insignificant trifles are so lovingly observed that they seem over life-size, and every detail becomes a whole world in itself. After this, the central subject of the chapter enters into the realm of Utopian projects, conveyed in the style of the moral weeklies.[36] In pseudoscientific detail the characters discuss various practical methods of controlling with mechanical perfection all the processes of intimacy. This latent Utopianism is conveyed through a number of tales which are intended to establish the illusion that these special cases actually happened in the lives of particular people. Through these stories, the reader is meant to accept as perfectly natural the life planned for him on a "national fertilising farm."[37] In order to bring about this acceptance, the style imitates the narrative form of the moral weeklies, which were designed to create intimate contact with the public. But here the style sets out projects which destroy all intimacy; again we have total incongruity.

The stylistic idiosyncrasies of the great eighteenth-century novelists offer plenty of variations on the love theme through the individualization of speech, while the nineteenth-century parodies nearly all hypostatize the moods and emotions associated with love. All these overblown treatments of the subject show an extremely one-sided view, for each style reveals a latent ideology, constantly reducing the reality to the scope of individual principles. In the language of Landor, the unseemly side of love is again glossed over, this time through the respectability of mythological characters.[38] There is a similar sweet innocence to be found in the homely Dickensian passage that follows a little later. Love is peace and domestic bliss.[39] But in between, there is a detailed section on sex determination and infant mortality that is couched in the scientific terminology of hygiene and biology, with the apparent claim of being able to define these phenomena within the theory of scientific positivism. Again, the relation between subject and treatment is grotesque, and the overall parody is enhanced here by the actual sequence of the styles. Next we come to theological interpretations in the style of Ruskin, Carlyle, and Newman, setting the world of appearances against its metaphysical background—though here, too, we have different definitions of love and the world under perception. After this series of rich and varied styles, the language at the end of the chapter seems to explode into a chaos of possibilities, and in this confused linguistic hodgepodge meaning finally seems to go by the board; it fades away in the elusiveness of language.

III

From these briefly sketched examples we may draw certain conclusions which together will give us a degree of insight into the Joycean technique of style. Although the various consequences are very closely connected with one another, we shall gain a clearer understanding of them by first examining them separately. To begin with, this stylistic historical tour of English literature is designed to grasp a particular subject through language. Each individual style projects a clearly recognizable idea of love, procreation, or birth. Joyce's style imitations therefore fulfill the demands summarized by John Middleton Murry as follows: "Style is a quality of language which communicates precisely emotions or thoughts, or a system of emotions or thoughts, peculiar to the author. . . . Style is perfect when the communication of the thought or emotion is exactly accomplished; its position in the scale of absolute greatness, however, will depend upon the comprehensiveness of the system of emotions and thoughts to which the reference is perceptible."[41] The styles imitated by Joyce are dominated by such thoughts or thought systems, and the predetermined, predetermining nature of all style is demonstrated quite unmistakably through the individual variations. The judgments inherent in each style create a uniform picture of the subject presented, choosing those elements of the given reality that correspond to the frame of reference essential to all observation.[42] The particular point of view, then, determines which individual phenomena out of all those present are, or are not to be presented. And this, for Joyce, is the whole problem of style. Presentability or nonpresentability is not a quality inherent to any observable reality, but has to be imposed on that reality by the observer. This involves a latent deformation of the object perceived, which in extreme cases is degraded to the level of a mere illustration of some given meaning. If now we go back to the beginning of the chapter, we notice not only the counter-point that exists between the introduction and the subsequent historical sequence of styles but also the richly contrasting tensions between the different types of presentation. At the start it seemed that banal objects could only be captured by a cryptic language, while the next passage showed that as language approached, reality seemed rather to withdraw than to come closer. The account was split up into a bewildering number of facets, with language attempting to comprehend the subject matter from every conceivable angle. To do this, it had to be freed from the normative restrictions of grammar and syntax, for only then could it sow all the nuances in the imagination of the reader. The account could contain no judgment, because otherwise it would not be presenting the object itself but the frame of reference in which the object was viewed. And it is such frames of references that are in fact presented by the ensuing series of imitations. Joyce's aim, however, was not solely to show up the limitations of all styles through the systems of thought underlying them but also to evoke those aspects of an object that are kept concealed by the perspective mode of observation. Hence the fact that virtually every chapter of *Ulysses* is written in a different style.[43] Herein lies a basic difference between Joyce and all other modern writers. Joyce wanted to bring out, if not actually to overcome, the inadequacy of style as regards the presentation of reality, by constant changes of style, for only by showing up the relativity of each form could he expose the intangibility and expansibility of observable reality. And so in "The Oxen of the Sun" we have the themes of love, procreation, and birth discussed in a series of historically sequent styles which each convey a single, one-sided viewpoint.

This leads us to the second conclusion to be drawn from the examples given. If style reproduces only aspects of reality and not—in contrast to its implicit claims—reality itself, then it must be failing in its intention. This idea is worked up through the element of parody in the stylistic impersonations. Joyce caricatures the formal restrictions of each style so that Leopold Bloom, the main character in the novel, finds himself taking on a corresponding variety of identities. The resultant distortion is one that the reader can scarcely ignore, since he already knows a good deal about Bloom's character from the preceding chapters. We find the same distortion in the treatment of the main theme of the chapter, for it is not love itself that is presented, but only the way in which Malory, Bunyan, Addison, and the other writers understood it. Indeed one has the impression that the different views presented by the different styles exclude rather than supplement one another. With each author, the theme takes on a different shape, but each treatment seems to assume that it is offering *the* reality. And so there emerges a latent naïveté underlying every style. One might perhaps wonder which of the views comes closest to the truth, but it is patently obvious that every one of the authors has cut reality to the shape of a particular meaning not inherent in that reality. By parodying the styles, Joyce has exposed their essentially manipulative character. The reader gradually becomes conscious of the fact that style fails to achieve its ends, in that it does not capture reality but imposes upon it an historically preconditioned form. The parody through which this process is set in motion contains a polemic element attacking this intrinsic tendency of style to edit observed realities. If now we think back to the invocation with which Joyce ended *A Portrait*, we must expect his meeting with reality to aim at an extension of experience beyond the frontiers of the already familiar. And for a presentation of this, there must, paradoxically, be total freedom from the restrictions of any one consistently sustained mode of presentation.

This brings us to our third conclusion. With his historical panoply of individual and period styles, Joyce exposes the characteristic quality of style—namely, that it imposes form on an essentially formless reality. Thus in the various views of love that are presented, the decisive influence is the historical conditions which shaped the understanding of the subject during the period concerned. Clearly, then, the theme itself is so multifarious that it can encompass every possible historical reflection of it, and the more clearly defined the judgment, the more historically conditioned is the style. Out of the series of parodies, then, emerges the fact that not only are the styles one-sided but they are also conditioned by sets of values that will change from period to period. In other words, the same subject (in this case, love) will take on a different form when viewed under different conditions or at different times. Which style can best capture the reality of the subject? The answer, clearly, is none, for all styles are relative to the historical conditions that shape them.

This brings us to a fourth and last conclusion: if the factors that shape a style are essentially historical, the resultant definition of the object to be described can only be a pragmatic one, since it depends on ever-changing historical conditions. But the pragmatic nature of style can only be exposed through some sort of comparative survey—in this case, the historical sequence—since none of the authors Joyce parodies would have regarded their own form of presentation as a merely pragmatic view of the subjects they were dealing with. Now if style can only accomplish a pragmatic definition, its function in illuminating observed reality must be figurative, or metaphorical, for the limited system of references that forms it is applied to the unlimited reality it is attempting to convey. This is the only way, of course, in which style can build up a uniform picture. But if style can only capture objects in a metaphorical manner, it must be counted simply as one of those rhetorical devices of which Lessing once said: "that they never stick strictly to the truth; that at one moment they say too much, and at another too little."[44] Joyce's chronological exhibition of styles shows clearly that they are all metaphorical and can only offer a preconditioned, one-sided view of their subject matter. The intrinsic aim of style is to capture a phenomenon as accurately as possible, but being only a metaphor, it cannot help but miss out a whole range of aspects of that phenomenon. Roman Ingarden, in describing the views that come to light through the style of a work of art, has said: "The views that we have during our experiences of one and the same thing change in different ways, and much that in an earlier view emerged only in the form of an unrealized quality will, in a later view, be present and transformed into a realized quality. But present in every view of an object are both realized and unrealized qualities, and it is intrinsically impossible ever to make the unrealized qualities disappear."[45] Joyce's parodies seek to change "unrealized qualities" into "realized," and with this process he shows us how the phenomenon itself begins to expand—for every definition excludes aspects which must themselves then be defined.

If we take up Goldberg's view of "The Oxen of the Sun" as the author's commentary on his novel,[46] we may reasonably extend our findings to the use of style throughout the whole book. While the theme of this one chapter is love, the theme of *Ulysses* itself is everyday human life, and the stylistic presentation of this varies from chapter to chapter, because it can never be grasped as a whole by any one individual style. Only by constantly varying the angle of approach is it possible to convey the potential range of the "real-life" world, but in literature the "approach" is what gives rise to the style. By constantly changing the style, Joyce not only conveys the preconditioned, one-sided nature of each approach but also seems to set both object and observer in motion, thus accumulating an assembly of mobile views that show the essential expansiveness of reality. In this sense, "The Oxen of the Sun" epitomizes the technique of the whole novel. The sequence of styles brings out the one-sidedness of each and the constant expansion of the subject. One aspect after another appears within the mirror of style, but "hey, presto, the mirror is breathed on" and that seemingly all-important facet "recedes, shrivels, to a tiny speck within the mist."[47] What Joyce says in this chapter about sins or evil memories is true also of these hidden aspects of reality, and in "The Oxen of the Sun," as throughout the novel, this insight is constantly developed: they are "hidden away by man in the darkest places of the heart but they abide there and wait. He may suffer their memory to grow dim, let them be as though they had not been and all but persuade himself that they were not or at least were otherwise. Yet a chance word will call them forth suddenly and they will rise up to confront him in the most various circumstances."[48]

Notes

1. T. S. Eliot, "Ulysses, Order, and Myth," in *James Joyce: Two Decades of Criticism*, ed. Seon Givens (New York, 1948), p. 201. (The essay was published originally in 1923).

2. T. S. Eliot, *Selected Essays* (London, ²1951), p. 145. (The "Hamlet" essay was published originally in 1919.)

3. A term used by H. Broch, *Dichten und Erkennen* (Zürich, 1955), p. 187, to describe June 16, 1904.

4. See, among others, Stuart Gilbert, *James Joyce's Ulysses* (New York, 1955, ¹1930); Frank Budgen, *James Joyce and the Making of Ulysses* (Bloomington, 1960, ¹1934): W. Y. Tindall, *A Reader's Guide to James Joyce* (London 1959), pp. 128 ff.; Richard Ellmann, *James Joyce* (New York, 1959), pp. 541 f.; Wylie Sypher, *Rococo to Cubism in Art and Literature* (New York, 1960), p. 285; Richard Ellmann, "Ulysses and the Odyssey,"*English Studies* 43 (1962): 423 ff. The idea of parallelism has also been extended beyond the *Odyssey*, for instance by Alan Dundes, "Re: Joyce—No in at the Womb," *Modern Fiction Studies* 8 (1962): 137 ff. There is a much more cautious but illuminating study of analogy and allusions by Robert Martin Adams, *Surface and Symbol: The Consistency of James Joyce's Ulysses* (New York, 1962). There is similar caution in some more recent studies of analogy. W. Y. Tindall, *James Joyce: His Way of Interpreting the Modern World* (New York, 1950), p. 102, rightly emphasizes that: "the Homeric pattern is only one level of the narrative Joyce composed." A. Walton Litz, *The Art of James Joyce* (London, 1961), p. 39, writes: "Similarly, there are many more Homeric references on the *Ulysses* note-sheets than ever made their way into the text, and we are forced to conclude that the parallel with the *Odyssey* was more useful to Joyce during the process of composition than it is to us while we read the book. Time and again he spoke of the comfort he derived from the narrative order of the *Odyssey*: it provided him—in his own words—with fixed 'ports of call.' The major parallels between the wanderings of Mr. Bloom and those of Ulysses are an important dimension of the novel, but in working out the trivial details of the Homeric correspondence Joyce was exploring his own materials, not preparing clues for future readers." Jackson I. Cope, "The Rhythmic Gesture: Image and Aesthetic in Joyce's *Ulysses*," *ELH* 29 (1962): 87, says the following about the parallelism: "If *Ulysses* is a novel of knowing, if its theme is the everpresence of recovered time in the creative form of the microcosm, we cannot forget that the most obvious mode of organization is the parallelism of mythic echo made living, like the sea in the shell, by being awakened in the protean rôles and memories of everyman."

5. See Richard Ellmann, "Ulysses: The Divine Nobody," in *Twelve Original Essays on Great English Novels*, ed. Ch. Shapiro (Detroit, 1960), pp. 244 ff.; the degree of controversy surrounding such a parallelism can be seen, for instance, in such statements as Arland Ussher's *Three Great Irishmen* (London, 1952), p. 121: "The life of Mr. Bloom, however, could hardly be described as an Odyssey ... any more than could that of the youthful Stephen Dedalus; though they had a good deal of an Athenian peripatos." Margaret Church, *Time and Reality: Studies in Contemporary Fiction* (Chapel Hill, 1962), p. 44, writes: "If Odysseus is representative of the heroic age and Bloom is representative of the human age, neither one acts as commentary on the other, for each is sufficient to his own age."

6. This concept has been discussed anew by Gottlieb Söhngen, *Analogie und Metapher: Kleine Philosophie und Theologie der Sprache* (Freiburg, 1962). Wallace Stevens, *The Necessary Angel* (New York, 1951), p. 130, ends his essay on "Effects of Analogy" with the following observation: "It is a transcendence achieved by means of the minor effects of figurations and the major effects of the poet's sense of of the world and of the motive music of his poems and it is the imaginative dynamism of all these analogies together. Thus poetry becomes and is a transcendent analogue composed of the particulars of reality, created by the poet's sense of

the world, that is to say, his attitude, as he intervenes and interposes the appearances of that sense."

7. See Ellmann, *Joyce*, p. 430.

8. See W. B. Stanford, *The Ulysses Theme* (Oxford, ²1963), who goes into the different nuances and variations in the continuity of the Homeric figure. Harry Levin, "What Was Modernism?" in *Varieties of Literary Experience*, ed. Stanley Burnshaw (New York, 1962), p. 322, writes: "It is the metamorphic impetus that provides this controlling device: the transmutation of Dublin citizens into mythical archetypes out of the *Odyssey*." Rudolf Sühnel, "Die literarischen Voraussetzungen von Joyces *Ulysses*," GRM, N.F. 12 (1962): 202 ff., rightly talks of this continuity as only a basis for studying the special qualities of *Ulysses*.

9. See, for instance, Ellmann, "Ulysses: The Divine Nobody," pp. 246 ff., and Broch, *Dichten und Erkennen*, p. 193.

10. James Joyce, *A Portrait of the Artist as a Young Man* (London, 1952), p. 288. Irene Henrdy, "Joyce's Epiphanies," in *James Joyce: Two Decades of Criticism*, ed. Seon Givens (New York, 1948), p. 39, calls this passage "the (final) epiphany in the *Portrait*."

11. Ernst Kreuder, *Das Unbeantwortbare: Die Aufgaben des modernen Romans* (Mainzer Akademie der Wissenschaften, Abhandlung der Klasse der Literatur, 1959, Nr. 2) (Wiesbaden, 1959), pp. 19, 25.

12. Harry Levin, *James Joyce: A Critical Introduction* (New York, 1960, ¹1941), p. 71.

13. It goes without saying that the Hamlet parallel also plays an important part for Stephen. But in principle the reference to Hamlet—or the elucidation of Stephen through Hamlet—serves to bring out his special situation, and so is very similar to the Homeric parallel.

14. See the statement reproduced in Ellmann's *Joyce*, p. 430.

15. S. L. Goldberg, *The Classical Temper: A Study of James Joyce's Ulysses* (London, 1961), p. 202.

16. Quoted by Ellmann in his introduction to Stanislaus Joyce, *My Brother's Keeper* (London, 1958), p. 23.

17. A typical negative judgment is given by Walter Allen, *Tradition and Dream* (London, 1964), p. 7. Less emphatic views are offered by, among others, Levin, *Joyce*, pp. 105 f.; Franz Stanzel, *Die typischen Erzählsituationen im Roman* (Wiener Beiträge zur Englischen Philologie, 63) (Vienna, 1955), p. 135; Litz, *The Art of James Joyce*, pp. 37 f. The stylistic experiments are very cautiously evaluated by M. Butor, *Repertoire* I, German transl. by Helmut Scheffel (Munich, no date), p. 108.

18. Goldberg, *The Classical Temper*, p. 288.

19. Ezra Pound, *Literary Essays*, ed. T. S. Eliot (London, 1960), p. 9.

20. For the purposes of this essay, the discussion is confined to the one central theme. Other themes are brought in from time to time, and these, too, have their form imposed on them by the style of the individual authors Joyce imitates.

21. James Joyce, *Ulysses* (London: Bodley Head, 1958), p. 366.

22. See also Gilbert, *James Joyce's Ulysses*, p. 296. For the purposes of this interpretation, discussion of the other parallels has deliberately been avoided.

23. See the interpretation given by E. R. Curtius, *Kritische Essays zur europäischen Literatur* (Berne, ²1954), pp. 309 ff., and Stanzel, *Erzählsituationen im Roman*, pp. 130 ff.

24. Joyce, *Ulysses*, p. 366.

25. See also Philip Toynbee, "A Study of Ulysses," in *Modern British Fiction*, ed. Mark Schorer (New York, 1961), pp. 347 f., and Levin, *Joyce*, pp. 105 f. and 111 f.

26. Broch, *Dichten und Erkennen*, p. 191. However, he does not discuss the subject any further.

27. See Gilbert, *James Joyce's Ulysses*, pp. 298 ff.

28. Goldberg, *The Classical Temper*, p. 212.

29. Joyce, *Ulysses*, p. 368.

30. Ibid., p. 369

31. Ibid., pp. 370 ff. For the key to the sequence of styles, see Gilbert, *James Joyce's Ulysses*, pp. 298 ff.; Budgen, *James Joyce*, pp. 215 ff., and Stanislaus Joyce, *My Brother's Keeper*, p. 104. No account has been taken here of the other parallels Gilbert mentions for this chapter. For an assessment of these, see especially Litz, *The Art of James Joyce*, pp. 34 f.

32. See, for instance, Joyce, *Ulysses*, p. 372: "But, gramercy, what of those Godpossibled souls that we nightly impossibilise, which is the sin against the Holy Ghost, Very God, Lord and Giver of Life?"

33. See Joyce, *Ulysses*, pp. 377 f.

34. Ibid., p. 378.

35. Ibid., p. 379.

36. Ibid., pp. 384 ff.

37. Ibid., p. 384.

38. Ibid., pp. 396 ff.

39. Ibid., pp. 402 ff.

40. Ibid., pp. 399 ff.

41. John Middleton Murry, *The Problem of Style* (Oxford, 1960; [1]1922), p. 65; see also F. L. Lucas, *Style* (London, [3]1956), pp. 14 ff. and Herbert Read, *English Prose Style* (Boston, 1961), pp. 183 f.

42. See Murry, *The Problem of Style*, p. 65.

43. See Jacques Mercanton, "The Hours of James Joyce. Part I," *Kenyon Review* 24 (1962): 701 f., who reproduces the following statement by Joyce concerning the style of *Ulysses*: "'The hallucinations in *Ulysses* are made up out of elements from the past, which the reader will recognize if he has read the book five, ten, or twenty times. Here is the unknown. There is no past, no future; everything flows in an eternal present. All the languages are present, for they have not yet been separated. It's a tower of Babel. Besides, in a dream, if somone speaks Norwegian to you, you are not suprised to understand it. The history of people is the history of language." Various observations on the problem of language are also to be found in Theodore Ziolkowski's essay "James Joyce's Epiphanie und die Überwindung der empirischen Welt in der modernen deutschen Prosa," *Deutsche Vierteljahrsschrift für Literaturwissenschaft und Geistesgeschichte* 35 (1961): 594 ff.; see also Heinz Decker, "Der Innere Monolog," *Akzente* 8 (1961): 107. Re the function of the experiments in style, see "Patterns of Communication in Joyce's *Ulysses*," [*The Implied Reader*], pp. 255 ff.

44. G. E. Lessing, *Gesammelte Werke*, VII, ed. Paul Rilla (Berlin, 1956), p. 233; Lucas, *Style*, p. 15, asks: "What, in fact, is 'style?' A dead metaphor." See also Joyce's remark on literature, reproduced by Stanislaus Joyce, *My Brother's Keeper*,

p. 105. On the pragmatic nature of metaphor, see Hans Blumenberg, *Paradigmen zu einer Metaphorologie* (Bonn, 1960), pp. 19 ff.

45. Roman Ingarden, *Das literarische Kunstwerk* (Tübingen, ²1960), p. 277.

46. See Goldberg, *The Classical Temper*, p. 288.

47. Joyce, *Ulysses*, p. 395.

48. Ibid., p. 403.

The Consequence of Deconstruction: A Technical Perspective of Joyce's *Finnegans Wake*   Margot C. Norris*

I

The attempt to assess the teleology of Joyce's *Finnegans Wake* has always presented critics with a dilemma: the choice between a radical and a conservative interpretation of the book. A radical interpretation would maintain that *Finnegans Wake* subverts not only the literary status quo, but the most cherished intellectual preconceptions of Western culture as well—a position most clearly maintained in the pioneer studies of the work. Yet in these early studies, such as *Our Exagmination*,[1] the weakness of the radical interpretation also becomes apparent. While proclaiming the revolutionary nature of *Work in Progress*, the writers lack scholarly pegs on which to hang their theories, and finally resort to *ad hoc* analogies to support their theses. In contrast, the conservative critics, who have dominated *Wake* criticism for the last thirty years, possess a small but scholarly arsenal: the stylistic and thematic conservatism of the early manuscript drafts, the inclusion of traditional, even arcane, literary material in the work, Joyce's admission that the work's structural and philosophical models were derived from a sixteenth-century metaphysician and an eighteenth-century philosopher, and finally, Joyce's own decidedly reactionary tastes.

Conservative criticism is characterized chiefly by a belief that the work contains fixed points of reference in the manner of the traditional novel. *A Skeleton Key to Finnegans Wake*, whose publication essentially initiated this critical trend, first outlined the complete naturalistic narrative level toward which the mythic elements in the work purportedly refer. By assigning this literal level as the point of reference in the work, the mythic events—fables, tales, legends, hallucinations, dreams within dreams, which comprise about one half of the book[2]—are rele-

*This essay first appeared in *ELH*, 41 (Spring 1974) and is reprinted with permission of The Johns Hopkins University Press.

gated to the subordinate function of illustrating, universalizing and in-
flating the naturalistic events. The pre-eminence of the novelistic plot
also demands traditional novelistic character analysis, which assumes
that character in fiction is a mirror of character in the world. Wakean
figures, however, like the "shape-shifters" of fairy tales, slip as easily
into animals, geographical features, household objects, edibles, and abstract concepts as into human guises. The demands of traditional point
of view—that is, the need to posit the vantage point of the narration in
a unitary consciousness—have been most difficult to satisfy in *Wake*
study as the "Who-is-the-dreamer" controversy[3] attests. Finally the assumption of an underlying point of reference has been extended to the
language of the work itself, reducing the fantastic, poly-semous words
to a simple message which has been "complicated" or "embroidered"[4]—
to the point of excrescence, according to some critics. After thirty years
of dominance in *Wake* studies, the limitation of this conservative, novelistic approach to the work is most evident in its lack of progress toward
establishing clearly the intellectual orientation of the work. Notwith-
standing the wealth of invaluable explication it has engendered, this
approach has not passed beyond defining *Finnegans Wake* as a profligate *Ulysses*.

In the light of recent evaluations of the status which the concept of structure has occupied in Western thought, it is now possible
to question altogether the relevance of the conservative approach to the
work, and to formulate a new critical direction which would historically
validate the radical axioms of the early *Wake* critics. When Samuel
Beckett, in *Our Exagmination,* called the book a purgatorial work for its
lack of any Absolute,[5] he was sensitive to the work's participation in the
"event" or "rupture" in the history of the concept of structure, which,
according to philosopher Jacques Derrida, took place in the history of
thought sometime in the late nineteenth and early twentieth century.
The destructive impact of this "event" becomes clear only in view of
the history of metaphysics, which Derrida characterizes as belief in being
as "presence": "the whole history of the concept of structure, before
the rupture I spoke of, must be thought of as a series of substitutions of
center for center, as a linked chain of determinations of the center."[6]

A clear illustration of this historic concept of structure can be found
in T. E. Hulme's influential work, *Speculations.* Hulme evaluated classicism and romanticism, whose dialectic he regarded as forming the
basis of the history of art, in terms of a single fundamental premise: that
belief in a Deity constituted the fixed part of man's nature.[7] Hulme
denounced romanticism as the displacement of that fixed belief in Deity
from the religious sphere, to which it properly belongs, to the human
sphere, that is, the belief in man as a god. Fundamental to Hulme's
tenets is therefore the notion of a center according to which man defines himself; the issue is merely who or what shall occupy that center.

The "rupture" in the history of structure—brought about, as Derrida says, by our being self-consciously forced to "think the structurality of structure"—results in the idea of a structure in which presence is not so much absent as unlocatable. The center is ex-centric, and the structure is determined not by presence but by freeplay. This "rupture" is manifested most purely in certain destructive discourses of the early twentieth century:

> Where and how does this decentering, this notion of the structurality of structure, occur? . . . I would probably cite the Nietzschean critique of metaphysics, the critique of the concepts of being and truth, for which were substituted the concepts of play, interpretation, and sign (sign without truth present); the Freudian critique of self-presence, that is, the critique of consciousness, of the subject, of self-identity and of self-proximity or self-possession; and, more radically, the Heideggerean destruction of metaphysics, of onto-theology, of the determination of being as presence.[8]

Among these destructive discourses of the early twentieth century, *Finnegans Wake* serves as a literary exemplar, and in doing so inaugurated a new concept of literary structure, which itself could not be deciphered so long as critical formalism was ruled by concepts like Hulme's.

II

The decentered structure of the work becomes apparent in the difficulty of locating a point of reference in any aspect of *Finnegans Wake*. The work is plotless insofar as events follow neither a temporal nor a causal sequence, and do not even occur on a single plane of reality. Instead, Wakean events are subject to multiple recapitulations on all narrative levels: in domestic situations, stories, fables, broadcasts, riddles—and, as in dream, they need not correspond to realized actions or historical happenings. The parricidal wishes of the sons are implicit in HCE's encounter with the cad (I.2), the ruination of HCE's reputation by the balladeers in I.2, the Butt and Taff radio skit (II.3), and the attack of the pub customers on HCE (II.3). The fraternal struggle, which duplicates the paternal conflict, is presented at an immediate narrative level in Shaun's virulent attack on Shem in I.7, elsewhere in the fables of the Ondt and the Gracehoper and the Mookse and Gripes. The brothers' quarreling over sister and / or mother appears in the tale of Burrus, Caseous, and Margareen (I.6), the exchange of blows in Cain-Abel tradition during the homework lesson of II.2, the washerwomen's bickering while gossiping about Anna Livia in I.8; the children's games of II.1, Jaun's sermon to the girls at St. Bride's in III.2. Father-son conflict over the family's women occurs in the Waterloo battle (I.1), the Tristan myth (II.4), and is implied in all other paternal conflicts. The characters who enact these events receive their identity not from a stability of form or personality, but rather from their position in a configuration of relationships. The figures who appear in such diverse situations as the children's games, the animal fables, the confrontation of primitives on the prehistoric mound, the radio vaudeville skit, the debate of justice and mercy, the homework lesson, or the nursery, are the same whether they are called Chuff and Glugg, Mookse and Gripes, Ondt and Gracehoper, Mutt and Jute, Butt and Taff, Justius and Mercius, Kev and Dolph, Jerry and Kevin, or Shem and Shaun. Furthermore, characters are subject to cross-identification. The family members and miscellaneous citizenry, fathers and sons, mothers and daughters, accusers and accused, gossipers and gossiped about, judges and judged— are all subject to interchange and substitution in the work. The *Wake* itself suggests the substitutability not only of characters, but of their speech and thoughts, as the Mime of II.1 announces: "nightly redistribution of parts and players by the puppetry producer and daily dubbing of ghosters" (219.7). Perhaps most important, because it marks a departure from the protagonistic subjectivism of the "stream of consciousness" technique, the point of view in *Finnegans Wake* is indeterminable. The origin of the discourse is no longer in the consciousness of speakers, but rather in a dialectic between the conscious and the unconscious—as manifested in the pervasive "double-talk" of Wakean figures. The single line of discourse, and often the single word, simultaneously contains expressed and repressed matter, banal and guilty sexual thoughts—suggesting that speakers are not what they say they are, or even what they think they are, and that the status of authentic self-knowledge in the work is indeterminable.

Finally, the expression of a decentered universe may be seen in the major themes of the work, particularly the disintegration of order and law subsequent to the fall of the father. Depicted naturalistically in the mutual disrespect and slovenliness of the household in Chapter Five of *Portrait*, the father's fall in *Finnegans Wake* also marks the unravelling of the family structure—but at the primal level of its foundation on taboos and kinship regulations. Incest and parricide rule the Earwickers until mothers and fathers, daughters and sons, are dislocated from their fixed positions in the family hierarchy, and are defined only by each other's desires. The fall of the father, by removing that principle which regulates and fixes the relationships of family members according to kinship laws and taboos, allows instead for a substitutability of love objects which brings daughter-mother-sister within the purview of the men's desires, and creates, in addition, numerous homosexual possibilities within the family.

This cursory summary should serve to indicate that the formal elements of the work, plot, character, and point of view, are not anchored to a single point of reference, do not refer back to a center. This condition produces that curious flux and uncertainty in the work which is sensed intuitively by the reader, and which the *Wake* itself describes as follows:

> every person, place and thing in the chaosmos of Alle anyway connected with the gobblydumped turkery was moving and changing every part of the time: the travelling inkhorn (possibly pot), the hare and turtle pen and paper, the continually more or less intermisunderstanding minds of the anticollaborators, the as time went on as it will variously inflected, differently pronounced, otherwise spelled, changeably meaning vocable scriptsigns. (118.21)

The substitutability of parts for one another, the variability and uncertainty of the work's structural and thematic elements, represent a decentered universe, one which lacks the center that defines, gives meaning, designates and holds the structure together—by holding it in immobility. The traditional concept of structure, which implied a center or presence, also implied a formal wholeness of the work of art, in which each of the particular elements referred always back to the center. Decentering of the structure, then suggests another, as yet uncategorizable sense of form—which modern poets often call "open" in contrast to "closed," but which is more conveniently defined here as "freeplay." Jacques Derrida describes this freeplay of a decentered system of language as follows:

> This field is in fact that of *freeplay*, that is to say, a field of infinite substitutions in the closure of a finite ensemble. This field permits these infinite substitutions only because it is finite, that is to say, because instead of being an inexhaustible field, as in the classical hypothesis, instead of being too large, there is something missing from it: a center which arrests and founds the freeplay of substitutions.[9]

The freeplay of elements in *Finnegans Wake* has long been recognized without pursuit of its implications for the total structure of the work. William Y. Tindall writes: "As God's world, created by the Word, is an endless arrangement and rearrangement of ninety-six elements—give or take a couple—so Joyce's closed system is an endless arrangement and rearrangement of a thousand and one elements that, whatever their multiplicity, are limited in number."[10]

Joyce's attempt to express a decentered universe in language required a technique which could effectively cope with the philosophical problems inherent in such a concept. The recent evidence of Benjamin Lee Whorf, and semanticists Korzybski and Hayakawa, increasingly demonstrate the extent to which the structure of a language expressed by a culture inherently contains the epistemology of that culture. Joyce, independently, by his own means, must have arrived at a discovery whose implications are only recently becoming understood: that the *Weltanschauung* of a writer is limited by the language he employs. A writer who would attempt to escape the epistemology of his culture is therefore confronted by a language embedded with inherited concepts; to criticize these concepts he must still make use of a language in which they are embedded. Jacques Derrida writes: "It is a question of putting expressly and systematically the problem of the status of a discourse which borrows from a heritage the resources necessary for the deconstruction of that heritage itself."[11] In using the standard English of the traditional novel to render a world without law, without fixed points of reference or a privileged "reality," without a stable consciousness lodged in its narrators and speakers, Joyce would have used a language which itself belied and contradicted everything he sought to express. The peculiar language of *Finnegans Wake,* which deviates from the English language code in respect to lexical items and consequently violates even the syntactical structure of English at times, represents Joyce's attempt to outflank the contradiction of critical language. In seeking to express a decentered universe Joyce needed to deconstruct the language itself. His challenge in writing *Finnegans Wake* consisted in communicating in language the deconstruction of language. Joyce's strategy in making the language of *Finnegans Wake* conform to its thematic and structural manifestations of a decentered universe, can be discussed in terms of two major techniques: the first might be called "imitative form," the second, "bricolage," borrowing a term from anthropologist Claude Lévi-Strauss, but adapting it here for a specific purpose.

III

Finnegans Wake includes those imitative techniques so successfully employed in *Ulysses*: the imitation of printed formats as in "Aeolus" and the "Triv and Quad" chapter (II.2), the imitations of sounds in "Sirens" and "Anna Livia Plurabelle" (I.8), the imitation of pedagogical modes as in the catechism of "Ithaca" and the quiz show of I.6. But the *Wake* language far surpasses the experiments of *Ulysses* as a type of verbal simulation. The stylistic incorporation of the novel's themes depends on the most fundamental correspondence between social and linguistic structures. The law of man and the law of language are homologous systems because they share an identical unconscious structure. The father's symbolic function as figure of the law is therefore analogous to the semantic function of language, which assigns to lexical items their meanings and their grammatical functions. The primordial law of the father, the incest taboo and the kinship regulations, function like those laws of phonological combination which permit certain sounds to be combined only in certain ways in the formation of words, and those laws of syntax which regulate the relationships of words in the formation of the sentence.[12] That the theme of the fallen father, the fallen God, has linguistic repercussions is suggested in the *Wake* itself:

"Gwds with gurs are gttrdmmrng. Hlls vlls. The timid hearts of words all exeomnosunt" (258.1). The vowels are here the "timid hearts of words" which flee with the defeated gods; the words can no longer be spoken, like many of the words in the *Wake*, and their meaning becomes dislocated, uncertain. The familial-linguistic correspondence is also revealed in the passage which describes the shooting of the Russian general, a type of parricide: *"The abnihilisation of the etym by the grisning of the grosning of the grinder of the grunder of the first lord of Hurtreford expolodotonates through Parsuralia with an ivanmorinthor-rorumble fragoromboassity amidwhiches general uttermosts confussion are perceivable moletons skaping with mulicules"* (353.22). The "etym," or word, is also "etymon," which, as the primary word from which a derivative is formed, corresponds to father. Although the construction of the phrase, "abnihilisation of the etym," is essentially ambiguous—it is not clear whether "etym" is the subject or object of the action implied in abnihilisation, or creation out of nothing—the implication is that in either case, the fall of the father creates first of all noise, an "ivanmorin-thorrorumble fragoromboassity." The equation of word and void occurs also in a parody of St. John's gospel prologue in II.2: "In the buginning is the woid, in the muddle is the sounddance and thereinofter you're in the unbewised again" (378.29). If the father signifies the semantic func-tion of language, the act of giving names to things or assigning meanings to words, then the fall of the father in *Finnegans Wake* signifies that severing of words from their referents which creates a linguistic free-play, a "sounddance," or "variously inflected, differently pronounced, otherwise spelled, changeably meaning vocable scriptsigns" (118.26), and therefore one is clearly in the "unbewised," the unproven, (German, *Beweis*), the uncertain, again. Hugh Kenner, after quoting a sentence from the *Wake*, remarks:

> It is worse than useless to push this toward one or the other of the meanings between which it hangs; to paraphrase it, for instance, in terms of porter being uncorked and poured. It is equally misleading to scan early drafts for the author's intentions, on the assumption that a "meaning" got buried by elaboration. Joyce worked seventeen years to push the work away from "meaning," adrift into language; nothing is to be gained by trying to push it back.[13]

If the ultimate meaningful word is the theological Logos, the Word of John's prologue, then its antithesis might be Stephen's recurrent notion in *Ulysses*: "God: noise in the street" (*Ulysses*, 186). The fall of the father, which marks the disjunction of word from meaning, results in noise, as the *Wake* passage cited earlier seemed to suggest. The *Wake* repeats Stephen's concept of God as a noise in the street, and amplifies it to thematic proportions. At the end of II.1, a litany is addressed to "Loud, hear us! / Loud, graciously hear us!" (258.25). The substitution of "Loud" for "Lord" is, of course, consistent with the Wakean proposition that the voice of God, the voice of the father (see the end of the tale of the Prankquean and the children's games) is the sound of thunder, and that the thunder announces the father's fall (cf. 3.15). Other associations of the father's fall with noise include reference to the tower of Babel: the fallen giant MacCool, marking with his body the geography of Dublin, is described as an "overgrown babeling" (6.31), a fallen tower of Babel or babbling baby. Both babble, the first speech of the infant man, and thunder, the first word of God to postlapsarian man, represent sound without meaning or signification.

The events of *Finnegans Wake* are steeped in noise, the crash of falling towers, bridges, men, Wall Street, civilizations; the clamor of countless battles; the boisterous happenings in Earwicker's pub; the angry invectives of quarreling antagonists. As someone says in the midst of the drunken shouting and raucous merrymaking at Finn MacCool's wake: "E'erawhere in this whorl would ye hear sich a din again?" (6.24). Furthermore, the gossip, rumor and slander discussed in the previous section illustrate an archaic definition of the word "noise" as "common talk, rumor, evil report or scandal"—a definition which still survives in the dual meaning of the word "report." In its perfect fusion of noise and rumor, *Finnegans Wake* resembles nothing so much as Chaucer's *The House of Fame*.

The noise which characterizes the thematic events of *Finnegans Wake* is expressed stylistically by a number of technical devices. There are many "voices" in the *Wake*—numerous utterances by the various figures, frequently unidentified, and often seeming to occur all at once, like many people shouting and clamoring simultaneously: "Mulo Mulelo! Homo Humilo! Dauncy a deady O! Dood dood dood! O Bawse! O Boese! O Muerther! O Mord!...Malawunga! Ser Oh Ser! See ah See! Hamovs! Hemoves! Mamor!" (499.5). In addition, any given utterance can be considered to contain a number of voices, as Clive Hart notes: "In theory, highly controlled choral speaking by a small group would be the only satisfactory solution to the problem of how to read *Finnegans Wake* aloud, each speaker adhering to one 'voice' of the counterpoint and using the appropriate accent and stress."[14] Stylistically, however, the *Wake* not only simulates the sound of "noise," as in the onomatopoetic thunder, but the concept of noise as an obstruction to the understanding of a message, as well. As a principle of information-theory, noise is any interference in the transmission of information: "whatever medium is used for the purpose of transmitting information, it will be subject to various unpredictable physical disturbances, which will obliterate or distort part of the message and thus lead to the loss of information. If the system were free of redundancy, the information lost would be irrecoverable."[15] If we grant that little information is transmitted to the reader of *Finnegans Wake* without either the interference generated by the labyrinthian progress of the narrative, or by the interference inherent in the linguistic distortions, another rationale for the work's length and extraordinary redundancy becomes apparent. Joyce clearly followed a sound principle of information theory in *Finnegans Wake*: a work with an unprecedented amount of "interference" requires an unprecedented amount of seemingly gratuitous repetition in compensation.

In regard to interference with a message, noise in *Finnegans Wake* is therefore not only something imaginatively "heard"—it can also be physically seen in the individual word on the page which is intentionally "misprinted" or "misspelled" and therefore no longer a part of the lexicon. The "meaning" of words depends on the existence of a language code, whose communal recognition and acceptance makes discourse in a society possible. The use of words which are not strictly part of that code, however much they resemble it, erects a barrier to the understanding of their "meanings," since it obscures their referents, the concepts they signify. The portmanteau word, one of the major lexical items in the work, is by definition a word that contains several meanings of which none can be assigned priority as a predominant or "true" referent.

Finnegans Wake is itself a symbolic act of parricide. The theme of the fallen father is stylistically incorporated into the anarchistic language of the work. In the familial configuration of the Wake, the fall of the father is co-existent with the violation of the incest taboo, creating the freeplay of family relationships that violates the orders, hierarchies, and combinations which govern kinship. If the stylistic imitation of the theme of the fallen father is expressed in the principle of "noise" in the work, in the dislocation and fragmentation of semantic units and their meanings, then the corresponding stylistic expression of incest calls for phonological and syntactical deviations from the norm of standard English.

The combinations of sounds which make up English words are governed by discernable laws. While these rules of permissible phonological combinations must account for all the actual words in the English lexicon, they also encompass words which are not, in fact, actualized in the language, but could be without violating these rules, for example, "dar," "fot," "sut." John Lyons notes the interesting applications of these "potential" words:

> Many of the non-occurrent combinations of phonemes would be accepted by native speakers as more 'normal' than others; they are, not only easily pronounceable, but in some way similar in form to other words of the language. . . . It is noticeable, for instance, and it has often been pointed out, that writers of nonsense verse (like Lewis Carroll or Edward Lear) will create 'words' which almost invariably conform to the phonological structure of actual words in the language; and the same is true of brand-names invented for manufactured products.[16]

The bulk of Joyce's nonsense words in the *Wake* consist of this potentially permissible type: for example, "escupement" (151.19), "wensum" (200.19), "foncey" (227.16), "hunnerable" (325.27), "flosting" (501.33), "ludubility" (607.3), "marracks" (15.36), and so on. Joyce, also, however, uses numerous words in *Finnegans Wake* whose phonemic order is clearly irregular in English, although perhaps not in other languages: for example "poingt" (50.2), "tuvavnr" (54.15), "dgiaour" (68.18), "stlongfella" (82.13), "trwth" (132.5), "dzoupgan" (199.18), "tsifengtse" (299.26), "remoltked" (333.13), "pszozlers" (415.14), "grianblachk" (503.23).

Besides taking liberties with the combinations of sound in words, Joyce also plays with the ways in which words combine to form sentences. Although the syntax of *Finnegans Wake* is predominantly regular, we can demonstrate with just a few simple examples the type of syntactic irregularities that do occur in the *Wake*:

> "Say it with missiles then and thus arabesque the page"
> (115.3) (noun in verbal position)
> "and show the widest federal in my cup"
> (443.13) (adjective in nominal position)
> "Lisp it slancy and crisp it quiet"
> (206.24) (adjective or noun in verbal position) [17]

Joyce once wrote of *Finnegans Wake*: "What the language will look like when I have finished, I don't know. But having declared war I shall go on *jusqu' au bout*."[18] If Joyce violates the laws of language, he does no more than to adapt the language to a vision in which law has been supplanted by play—a linguistic freeplay which is the fertile ground for new semantic and syntactic forms, for a thoroughgoing linguistic originality.

IV

Although *Finnegans Wake* is thoroughly original—even the most casual reader of the *Wake* would recognize any given passages as belonging to it—it may also be the most self-consciously unoriginal work in the language. In its distorted, fragmented language are lodged all of Joyce's immense, but thoroughly familiar preoccupations: the Dublin of his youth, familial relationships, sexual obsessions, bits of military and political history, allusions to a multitude of literary works, sacred books, arcane writing, old myths, fables, fairy tales, children's games, songs, riddles, and great quantities of talk. Joyce's incorporated literary forms are in some respects no newer than his matter; Shem himself provides an amusing catalogue of them in I.7: "twisted quills, painful digests, magnifying wineglasses, solid objects cast at goblins, once current puns, quashed quotatoes, messes of mottage, unquestionable issue papers, seedy ejaculations, limerick damns, crocodile tears, spilt ink, blasphematory spits, stale shestnuts...." (183.20). As Ellmann aptly describes *Finnegans Wake*, "It was a wholly new book based upon the premise that there is nothing new under the sun."[19] This paradox is clearly the crux of the philosophical problem which Joyce set out to solve technically in *Finnegans Wake*. Hart and Atherton attribute Joyce's artistic dependence on the inherited matter of the cultural and personal past to a sense of religious prohibition, a guilt which Joyce associated with the creative process: "Joyce was always an arranger rather than a creator, for, like a medieval artist, he seems superstitiously to have feared the presumption of human attempts at creation. The mediaeval notion that the artist may organise but cannot under any circumstances create something really new is, of course, capable of universal application but it is more than usually relevant to Joyce."[20] Hart and Atherton, however, appear to minimize grossly the extent to which this paradox of artistic creation is at issue in Joyce's work, as well as in that of contemporary writers.[21] Current work in comparative mythology had created an awareness that all literature is finally the plunder of language and of other literatures —the *Wake* at least straightforwardly so, as Joyce plumbs old and new myths, rummages through a vast assortment of books, including his own, and writes down snatches of conversations which find their way into the work.

However individual the experience of the artist, once committed to language that experience is given over to "otherness," since language is never a private property. In fact, that to which language belongs has been described by psychoanalyst-philosopher Jacques Lacan as "the Other," which may be rudimentarily defined as "a treasury of words (or better signifiers) from which the subject must borrow when he speaks."[22] Joyce grandly acknowledges the debt, calling *Finnegans Wake* an "epical forged cheque" (181.16), and "the last word in stolentelling" (424.35).

By admitting his debt to language and literature, and therefore to the intellectual and cultural traditions which they embody, Joyce betrays a conscious recognition of the fact that he cannot do without that which he seeks to oppose. This, of course, is the dilemma of critical languages, of the destructive discourses of the twentieth century which are engaged in the destruction of the history of metaphysics, according to Derrida: "We have no language—no syntax and no lexicon—which is alien to this history; we cannot utter a single destructive proposition which has not already slipped into the form, the logic, and the implicit postulations of precisely what it seeks to contest."[23] In declaring war on language, Joyce must use language—not "new" or hybrid language like Esperanto and Volapuk. The language of *Finnegans Wake* is still finally the English language, albeit "jinglish janglage" (275.f.6).

To confront this dilemma, Joyce resorts to a technical method which critics have already identified in their comparisons of *Finnegans Wake* to the "objet trouvé" collage: "Bits and pieces are picked up and incorporated into the texture with little modification, while the precise nature of each individual fragment is not always of great importance."[24] Borrowing a term which Lévi-Strauss applies to mythical thought and mythological activity in *The Savage Mind*, this practice of using bits and pieces of heterogeneous materials without regard to their specific function, may be called "bricolage." Joyce once asked his Aunt Josephine to send "any news you like, programmes, pawntickets, press cuttings, handbills. I like reading them";[25] he is like Lévi-Strauss' "bricoleur," collecting and saving things "on the principle that 'they may always come in handy.'"[26] That Joyce's method certainly approximated that of the bricoleur is most evident in his voluminous working notebooks for the *Wake*, crammed as these are with list upon list of apparently unrelated words, phrases, snatches of thought, bits of data.[27]

More important than Joyce's writing practice, however, is the way in which this method of bricolage allows Joyce to liberate materials from their old contexts, to juxtapose them freely and allow them to enter into new and unexpected combinations with each other. Lévi-Strauss writes of the bricoleur: "Now, the characteristic feature of mythical thought, as of 'bricolage' on the practical plane, is that it builds up structured sets, not directly with other structured sets but by using the remains and debris of events: in French 'des bribes et des morceaux,' or odds and ends in English, fossilized evidence of the history of an individual or a society."[28] An understanding of Joyce's use of the battle of Waterloo will be little improved by checking up on the facts in a history book. Such a historical account itself would only be the debris of the event, a bit of rubbish in Kate's museum, the tale of an old charwoman in which the words left over from the event (Waterloo as the site of urinating girls as well as the battle) are more important than any concept of the great battle's influence on the course of history. The Crash of Wall Street reminds Joyce of Humpty Dumpty's fall from another wall, and all that remains of the subsequent Great Depression is the imprint of the fallen giant's body on the topography of Dublin. For Joyce, all of Western civilization is finally reducible to a great rubbish heap of words, with bits of wornout concepts still adhering to them, bound together in clichéd and stratified relationships: "jetsam litterage of convolvuli of times lost or strayed, of lands derelict and of tongues laggin too" (292.15). By taking as his elements the disparate odds and ends of this debris of words, fragmenting them further when necessary, and putting them together again, not with an eye to their old functions, but as they appear useful for the purpose of the moment, Joyce infuses them with new vitality, lets them sparkle in the setting of wholly unexpected contexts and associations. William Carlos Williams wrote of Joyce's style in *Work in Progress*: "If to achieve truth we work with words purely, as a writer must, and all the words are dead or beautiful, how then shall we succeed any better than might a philosopher with dead abstractions or their configurations? . . . There must be something new done with words. Leave beauty out, or conceivably, one might break them up to let the staleness out of them as Joyce, I think, has done."[29]

Joyce's method in creating the *Wake* is exemplified by the ALP-hen, gathering spoiled goods into her nabsack, distributing them not according to design but as they come to hand, enriching and restoring them by new contexts and novel functions. The bricoleur does not begin, like the engineer, with a fully conceived project, a detailed model whose actualization depends on the procurement of tools and materials precisely designed for the purposes of the project. The bricoleur uses whatever is at hand for his tools and materials, and the result of his labors will never conform exactly to his original aim, which is sketchy at best.[30] As a result the project of the bricoleur proceeds like an organic growth; Joyce often spoke of *Finnegans Wake* as though it had an independent life of its own, as though it achieved its form without his direction or intervention.[31] Perhaps the difference between Joyce's method in *Portrait* and in *Finnegans Wake* can be described by the different meanings which the important word "forge" holds for each work: in *Portrait*, Joyce fashions and tempers his elements into an impeccably designed artifact; in the *Wake* he used essentially devious means, compared with those of the artisan, to create an impressively original design, which on closer inspection consists of unaltered and familiar pieces of junk, borrowed or stolen from the smithies of countless others: "The prouts who will invent a writing there ultimately is the poeta, still more learned, who discovered the raiding there originally. That's the point of eschatology our book of kills reaches for now in soandso many counterpoint words. What can't be coded can be decorded if an ear aye sieze what no eye ere grieved for" (482.31). Like the *Book of Kells*, which weaves an imaginative graphic text from the pre-text of the Gospels, *Finnegans Wake* is woven from a multitude of earlier literatures. Implied in this process is a plunder, "the raiding there originally." The poet, like the Egyptian god Thoth, must invent a writing, but by discovering that all literature is a plunder of language and of previous literatures. Centuries of such plunder result in stale repetition, from which the artist can escape only by a mode of literary violence. *Finnegans Wake* is therefore a "book of kills"; it goes beyond the plunder of language to destroy it, in order that we may see how it is created. Joyce breaks language down toward its origin, then re-appropriates it originally, at the level of phonemic play. By deconstructing the language and literary traditions, the artist starts again at the beginning, by discovering a "reading" there originally, in the full sense of the German word "lese": both a reading and a gathering, a putting one thing with another as it comes to hand, like the child who first learns to read: "We are once amore as babes awondering in a wold made fresh where with the hen in the storyaboot we start from scratch" (336.16).

By writing *Finnegans Wake* as he did, Joyce attests to the impossibility of metalanguage, that is, the failure of making a critique in language of the epistemology embedded in language. To some extent this paradox applies to talking or writing about the *Wake* as well: our standard, conventional language is ill-suited to describing the work, to saying anything meaningful about it. I believe that Joyce recognized the problems inherent in *Wake* criticism, and that as a result he planned critical studies as a kind of sequel to the work. The evidence which points to this is the title of *Our Exagmination Round His Factification for Incamination of Work in Progress*; the inclusion of a bogus letter written by himself under the name Vladimir Dixon, which imitates the cross-identification of characters in the *Wake*; the designation of *Our Exagmination* as O, and another projected collection of essays as X, echoing the notations with which he designated the title and figures of *Finnegans Wake*; the correspondence of the twelve essays in *Our Exagmination* with the twelve customers in Earwicker's pub, the twelve apostles, and so on, and the correspondence of the projected work of four essays with the four evangelists, historians, commentators in *Finnegans Wake*. It seems as though Joyce thought of critical studies of the *Wake* as simply more commentaries on ALP's letter, further investigations into the "true facts" of the Phoenix Park incident—the continuation in the real world of the spiral of futile interpretations which is *Finnegans Wake*.

Notes

1. Samuel Beckett, W. C. Williams and others, *Our Exagmination Round His Factification for Incamination of Work in Progress* (Paris: Shakespeare and Co., 1929). This small volume, written under Joyce's supervision and with his explicit approval, is still perhaps the most radical critique of the work available.

2. See Clive Hart's plan of *Finnegans Wake* as based on the scheme of *Ulysses* in *Structure and Motif in Finnegans Wake* (Evanston: Northwestern University Press, 1962), p. 17 and Chapter 3. Hart proposes that *Finnegans Wake* is structured in terms of three layers of dream: the first comprises the literal narrative of HCE's Dublin existence; the second, HCE's dream of Shaun (Book III); the third, HCE's dream about Shaun's dream about HCE and ALP in III.4. Additional interpolations in the literal narrative include most of Book I, which is viewed as stories told by the drunken customers, and II.4, the Tristan myth, which is designated as a transitional hallucination of HCE's half-dreaming, half-waking state at the end of II.3. This leaves only parts of Book II, the short segment of Book IV, and parts of Book I to support the literal narrative of the work.

3. Hart, p. 72.

4. See Edmund Wilson, *Axel's Castle* (New York: Charles Scribner's Sons, 1959), pp. 34–35; also William Y. Tindall, *A Reader's Guide to Finnegans Wake* (New York: Farrar, Straus and Giroux, 1969), p. 13; and Hart, p. 31.

5. Beckett, *Our Exagmination*, p. 16.

6. Jacques Derrida, "Structure, Sign, and Play in the Discourse of the Human Sciences," in *The Languages of Criticism and the Sciences of Man: The Structuralist Controversy*, ed. Richard Macksey and Eugenio Donato (Baltimore: Johns Hopkins Press, 1970), p. 249.

7. T. E. Hulme, *Speculations*, ed. Herbert Read (New York: Harcourt, Brace and Co., 1924), p. 117.

8. Derrida, p. 249.

9. Derrida, p. 260.

10. Tindall, p. 15.

11. Derrida, p. 252.

12. For a fuller discussion of the concept of the familial-linguistic correspondence see Jacques Lacan, "The Function of Language in Psychoanalysis" in *The Language of the Self*, tr. Anthony Wilden (Baltimore: Johns Hopkins Press, 1968), pp. 39–47. Lacan notes, "This law, therefore (the incest prohibition), is revealed clearly enough as identical to an order of Language. For without kinship nominations, no power is capable of instituting the order of preferences and taboos which bind and weave the yarn of lineage down through succeeding generations."

13. Hugh Kenner, *Dublin's Joyce* (Boston: Beacon Press, 1956), p. 304.

14. Hart, p. 36.

15. John Lyons, *Introduction to Theoretical Linguistics* (Cambridge: University Press, 1969), p. 88.

16. Lyons, p. 120.

17. Structural grammars, of course, do distinguish parts of speech and their "normal" sentence positions, and point out that several parts of speech may occupy a given sentence position. The *Wake* examples cited are not permissible, however, particularly since the verbal position is restricted to verbs and auxiliaries.

18. *Letters of James Joyce*, Vol. 1, ed. Stuart Gilbert (New York: Viking Press, 1957), 237. Letter addressed to Harriet Shaw Weaver dated November 11, 1925.

19. Richard Ellmann, *James Joyce* (New York: Oxford University Press, 1959), p. 558.

20. Hart, p. 44.

21. William Carlos Williams in *Spring and All* describes the frustration of the artist who imaginatively annihilates the universe to create it anew, only to discover that "EVOLUTION HAS REPEATED ITSELF FROM THE BEGINNING. . . . In fact now, for the first time, everything IS new. . . . The terms 'veracity,' 'actuality,' 'real,' 'natural,' 'sincere' are being discussed at length, every word in the discussion being evolved from an identical discussion which took place the day before yesterday" (*Imaginations*, ed. Webster Schott [New York: New Directions, 1970], p. 93).

22. Stuart Schneiderman, "Afloat with Jacques Lacan," *Diacritics*, 1 (Winter, 1971) 28.

23. Derrida, p. 250.

24. Hart, p. 35.

25. *Letters*, I, 194. Letter to Mrs. William Murray dated November 10, 1922.

26. Claude Lévi-Strauss, *The Savage Mind* (Chicago: University of Chicago Press, 1969), p. 18.

27. David Hayman has noted that late in his work on the *Wake*, Joyce wrote a draft for the introduction of II.2, working directly from the notes in his workbook: "Returning to his Scribblehehobble notebook he began to write an introduction for 'The Muddest Thick,' drawing systematically upon each of the first fourteen pages

of his notes, revising only slightly but adding heavily from the notes as he went. Of the 266 words in the completed first draft, approximately 132 can be traced directly to the notes" ("'Scribbledehobbles' and How They Grew: A Turning Point in the Development of a Chapter," in *Twelve and a Tilly*, ed. Jack P. Dalton and Clive Hart [Evanston: Northwestern University Press, 1965], p. 110).

28. Lévi-Strauss, p. 21.

29. "William Carlos Williams on Joyce's Style" in *James Joyce: The Critical Heritage*, ed. Robert Deming (New York: Barnes and Noble, 1970), I, 377.

30. Lévi-Strauss, p. 21.

31. *Letters*, I, 204. Letter to Harriet Shaw Weaver dated October 9, 1923: "I work as much as I can because these are not fragments but active elements and when they are more and a little older they will begin to fuse of themselves."

Nightletters: Woman's Writing in the *Wake*

Shari Benstock*

This essay circumscribes the "feminine position" of *Finnegans Wake*. It is an attempt to place woman at the scene of *Wake* writing, a participant in what has traditionally been seen as a male enterprise. To follow the trajectory of *Finnegans Wake* letters—in their functions as alphabetic symbols and as epistolary communications—is to discover a pattern of relationships between scripture and storytelling, between writing and dreaming.[1] Such a process focuses on two sets of critical assumptions that have, until very recently, structured our response to the *Wake*: that spoken language is privileged ("every telling has a taling"—213.12)[2] in the rendering of a dream ("his dream monologue"—474.4)[3] whose meanings become available only through a process of linguistic *scripture* ("wipe your glosses with what you know"—304, fn. 3).[4] In an effort to displace these assumptions, this study isolates certain textual displacements in *Finnegans Wake*—first, of written communications that shuttle between a variety of writers and readers (ALP, HCE, Shem, Shaun, and Issy); next of alphabetic symbols (SP / pp) that juxtapose and duplicate each other; finally, of women, whose place in the text is defined by the movement of its letters.

THE SCENE OF THE WRITING

The lessons chapter of *Finnegans Wake* (10) describes the general condition under which letters are composed and relayed from writer to reader:

*This essay was written specifically for this volume and is published here for the first time by permission of the author.

All the world's in want and is writing a letters.[5] A letters from a person to a place about a thing. And all the world's on wish to be carrying a letters. A letter to a king about a treasure from a cat.[6] When men want to write a letters. Ten men, ton men, pen men, pun men, wont to rise a ladder. . . . Is then any lettersday from many peoples. . . ? A posy cord. Plece.

----

[5]To be slipped on, to be slept by, to be conned to, to be kept up. And when you're done push the chain.
    [6]With her modesties office. (278.13–20)

This analysis suggests that the need to write letters is generalized, that letters themselves share certain properties ("a letters from a person to a place about a thing"), and that, in particular, the letters here are to a "king about a treasure from a cat." The king designates Earwicker whose occupation (as Tim Finnegan) is "to rise a ladder," that is, to write a letter. "Pen men" and "pun men" embody the elements of the writing trade (pens and puns), suggesting that writing is a male task. The footnotes, written by Issy, constitute a "lady's postscript" (42.9), a marginal commentary on the primary text as well as a parallel text to the story the chapter tells.[5] These notes delineate the connections between letters and desire, between psychoanalysis and dreams: the letters are "slipped on" (as in Freudian "slips"), "slept by" (the impetus to dream), they serve as blackmail weapons ("to be conned to") as well as phallic symbols ("to be kept up"). The link between writing and defecation, the use of body excrement as ink, is apparent in Shem's ability to make "encostive inkum out of the last of his lavings" (27.9–10), but is suggested here in the pushing of the "chain" that will start the letter on its way through the postal (sewage) system. This particular letter—to a king from a cat—is from Issy (the cat) to her father (his majesty, who is here her literary "subject") about a treasure (probably her "pussy"), the object of his desire that initiates the letterwriting, that makes letters jump back and forth across the abyss of repressed desire. As a writer, she occupies a "modesties office" (that is also a "majesty's service," which includes the postal system that delivers the letters' "treasure"), but one that is potentially threatening to the majesty's authority: through the letter, through the action of desire, she can reverse his "rise" on the ladder, undermine that (sexual) power of his authority. She utilizes a "posy cord," a postcard.[6]

The right of authorship is the rite of authority; it is writing. While the major threat to the king's authority would seem to be from his sons, who wish to dispossess him of his control over language, in fact the most imminent menace is from the daughter, who has knowledge of his sin, whose letter can serve as witness against him. As Issy learns to write letters (following the model set forth by her mother's letters) she retraces the father's sin, remembers an act in which she was a complicit witness; her writing is the return of the repressed, it is the "trace" of desire. The sin is incest, the desire to make a contract with the object of desire, to bridge the gap between Self and Other. In *Finnegans Wake* this desire runs a doubled route—between father and daughter, between daughter and father. Earwicker plays out the multiple occasions of his desire through the dream; Issy plays out the multiple possibilities of her desire while seated at the mirror, writing to her "double," her mirror image, through whom she translates the manifestations of desire. Issy's writing exists in this space split by the mirror.

The lessons chapter presents examples of the Earwicker children learning to write letters, scripting them from a copybook model that bears many resemblances to Anna Livia's letter as it appears toward the close of the *Wake*. "Dear and he went on to scripple gentlemine born, milady bread. . . . And how are you, waggy?" (301.10–15) begins Shaun's effort, a close match for his mother's ("Dear. And we go on to Dirtdump"—615.2) and his sister's:

> Dear (name of desired subject, A.N.), well, and I go on to. Shlicksher.
> I and we (tender condolences for happy funeral, one if) so sorry to
> (mention person suppressed for the moment, F. M.). Well (enquiries
> after allhealths) how are you (question maggy). A lovely (introduce
> to domestic circles) pershan of cates. Shrubsher. Those pothooks mostly
> she hawks from Poppa Vere Foster but these curly mequeues are of
> Mippa's moulding. Shrubsheruthr. (Wave gently in the ere turning
> ptover). Well, mabby (consolation of shopes) to soon air. With best
> from cinder Christinette if prints chumming, can be when desires
> Soldi, for asamples, backfronted or, if all, peethrolio or Get my Prize,
> using her flower or perfume or, if veryveryvery chumming, in other-
> wards, who she supposed adeal, kississts my exits. Shlicksheruthr. From
> Auburn chenlemagne. (280.9–28)

At one level this letter is the kind of chatty, informal "introduction to domestic circles" that the young Issy writes under the guidance (under the dictation) of her mother, who provides the homemaker model, one of whose duties is to establish correspondence, to write letters—of condolence, congratulation, acknowledgement, appreciation, etc. Indeed, it is the mother (as A.N., Nourse Asa, a type of Anna Livia, from whom Issy admits to having "learned all the runes of the gamest game ever"—279, fn. 1) who is addressed by the letter. And it is the mother who signs (under the name of "Auburn chenlemagne. *P*ious and *p*ure *f*air one" —280.27–28) the letter, this missive duplicating and enclosing aspects of Anna Livia as mother, daughter, lover, mistress, sister under its salutation and signature.[7]

But the letter also incorporates various elements of Issy's seductive nature, exploiting a provocative vocabulary that reveals—without specifically addressing (that is, naming)—the object of desire: F.M., Father Michael, the parish priest (pp), who serves both as a representative of

God the Father (and therefore is a figure of Earwicker) and in the place of Brother Mick (Shaun, who plays at various times the roles of priest, postman and policeman—a representative of the law, a figure of authority), the "prints chumming" for whom Christinette "can be when desires Soldi" (that is, exchanged, sold as the double). Issy's letter follows an extended footnote (p. 279) that usurps the scripted narrative and explores the same conflation of the old / young lovers (here Mark of Cornwall and Tristram) as Issy doubles as Isolde, writing an erotic letter to her teacher: "The good fother with the twingling in his eye will always have cakes in his pocket to bethroat us with for our allmichael good." The doubled object of desire ("fother / allmichael") is counterbalanced by the divided Issy, present as the Maggies (of the rhyme in which the brothers play Mick and Nick and of the park scene where the two young girls tempt Earwicker) and as Christine Beauchamp whose schizophrenia split her into Chris and her letterwriting opposite, Sally. The division of Self and Other is evident in Issy's letter in the double entendres of its language ("kissists my exits") which suggest that Issy's Other knows a great deal about the "desired subject" and "suppressed" object, apparent even in the grammatical distinctions between the first and second persons of the writing ("I" and "you") and in the separate, third-person description of the writers' actions, actions that duplicate the sexual stimulus implicit in her linguistic gestures: "Shlicksher. . . . Shrusbsher. . . . Shlicksheruthr." This descriptive voice mimics Issy's lisp, the clue to her presence in various *Wake* texts in a "little language" of seduction that doubles consonants to divide her into "pepette" (pp), the counterpart of her twin brothers, the penman and postman.[8]

In an effort to discover the basis of this double female, the *Wake* traces Issy's psychic and sexual development through writing to preverbal states, following a path through the dream to the cradle. Issy's practice letter is linked to this dream pathway, littered with letters: her model letter to A.N. is introduced by a dream sequence that suggests she can write the scene her father hopes she cannot remember: "A scene at sight. Or dreamoneire. Which they shall memorise. By her freewritten Hopely for ear that annalykeses if scares for eye that sumns. Is it in the now woodwordings . . . then will singingsing tomorrows gone and yesters outcome?" (280.1–7). The letters of the *Wake* form a *traumscrapt*, a transcript of a dream. Issy's letters are particularly important in solving the central mystery of the dream, in recovering the ambiguous origins of the story, because they suggest in the "woodwordings" her presence in the park, her complicity in the primal scene. She writes, then, from knowledge, but a knowledge that is recovered "for eye that sumns" *as* she writes: "All schwants (schwrites) ischt tell the cock's trootabout him. . . . He had to see life foully the plak and the smut, (schwrites). . . . Yours very truthful. Add dapple inn" (113.11–18). This letter of accusation is written in Issy's language but signed under her mother's initials, making it appear that Anna Livia has somehow authorized this account, that perhaps it was written under her dictation. Anna Livia, however, seeks to exonerate Earwicker, to protect the "Reverend" by obliterating—wiping the written slate clean of—indiscretions that might incriminate him: "the mother of the book with a dustwhisk tabularasing his obliteration done upon her involucrum" (50.11–13). The attempted cover-up is always an uncovering, a revelation to be feared both for Anna Livia and for Earwicker: "my deeply forfear revebereared, who is costing us mostfortunes which I am writing in mepetition" (492.27–28).

The daughter's desire to expose her father by disclosing his sin ("I'll be the mort of him"—460.22) is also her effort to recover an elusive piece of information about her own past, to read the transcript of her unconscious, to discover her presence in the father's dream. One part of her suspects an occurrence ("Something happened that time I was asleep, torn letters or was there snow?"—307, fn. 5), while another part of her knows the circumstances of its appearance: "Of course I know you are a viry vikid girl to go in the dreemplace and at that time of the draym and it was a very wrong thing to do, even under the dark flush of night, dare all grandpassia!" (527.5–8). What is it that the Other has witnessed in the father's dream? Could it be his incestuous longings for the daughter? Such a suspicion drives the writing act, involving both Self and Other in a search for language in which to tell (write) the story, a story whose origin may rest in the preverbal event of the daughter's observance of the father's erection: "The infant Isabella from her coign to do obeisance toward the duffgerent, as first futherer with drawn brand. Then the court to come in to full morning" (566.23–25). Self and Other try to bring unconscious events in consciousness through language; the Other (dream / mirror image) tries to tell the Self what she knows. It is through the mirror that these two counterparts find a means of communication.

—That letter selfpenned to one's other, that neverperfect everplanned?
—This nonday diary, this allnights newseryreel. (489.33–35)

The setting of nursery and bedroom, the acts of writing and dreaming, coincide as young Issy, seated at her mother's vanity table (and pretending to *be* her mother as she plays at grown-up with face creams and make-up), converses with her mirror image. This scene duplicates a dialogue begun in the cradle when Issy would "talk petnames with her little playfilly," the image of herself in the "shellback thimblecasket mirror" that showed "her dearest friendeen" (561.16–36)—that is, her own image. The passage exploits a purposeful ambiguity of spoken and written language, marking the intrusion of Issy into the series of riddles posed of Shaun by Shem. This question involves the desire for the absent lover: "What bitter's love but yurning, what' sour lovemutch but a bref burning till shee that drawes dothe smoake retourne?" (143.29–

30). The answer posits a dialogue between pepette (pette, pitounette, pipetta) and her mirror opposite, with whom she is jealously competitive, concerning the seduction of a man ("you lovely fellow of my dreams"—146.6) who is either Shem, Shaun, or the father ("old somebooby"). The mother is a third (and, like the men, absent) party to the scripting of this scene, referred to always in the third-person while the two doubles exist as "I" and "you." The "I" of this correspondence tries to extract information about sexual practices from the "you": "I thought ye knew all and more, ye aucthor, to explique to ones the significat of their exsystems with your nieu nivulon lead" (148.16–18). The mirror image is both author and actor ("Aucthor"), the one whose authority is needed to sustain the writing. The literary setting for this scene is taken from Swift's *Journal to Stella*, the psychological background from Morton Prince's case history of Christine Beauchamp in *The Dissociation of a Personality*. Both of these works describe clandestine writings between lovers / enemies who employ petnames and pseudonyms to hide identities and exchange roles as the writers and receivers of letters. The alliance of Self and Other in the writing act is a collaboration that breeds both narcissistic love and hate ("I hate the very thought of the thought of you and because, dearling, of course, adorest . . . when we do and contract with encho tencho solver when you are married to reading and writing"—146.18–22). The marriage of reading and writing is a contract whose authority is both broken and sustained by the process of reading and writing, an authority that is tested here as the mother's image is both recreated and resisted by the mirror doubles.

But to discover the complicated ways in which authority manifests itself in *Wake* documents, we must return to that unremembered scene in the nursery where the infant Isabella sees her father's erect penis. We are told she does "obeisance" to him and that his act (of erection) will result in the "court" (both as tribunal and as a method of seduction) "to come in to full morning" (566.23–25). The setting is the royal court in which Earwicker is the majesty to whom Issy is a subject, whose obedience and loyalty are demanded. Earwicker here both embodies the law and is exposed by it; the one who is in a position to expose him to the effects of the law is precisely the one who has been required to pay obeisance to his erect phallus—the daughter. Earwicker is caught in the double bind of his authoritarian role, simultaneously wanting to remain innocent of the knowledge of his power and to be apprised of it; he both represents censorship (which *is* the law) and applies that censorship to his own condition. Anna Livia, in desiring to clear her husband's name of any hint of guilt, acts as a censor as well, censoring ("tabularasing") her letter that is written to Earwicker and about him. Issy's letters, which also concern her father, demand a language of double entendre precisely because they are doubly censored: addressed to the mother (or her sister, Maggy), they concern the father (Majesty) and are signed by his wife (a signature that may well be a forgery, stolen from the mother by the daughter as she tries to usurp the mother's position in the family); these letters are then incorporated into the mother's letter to the father, their contents altered so that they respect *his* authority, do obeisance to *his* majesty, show respect for *his* name.

Thus, the relationship between the *Wake* dream and its letters exactly duplicates the relationship between the unconscious and the conscious, that is, between the unconscious and the law—the double bind of censorship inherent in all writing. The letters of the *Wake* are written to one censor (the ultimate censor, HCE) and conveyed through (the writing of) another censor (ALP). Their progress from writer to reader effectively blocks off the crucial events of the dream—of the letter—allowing the censor no access to that which he has censored. Moreover, the action of censorship (and the transference of censorship) is the action of love—Anna Livia loves her husband; she does not want (him) to know the ways in which he loves his daughter (her own youthful mirror image). It is love letters that the *Wake* censors and silences.

SUIVEZ LA PISTE

—Let us consider letters—how they come at breakfast, and at night, with their yellow stamps and their green stamps, immortalized by the postmark—for to see one's own envelope on another's table is to realize how soon deeds sever and become alien.[9]

The point about letters in the *Wake* is that they are feared to exist. Indeed, the nagging worry that a written document attesting to a crime may be circulated among citizenry, dug up by a prying gossip, published in the local newspaper, used as a blackmail device, to be appropriated, counterfeited, stolen, forged, or sent astray, accounts for Earwicker's troublesome dream of the events in Phoenix Park.[10] Whatever the content of such a letter (enclosed in "a quite everydaylooking stamped addressed envelope"—109.7–8), however it was written, to whomever it may be addressed, its threat lies in its suspected existence. Although the presumed recipient, Earwicker seems unaware that he is also the avowed subject of the letter. The effort to discover the identities of sender and receiver, to follow the route taken by the postal service that attempts to deliver the letter, generates the *Wake* action—action that can be read at another level as the plot of the dream.

Because the five family members subsume the multitude of characters present in the *Wake* world, the possible choices for writers and readers of the letter are limited, making its displacement through the postal system the pathway to incestuous desire. The letter is entrusted to Shaun the Post, who—as priest and policeman—is also the embodiment of canonical and common law, that is, the laws of censorship. These double roles catch him in a double bind: the need to deliver the letter

is countered by the desire to suppress it. To implement this law of repressed desire, he delivers the letter always into the wrong hands (which
are also the right hands), insuring that the letter is continually deflected
from its real destination—diverted, displaced, detoured. The letter's potential for "possibly-not-arriving" at the correct destination worries Earwicker, preventing him from knowing his own secret desire.[11] This condition is inherent in the postal system itself, a central component of His
Majesty's (Secret) Service: the diverted plot and scrambled discourse of
the *Wake* dream are the *effects* of the letter's non-arrival.

> No such parson. No such fender.
> No such lumber. No such race. (63.11–12)

As the letter is carried along the pathway to its destination, it meets
every possible form of resistance to delivery. Ultimately, the letter cannot be delivered, for reasons stamped on its envelope: "No such no.";
"None so strait"; "Overwayed. Understrumped"; "Too Let. To be Soiled";
"Vacant." The occupants of the various Dublin addresses tracked by the
postal system (addresses that once belonged to James Joyce) meet similar fates: "Noon sick parson"; "Exbelled from 1014 d."; "Dining with
the Danes"; "Arrusted"; "Drowned in the Laffey"; "Salved. All reddy
buried"; "Cohabited by Unfortunates." The letter follows a circuit that
either begins or should terminate at "29 Hardware Saint. . . . Baile-Atha-
Cliath," but even its message despairs of delivery: "Nave unlodgeable.
Loved noa's dress. Sinned, Jetty Pierrse." The letter has been opened by
"Miss Take," its address "Wrongly spilled," and has been sent "Back to
the P.O. Kaer of" (420.17–421.14). The signature, while nearly illegible,
admits responsibility for having "sinned" and "signed," while the name
suggests both Jerry (Shem) and HCE, among whose doubles is Persse
O'Reilly.

The postal system itself has certain claims on this letter. It has become the property of the post (and Shaun will claim authorship of it),
its final resting place to be the Dead Letter Office (the midden heap),
where its "penmarks used out in sinscript with such hesitancy by [the]
cerebrated brother" (421.18–19) will be pecked at by Biddy the hen.
Interrogated here by the girls from St. Bride's school (incarnations of
Issy), Shaun first denounces the letter as belonging to "Mr O'Shem the
Draper," who put his mother up to writing it ("She, the mammy far,
was put up to it by him"—421.35–36), for which Shem should be "de-
praved of his libertins to be silenced, sackclothed and suspended"
(421.36–422.1)

As his twin, Shaun claims credit for the letter ("Well it is partly
my own, isn't it?"—422.23), accusing his "celebrAted" brother of stealing
it from him ("Every dimmed letter in it is a copy. . . . The last word in
stolentelling!"—424.32,35). Angered by this thievery ("As he was rising
my lather"—424.36–425.1—that is, as he was writing my letter), Shaun

recognizes the hand of his brother in the letter's "hesitency," whose subject is "HeCitEncy," his excellency, HCE. The letter tells again the episode in the park which here conflates the sin of the father with the writing of the letter, as though "righting his name for him . . . after laying out his litterery bed" (422.34–35) were the equivalent of the sexual sin the letter describes. Claiming the authority of the letter for himself, Shaun disclaims his responsibilities as the postman ("innocent of disseminating the foul emanation"—425.10–11), claiming that under the law he "will commission to the flames any incendiarist whosoever . . . would endeavour to set ever annyma roner moother of mine on fire" (426.2–4). The letter is "incendiary" to the extent that it writes of consuming desire of the father for the daughter and here of the son (Shem) for the mother.

The *Wake* constructs its postal system of desire on the body of Anna Livia, the River Liffey, tracing its route from Sallygap to Dublin Bay. Along this canal the Viking invaders made their way into Ireland—up the vagina of Anna Livia. The sigla of this postal code include the letters of characters' names (HCE, ALP, S / S and p / p) as well as the mirror opposites (b / p; p / q). The letters are a sexual code as well—the doubled "p" marking the threat of the twin sons and the double identity of the daughter; the "S" and "p" marking the penis in its flaccid and erect forms; the "S" tracing the spiral cone of the vagina, the "commodius vicus of recirculation" (3.2) of the river. The letter / dream of desire starts and ends in the woman's body—in the River Liffey—the keys to which are given by Anna Livia through her "Lps." located at the mouth of the river, in the labia of the vaginal canal. Riding the river's wave, the letter rests in the "Gyre O" of the vagina and is buried in the midden heap, the "midden wedge of the stream's your muddy old triagonal delta" (297.23–24), a letter that was never mailed but is nonetheless constantly moving through the postal system, tracing the map of desire, in "appia lippia pluvaville."

THE SCENE OF THE READING

> Closer inspection of the *bordereau* would reveal a multiplicity of personalities inflicted on the documents. . . . In fact, under the closed eyes of the inspectors the traits featuring the *chiaroscuro* coalesce, their contrarieties eliminated, in one stable somebody. (107.23–30)

How do we go about reading *Wake* language then? Philippe Sollers suggests that "Joyce dreams of a book that will be inseparably dream and interpretation, ceaseless crossing of borders—precisely a *waking*."[12] But who can read its message? *Wake* writing poses its riddle of femininity in the woman's body; the secret of the *Wake* postal system rests with woman—a riddle whose secret remains unintelligible (that is, unreadable) to man. Interpretation of this text has often followed Shaun's failed attempt to read the "eternal geomater," a misconstruing or a misplacement of the parts; or, the reading method, like that of the autocrat of the breakfast table, has been an authoritarian effort at rewriting the text by obliterating parts of it, by puncturing it with a pronged instrument so that it can be "correctly understood to mean stop, please stop, do please stop" (124.4–5). When man has tried to read the riddle, he has stripped woman of her complexity, emptied her of significance. By privileging the "telling" of the *Wake*, the giving of priority to its spoken language, critics have silenced whole portions of *Wake* language in the denial of the link between woman and writing. The reader's effort is similar to Earwicker's: to possess knowledge (of his sin) by limiting that knowledge; to put a stop to the dissemination of the letter through the postal system; to deny desire and its effects; to censure the fear of castration that desire brings in its wake.

Anna Livia insures that Earwicker's secret is safe by hiding the letter in the one place he would not think to look, a place he knows *too* well, and one he assumes can only be filled by him, a place that marks the very failure of the postal system to read the writing of woman: her vagina. And here the letter remains—unreadable because never delivered—hidden from prying eyes in warm recesses of the midden heap. The document dug up on the midden by Belinda of the Dorans is Anna Livia's "untitled mamafesta memorialising the Mosthighest" (104.4), a tribute to HCE and a testimony that has, like its subject, "gone by many names at disjointed times" (104.5); the letter's message is another version of the Maggy / Majesty letter dictated to Shem by ALP and practiced by the children at their lessons. Residence on the midden has subjected the letter to a chemical / historical process of melting and merging, however, that has produced a mutation of its elements, developing a negative message from its positive, blurring the distinctions between sign and substance, inverting the intentions of its author. This second text, the negative of the original, presents a second incarnation of woman, a double concealment of woman effected first by the covering of the "everydaylooking stamped addressed envelope" and then by her "feminine cloithering" (109.31). In order to read the letter's message, the reader must first strip the woman and next penetrate her body; the envelope must be torn and the letter removed; the "nakedness [that] may happen to tuck itself under its flap" (109.11–12) must be revealed; that which is "inside" must be opened to the "outside." Such a process violates the hymeneal covering of the vagina where the letter is lodged, ruptures its protective layers, an infringement that—rather than rendering the clarity of the message—opens the letter to ambiguity, destroying the inviolate nature of its authority. The double language of the letter is doubly exposed, collapsing the distinction between "sin" and "sign." The double signatures of dream and letter become a single element in the waking / reading process that would recover them by violating them.

In the double hiding place of the letter—in the double invagination of the text that supports the tension between "sin" and "sign," between Self and Other, between mother and daughter, between brother and sister—the secret is safe and all the metaphors of duality, all the protective layers of language and clothing, are maintained.

Whose dream is this? To whom do the letters belong? The answers to these questions are both multiple and non-existent, they both circumscribe and extend the boundaries of authority. But if it is desire that makes the postal system of the *Wake* run, then it is desire—as invested in woman—that cannot be possessed. This elusive yet essential element exists outside the laws of authority or censorship, outside the bounds of language. Only its movements can be mapped, the trace of these movements the signature *of* desire. This double bind of being both within and beyond writing is precisely the condition of *Wake* writing, writing that has always been considered "mad," outside the bounds of literature. This writing is borne of woman, who writes even though she has no "member" for writing, even though she holds no membership in the writing community. The *Finnegans Wake* dream is inscribed by her and through her, is contained in her body, even as she remains outside the dream, beyond knowledge of its actions. This writing displaces desire while constantly repeating the *notion of* desire; this dream displaces the sexual crime while constantly repeating the notion of that crime.

The writing of *Finnegans Wake* both inhabits and is inhabited by woman, by ALP and Issy, who are present in the transparent space of the hymeneal folds, in the silences of the historically interweaved, overlapped, and spiralling story, who constitute the absent center of the *Wake* universe, who are to be found inside the mirror, in the bar between the conscious and the unconscious, between dreaming and waking, between signifier and signified—both inside and outside the fabric they weave. These two—who are one in desire—are capable of providing the origin of the text that exists outside the text, the frame for the dreamstory that is both ouside and within itself: they are the letter (of desire) that violates and is violated.

Notes

1. Portions of this essay are included in "The Letter of the Law: *La Carte Postale* in *Finnegans Wake*," *Philological Quarterly* 63 (Sp. 1984), 163–85). My current work on *Finnegans Wake* is heavily indebted to a reading of works by Jacques Derrida, particularly his examination of *Wake* alphabetic symbols included in the "Envois" of *La Carte Postale*.

2. All references to *Finnegans Wake* are to the Viking Press edition (New York, 1947), page and line numbers supplied parenthetically.

3. The priviliged spoken word of the *Wake* is examined by Philippie Sollers in "*Comme si le vieil Homère*," *Nouvel Observateur*, 6 February 1982, 73–74. But the notion that the *Wake* is somehow more available, more understandable, when

read aloud, that its language frequently empowers aural rather than visual techniques of wordplay, has been a long and commonly held assumption. Indeed, a standard method of teaching *Finnegans Wake* is to read it aloud, suggesting that what is *heard* in the *Wake* may be more evident, even more trustworthy, than what is *seen*. Skepticism about such a privileging of the spoken over the written word of the *Wake* is at the center of my investigation of its language.

4. Until very recently, *Finnegans Wake* scholarship has concentrated on close readings of the text, employing a method of linguistic detection that stripped away lexical ambiguities, rendering the *Wake* readable, essentially, in English. (Not surprisingly, this method has been best and longest practiced by American and English readers of Joyce's text.) Emphasis has been placed on accounting for the various languages present at the *Wake*, in examining the common properties of those languages, in breaking down allusions and puns, and in attempting to read a literal—that is, realistic—level of events in the *Wake* to decode its surface. Recent developments in European critical theory and, in particular, French response to *Finnegans Wake*, have replaced this emphasis on critical *stripture* with a more theoretical approach to linguistic and narrative structures in the *Wake* in an effort to preserve the play of language at all levels. It is precisely the kinds of transferences, exchanges, and correspondences available in the "play" of *Wake* language that interest me here, so that my reading of its movement attempts to preserve multiplicities rather than to render an unequivocal synopsis.

5. I discuss this phenomenon at length in "At the Margin of Discourse: Footnotes in the Fictional Text," *PMLA*, 98 (1983), 204–25. Overlooked by traditional *Wake* critical approaches, writing by women of the *Wake*—particularly Anna Livia and Issy—is viewed in this essay as constituting the *hymeneal* writing described by Derrida in "La loi du genre / The Law of Genre," *Glyph*, 7 (1980), 176–232.

6. The publication of Jacques Derrida's *La Carte Postale* (Paris: Flammarion, 1980) has drawn attention to the postcard as illustrating the principle on which the postal system of communication rests and as a sign of sexual desire that moves the card within the system. As a variously framed and contained example of a writing effect (of sexual desire), the postcard calls attention to the ways in which written language both extends and escapes its own boundaries.

7. The circular structure of *Finnegans Wake* encloses both the letterwriting (by ALP) and the letterreading (by HCE) incorporated in the "wake" and "awakening" that the story tells. The narrative dictated by ALP is both a loveletter and a deathletter, written to and about the subject whose love and death provide its plot. The letter is "the nightmail afarfrom morning nears" (565.32) that tells HCE "You were dreamend, dear" (568.18)—he was "dreamed" by and "dreaming" of his wife. Since the cycle of life and death, of dreaming and awakening, encloses both HCE and ALP, it is possible that the wife's testament—the *Wake*— is both written and read as the River Liffey makes its way toward death in the sea, in the "riverrun" of Anna Livia's own death in the arms of her father (628.1–4). It is death, for which sleep is an analogue, that initiates and moves the story; writing is the ghostly effect of this death-initiation, the effects of desire whose final destination is death. The relationship between writer and reader, between writer and dreamer, between death and dreaming, is at the center of the *Wake* writing cycle.

8. The important series of alphabetic doubles in *La Carte Postale* are: S (Socrates), P (Plato), and PP (postal principal / pleasure principle). These initials have their important counterparts in the *Wake* as well in Shem the Penman, Shaun the Postman, and in pepette (who frequently appears in the narrative under the designation "pp"). The "s" sounds of the *Wake* are associated with Issy's lisp, with the "slithering of snakes in the grass and the swish of temptresses' skirts. . . . The

pattern of 'p' and 'q' (found in the Pankquean's name) suggest the broken dictum of propriety brought about by the park incident, the urinary suggestion of 'pee' and the visual presence of mirror opposites (Issy and her double, the two temptresses in the park)." See Bernard Benstock, *Joyce-again's Wake* (Seattle: University of Washington Press, 1965), pp. 148–54. This combination of consonants is usually associated with the girls, but the presence of "p" in penman, postman (policeman, priest), and Phoenix Park suggest an alliance with the men of the *Wake* as well and, particularly, with the penis as the instrument of writing.

9. Quoted from Virginia Woolf, *Jacob's Room* (New York: Harcourt, Brace and World, 1923), p. 92.

10. The scratching of the dry tree branch against the bedroom window has often been cited as the more imminent and literal irritation to sleep that initiates the dream. But this tree branch is a figure of a pen scratching its message on the window, the sound of its scripture ("Tip.") duplicating the scratchy whisper of voices (like those of the washerwomen) telling the story of the indiscretion.

11. The phase "possibly-not-arriving" refers, of course, to the famous difference of opinion between Jacques Derrida and the late Jacques Lacan concerning the final destination of the purloined letter in Poe's story of the same name. Lacan claims that "a letter always arrives at its destination" (see "Seminar on 'The Purloined Letter,'" trans. Jeffrey Mehlman, *Yale French Studies*, 48 [1972], 38–72), while Derrida suggests that "a letter does *not always* arrive at its destination, and since this belongs to its structure, it can be said that it never really arrives there, that when it arrives, its possibly-not-arriving torments it with an internal divergence" (see "The Purveyor of Truth," trans. Willis Domingo et al., *Yale French Studies*, 52 [1975], 107). For purposes of this study of *Finnegans Wake*, Derrida's position on the destination of the letter is the only tenable one. Joyce's text provides almost encyclopedic evidence of all the various ways in which the letter cannot and does not arrive at its destination(s) precisely because it is prevented from doing so by the internal laws of its own censorship.

12. See Philippe Sollers, "Joyce and Co.," *In the Wake of the Wake*, ed. David Hayman *TriQuarterly*, 38, (1977) 107–08.

INDEX